SOUL JAZZ

SOUL JAZZ

Jazz in The Black Community, 1945-1975

BOB PORTER

Copyright © 2016 by Bob Porter.

Library of Congress Control Number: 2016916379
ISBN: Hardcover   978-1-5245-4787-5
           Softcover   978-1-5245-4786-8
           eBook   978-1-5245-4785-1

All rights reserved. No part of this book may be reproduced or transmitted in any form or by any means, electronic or mechanical, including photocopying, recording, or by any information storage and retrieval system, without permission in writing from the copyright owner.

Any people depicted in stock imagery provided by Thinkstock are models, and such images are being used for illustrative purposes only.
Certain stock imagery © Thinkstock.

Print information available on the last page.

Rev. date: 12/05/2016

To order additional copies of this book, contact:
Xlibris
1-888-795-4274
www.Xlibris.com
Orders@Xlibris.com
742348

CONTENTS

PREFACE ix

INTRODUCTION xi

RACE MUSIC 1
As America emerges from twenty-five years of prohibition, depression, and war, new opportunities present themselves in the fields of radio; concert promotion; and production, distribution, and sales of phonograph records. These may prove to be a benefit to black musicians who continue to face the same social roadblocks as segregation is the rule of the day. Music is changing: danceable swing is still the most popular; yet bebop, the New Orleans revival, and a decided preference for vocal records are on the horizon. The decline of the big band and the rise of small combos seem to be inevitable.

ILLINOIS JACQUET 47
Jacquet was the first star instrumentalist to emerge since the end of World War II. A singular stylist on the tenor saxophone, his work influenced hundreds of other musicians. His famous solo on Lionel Hampton's "Flyin' Home" is probably the most duplicated solo of all time. His first seven-piece band serves as a model for dozens of others.

RHYTHM AND BLUES 57
The rise of disc jockeys, independent record companies, and a new bluesy sound serves to propel R&B to the front of the sales pack. Thus begins the separation from jazz in the mind of the music industry. There are new speeds for phonograph records, as well as new stars, new trends, and new dances. The saxophone dominates, and the jukebox gets new life. Black radio formats begin to emerge. Musical performances begin to develop regional characteristics. Count Basie folds his old band and forms a new one. Duke Ellington loses an old drummer and finds a new one. Moondog gets hot in Ohio.

GENE AMMONS 105
The second-generation, Chicago-based jazzman was a tenor sax star who sparked black bands (Billy Eckstine) and white bands (Woody Herman) and made hit recordings in every decade covered by this book. And he did it with ballads, blues, Latin material, organ groups, and funk. Ammons was a stylist of the first rank and one whose work combined the best influences of his predecessors.

THE BIG BEAT 113
R&B gets renamed rock 'n' roll. Alan Freed gets to be a superstar. Count Basie gets a new singer. Duke Ellington gets a magazine cover. Norman Granz folds up the tent. Jazz festivals become a big deal. The 12" LP wins the battle of sizes, and the payola scandals are on the horizon. Jonah Jones and Cozy Cole, a couple of swing stars, still know how to do it. The Hammond organ is a part of the entertainment mix in most black neighborhoods

HANK CRAWFORD 149
An alto saxophonist with a unique, singing, sound, and singular approach, Crawford is also the architect of the Ray Charles sound during his (1958–1963) tenure with Charles. His arrangements with their distinctive voicings prove to be horn section sound favored by most contemporary bluesmen. Late in his career, he embraces the organ sound and finds a new audience.

SOUL JAZZ 157
The surging popularity of the organ combo provides new life for jazz. Jimmy Smith becomes a superstar. Jack McDuff, Jimmy McGriff, and Groove Holmes have big hits. The rise of FM radio and stereophonic sound means fresh listening experiences and improved audio. Saxophonists such as Lou Donaldson, Stanley Turrentine, and Sonny Stitt prefer organ in the rhythm section. Consolidation among the independent record labels begins. The rise and fall of MGM/Verve records presages problems for the future. Rudy Van Gelder builds his new studio.

GRANT GREEN 201
The St. Louis guitarist is brought to Blue Note Records by Lou Donaldson and quickly becomes a ubiquitous sideman. He records his own albums but appears on hit albums by Lou Donaldson, Lee Morgan, Herbie Hancock, and others. His professional advancement is held up by a personal drug problem. After a hiatus, he returns to Blue Note with new ideas that take hold in the marketplace.

FUNK AND FUSION 211
Jazz becomes more commercial with big hits selling like pop records. Creed Taylor, at Verve, A&M, and finally his own CTI/Kudu operation, is the man who knows his audience. Jazz stars become celebrities in the black community. Electric pianos and electric saxophones are now part of the band. Pianists manage to survive in different ways. There will be no more mono albums released, and straight-ahead jazz sales take a big dive. Label consolidation continues, and there are fewer players in the game.

GROVER WASHINGTON JR. 247
This versatile multi-instrumentalist goes from sideman to superstar in a very short time. He makes the most of every break that comes his way. His popularity soon becomes the equal of any musician of the 1970s, while his playing is a veritable definition of the new radio format "smooth jazz," and he is savvy enough on the business side to ensure his long-term success.

THE PRODUCERS 255
Employment details and major successes of the independent producers whose work makes up much of the subject matter of this book.

EPILOGUE 261
One great soul jazz moment.

ACKNOWLEDGMENTS 263

INDEX 265

For Constance Kavanagh Porter, whose love of music inspired my own and, of course, Linda.

PREFACE

THIS IS A BOOK ABOUT black jazz musicians and singers who emerged from the big bands of the swing era—from the end of World War II when the big band business was beginning to unravel to the end of the Vietnam War and the coming of disco. It contains references to many musicians whose popularity was largely contained within the black community.

While jazz writers have routinely dealt with musicians of all races, their work has generally reflected the point of view of an integrated community. In an ideal world, perhaps that is the way it should be. But that is not the way it was in the period covered by this book. The America of 1945 was a segregated country, and while the legal underpinnings of discrimination would fall during this time, the effects of those policies would linger. Black communities had their own heroes, and black fans of jazz had their own way of responding to the music. Those attitudes rarely reflected the values represented in the jazz press: most jazz writers of the fifties and sixties did not come to Harlem to hear music.

You can find contemporary jazz history texts with no mention of Buddy Johnson, Illinois Jacquet, Gene Ammons, or Donald Byrd: successful jazz musicians whose popularity drew largely from the black community. And this situation seems likely to continue: there is little variance in the telling of jazz history. I have helped dozens of researchers and writers through the years, and I always hoped that one of them would tackle this untold story. Nobody did, and now most of the greatest players are gone. Thus, I decided to do this myself.

SOUL JAZZ is a book that seeks to correct this imbalance. My personal interest in the music of many players discussed here is the result of lengthy periods of digging through discographies and articles from the black press. And listening, lots of listening! This is a book that I wish had existed when I was first coming into contact with jazz in my teens.

SOUL JAZZ spends a great deal of time on radio and records. Records are facts: a recorded history of what was played at a given moment. In the black community, success involved radio play and record sales. The musicians covered in *SOUL JAZZ* tend to be the ones who had the hit records and became the biggest stars.

Soul jazz is the music of the organ groups, funky piano trios, and tenor sax men of the fifties, sixties, and early 1970s. Not all labels recorded jazz, and not all jazz labels recorded soul jazz. There were five or six labels that did most of the recording, and those are covered in depth. I have included material on prominent record producers of the time. These men had a considerable say in who was recorded and what kinds of records were made.

In my career as a record producer, I was fortunate enough to have worked with many of these musicians. I have included individual portraits of five men who made a considerable impact on the scene whom I worked with directly in the recording studio. Others I had the opportunity to meet or hang out with. All of them have my admiration for the music they performed and left for us via recordings.

Finally, I have included material on figures and events involved in the worlds of sports and politics. Jazz does not exist in a vacuum, and the events of the times often inspired music with related themes.

SOUL JAZZ is devoted to a time that has long since passed. The musicians, the clubs, the radio stations, and the record labels are all memories now. The best way to experience the music as it was is on recordings. At this point, when there are few CD stores and much of the great music is out of print, finding the music will not be easy. But each discovery will be rewarding.

In time, perhaps you will hear what I heard many years ago: great jazz played by musicians who are not well documented but whose gifts will thrill you in a way no other jazz can.

INTRODUCTION

JAZZ HAS BEEN DESCRIBED ANY number of times as the great American art form. It is certainly that, but it is also a way to make a living. In order to present his art to the world, a musician must first find a way to put bread on the table and a roof over his head.

Jazz musicians coming of age in the 1940s tended to be specialists. They studied, practiced, and adopted a style, often with a particular role model in mind. With luck, they found a teacher or an older player who could mentor them, sponsor them, and provide helpful suggestions. Aspiring jazz musicians could choose to pursue a swing style or something akin to Chicago style, itself an outgrowth of traditional New Orleans jazz. As the music evolved, more choices emerged: bebop and rhythm and blues foremost among them. Regardless of the approach a player chooses, the business of music is identical to all.

A bandleader is responsible for everyone in the group. A leader, or his representatives, must do all the booking; arrange for travel, promotion, and publicity; and produce the payroll. They must also negotiate recording contracts and publishing agreements and make musical decisions. Many bandleaders also write and arrange and are thus responsible for the majority of the organization's music while others derive the musical direction from staff writers or freelance arrangers. Prominent sidemen are capable of having recording contracts and developing a fan base of their own. Arrangers are employed by leaders of large or small ensembles to provide material for performances or record dates.

Composers can be leaders, sidemen, arrangers, or professional songwriters. Composers split their money with publishers who administrate the catalog of the composers. Some writers are their own publisher, which can mean twice the income of a writer who is not a publisher. Most record labels, large or small, have in-house publishing companies. For many years, it was common practice for leaders to give themselves a cowriter credit on songs they introduced whether or not they had a hand in the actual composition. During the early years covered in this book, we will find some owners of small record labels doing the same thing. Writer or cowriter credits can act as currency, and it is not a rare occurrence for composers to sell songs outright to publishers. Additional income is available through royalties distributed by performing rights organizations such as ASCAP, BMI, or SESAC.

The record business is set up to reward leaders who have a royalty built into their contracts. Arrangers and sidemen are paid flat fees. In the record business, everything is negotiable. Union scale wages are the dead minimum for recording work, and royalty rates paid to music publishers by record labels are predetermined unless other arrangements have been made.

The black musician who returned from World War II (WWII) faced a series of legal and social roadblocks that were designed to keep him from achieving success or to make it infinitely more difficult to attain. In order to have a career, building a following within the black community was the first order of business. Ranking members of the church, doctors, lawyers, educators, and businesspeople could be viewed as important contributors to the local black community; but great jazz musicians were kings and counts and dukes. A jazz musician with a fan base and a recording contract could be a star to his people.

A crossover to acceptance within the white community was a far more difficult task to accomplish and one that never entered the mind of many talented musicians.

In 1945, racist policies decreed that there were no black baseball players in the major leagues and precious few football players in the National Football League (a league struggling to stay alive) while the National Basketball Association did not exist. The major sport of interest to the black community was boxing. Past champions such as Jack Johnson and Henry Armstrong had been hugely popular in black neighborhoods. But the most important single figure to black people was the heavyweight champion Joe Louis. Radio had played an important part in building the Joe Louis legend. People bought radios to hear his fights, and those radios could be heard all over the neighborhood when the champ was defending his title and the fight was being broadcast. When the Count Basie Orchestra recorded "King Joe Parts 1 and 2," one did not need to hear the song to know to know the identity of its subject.

In the segregated United States of 1945, there was relatively little opportunity for black music to be heard on the radio, outside of a few large cities. Radio was 100 percent white owned and dominated by the networks. The few disc jockeys were heard on independent stations, often those with low power and limited range. There was no FM band. In the coming years, the growth of radio paralleled the growth of the record industry. Black music played a significant part in this growth.

The black audience bought records in large quantities. Labels that recorded music for the black audience could find immediate acceptance if they had the right material. Those labels that could maintain the popularity of their recordings could be successful long-term enterprises. Much more often, record labels were not successful. They were almost always undercapitalized, and the enthusiasm for the business end did not match the interest in the music or vice versa.

At this time, wholesale record distribution was in its infancy. Black music would spur the growth of distributors throughout the country. But making a correct decision on which distributor to use in which territory was often crucial in creating the cash flow for a label to sustain itself between hits.

In its musical tastes, the black audience was often quick to embrace new trends and quicker still to abandon music that was perceived as old hat. Beginning in 1949 with "The Hucklebuck," new dance steps came out of the black community with astonishing frequency. There would usually be one singular song to introduce the beat of the latest step. In some cases, dozens of songs followed, all using the new dance as part of the title. Much of black popular music in the decades that followed was built around dances. In a sense, this was a carryover from the swing era, yet it also demonstrated the widening separation between black popular music and modern jazz. There were no dance steps associated with bebop.

If the mass black community would leave much modern jazz behind while embracing R&B, a smaller audience would emerge that revered modern jazz and excluded most R&B. Soul jazz would emphasize the solid beat and the blues feeling of R&B with the instrumentation and modern jazz improvisational context, thereby creating a common ground that appealed to both groups. While still unknown to many white listeners, musicians such as Gene Ammons or Jimmy Smith had a strong following in both camps.

Underneath everything else over the course of this book was the desire for equal opportunity. It had been the overriding concern of the black community since emancipation. The 1896 *Plessy v. Ferguson* decision by the US Supreme Court had endorsed segregation and the concept of "separate but equal." The battle to obtain civil rights for black people was well under way in 1945 but had suffered some significant setbacks.

The Fair Employment Practices Committee (FEPC) had been created by President Roosevelt in 1941. The FEPC mandated certain percentages be set aside for black employment on federally funded work. The dictum was ignored in the South and never fully supported by the administration. Racial violence broke out in Alabama and Texas when attempts to enforce mandates were undertaken. There was a lengthy strike at the Ford Motor Company in Detroit, and there were other trouble spots across the country. There were similar problems in the military.

Prior to the outbreak of WWII, there were no black marines and none in the army air corps. Those in the navy were relegated to such menial positions as cooks and servants. The commandant of the Marine Corps stated that blacks were attempting to gain entry to a club that didn't want them. In 1940, with war on the horizon, things began to change. The army was required by the Roosevelt administration to bring the number of troops in line with the actual percentage of the country's population—about 10 percent—and the army began to train black officers. The army air corps established an airfield at Tuskegee, Alabama, to train black pilots. Beginning in 1942, black musicians were welcomed into the navy band via the Great Lakes Naval Training Center in Illinois.

This book is about musical change: the different methods of playing the music, the differing attitudes toward the music coming from the black community, the comings and goings in the music business and media, and, finally, the adjustments of the musicians themselves.

Each change in the music business, each new direction, each hot new sound, each new personnel lineup, brought fresh opportunity. These changes also meant that the old way of doing things would not be the same.

The new innovations in music frequently mirrored the changes in the fight for equality. In 1948, President Truman ordered the desegregation of the American military.

In 1954, the US Supreme Court reversed its separate but equal decision. In the mid-'60s would come the Voting Rights Act and the Civil Rights Act. The attitudes of the American people, as a whole, changed drastically, if slowly, over the time span of this book. There was a great deal of nonmilitary, racially inspired bloodshed in America during the years between the end of WWII and the end of the Vietnam War. Some musicians manned the barricades while others sat on the sidelines in the pursuit of equality. But by 1975, the United States was a very different place.

RACE MUSIC

AT THE END OF WORLD War II (WWII), the music business was just coming out of a lengthy strike against record labels by the American Federation of Musicians that began July 1, 1942. Decca was the first of the big labels to settle with the union, and by the end of 1943, they were recording again. Columbia and RCA, the two other big labels, held out until November 1944. In those intervening months, dozens of little labels had filled the vacuum by agreeing to the same terms as Decca.

America was a segregated country, some areas by law and others by custom. Musical descriptions tended to reflect this. White orchestras such as Benny Goodman, Artie Shaw, and Tommy Dorsey were considered dance bands. Recordings with any measure of appeal to white, rural audiences were labeled hillbilly. All black music, whether it be country blues or jazz, with the exception of spirituals, was designated race music.

It was still the big band era in 1945. Major black performers were bandleaders for the most part. The ballrooms, theaters, and large nightclubs that had played such an important part in the swing era were coming under increasing pressure from unemployment, inflation, and television as well as the changing tastes of the audience. This meant fewer places to play. There would be many more successful new combos, along the lines of the King Cole Trio or Louis Jordan's Tympany Five, by the end of the decade. These small combos often had extended engagements at a local nightspot and did little traveling.

It is important to note that the road to success in the big band field included such important areas as a recording contract preferably with one of the major labels of the time as well as agency and management representation for the purposes of arranging tours and creating publicity. Without an affiliation with a major booking agency, a big band could not organize lengthy tours. A string of one-nighters on the road was an absolute necessity for a big band. This is where the real money was made. Movie appearances were available only to the biggest stars, but locations equipped for radio broadcasts were a vital part of the publicity and promotional effort, so it was important to play the right spots.

THE BIG BANDS

Count Basie (1904–1984) had the premier Kansas City–style swing band, formed in 1936. It featured piano by the leader, a rock-solid rhythm section, and excellent jazz soloists. The summer 1945 edition featured trumpet player Sweets Edison, trombonists Dickie Wells and J. J. Johnson, saxophonists Buddy Tate and Lucky Thompson, and vocalist Jimmy Rushing. Many of his original stars were either in the military (Buck Clayton, Lester Young, Jo Jones) or had passed on (Herschel Evans), but Basie managed to keep the essence of his band together. He had recorded for Columbia since 1939 and was booked by William Morris, a major talent agency. Basie was a national attraction and appeared in venues coast to coast.

Duke Ellington (1899–1974) was a pianist, composer-arranger, and bandleader and had formed his first group in 1923. He gained great celebrity during his 1927–1931 association with the Cotton Club in New York. The engagement permitted him to form a big band and be heard on the radio. In 1943, he began a series of annual concerts at Carnegie Hall and introduced new, longer works.

Ellington's enormous wartime popularity was partly caused by his five #1 hits on the Race Record charts (beginning in May 1943), some of which had been recorded as early as 1940. Also of importance was a weekly radio show **Your Saturday Date with the Duke**, which began in April 1945. Ellington was booked by William Morris and recorded for RCA Victor. His current band featured Taft Jordan, Rex Stewart, and Cat Anderson among the trumpets and Tricky Sam Nanton and Lawrence Brown on trombone with Johnny Hodges (alto sax), Jimmy Hamilton (clarinet/tenor sax), and Harry Carney (baritone sax) in the reed section. Al Hibbler was his male vocalist.

Ellington was especially adept at finding replacements for key men. When Cootie Williams and Ben Webster left the band to head their own groups, a Ray Nance or an Al Sears came in and created playing that, while clearly different from their predecessors, was fully in keeping with the overall sound of the band.

Lionel Hampton's (1908–2002) great ability on vibraharp and occasionally as pianist, drummer, and vocalist was established via a series of small band recordings for RCA Victor from 1937 to 1941 and his appearances with various Benny Goodman combos from 1936 to 1940. His big band was formed in Los Angeles in the fall of 1940. The original unit that included such budding stars as Ernie Royal and Joe Newman on trumpets, as well as Marshall Royal, Dexter Gordon, Illinois Jacquet, and Jack McVea on reeds, had only pianist Milt Buckner left by the summer of 1945. The combination of low pay and the relentlessly frantic pace of performance dictated by the leader led to considerable personnel turnover in the Hampton band. Cat Anderson, Earl Bostic, and Al Sears had recorded with Hampton the previous year; but the current edition featured two emerging stars: tenor saxophonist Arnett Cobb and vocalist Dinah Washington. In keeping with the Hampton tradition, there were more changes before the end of the year. Hampton recorded for Decca, was managed by Joe Glaser (although his wife, Gladys, was deeply involved), and booked by Associated Booking Corporation. Hampton was coming off a #1 Race Records hit with "Hamp's Boogie Woogie" from 1944.

Erskine Hawkins (1914–1993) assumed leadership of the 'Bama State Collegians in 1934. The band came to New York in 1936 and in 1938 became, officially, the Erskine Hawkins Orchestra. While Hawkins was a high-note trumpet specialist, he was also an exceptional bandleader who kept his key people for many years. The band was built around the arranging talents of Sammy Lowe. Key soloists were alto saxophonist Bobby Smith, tenor saxophonist Julian Dash, baritone saxophonist Heywood Henry, and vocalist Jimmy Mitchelle. Former members who were important contributors were trumpeter Dud Bascomb, his brother tenor saxophonist Paul Bascomb, and pianist/arranger Avery Parrish.

The Hawkins band was managed by Moe Gale, booked by the Gale Agency, and recorded for RCA Victor. Since Gale was also the owner of New York's Savoy Ballroom, the band was virtually guaranteed several annual engagements at black America's most famous dance emporium. They had a solid stream of hit records beginning with "Tuxedo Junction" (1939), "After Hours" (1940), and a huge #1 Race Records hit from 1943, "Don't Cry, Baby."

The abilities of Buddy Johnson (1915–1977) as a pianist and bandleader were obscured in the long run by his songwriting. Johnson was a master of the blue ballad, and his songs have been performed by countless singers through the years. Johnson's final Decca session before the 1942 ban featured a nine-piece band while his first after the ban featured sixteen pieces. The increased bookings at military posts created the opening to expand. Originally from South Carolina, Johnson knew the Southern audience better than most, and this young band found an instant following in the black community. The band also had hits such as "Let's Beat Out Some Love" and "When My Man Comes Home" (a #1 Race Records hit in 1944) and their latest release "That's the Stuff You Gotta Watch." Buddy himself contributed the vocal to "Let's Beat Out Some Love," but the other two hits had vocals by Buddy's sister Ella Johnson, who handled most of the blues vocals. Arthur Prysock was the male vocalist in the band, and his specialties were romantic ballads. It was those romantic ballads that gave Buddy Johnson an edge. While he had his share of novelty and blues hits, many Buddy Johnson's songs had an appeal to women not found in all the black bands.

The Johnson band was booked by the Gale Agency and was a regular attraction at the Savoy Ballroom. David Van Dyke was given most of the tenor sax solos, but because of the emphasis on the vocalists, this was a band where solos were less important than a good song and a solid beat.

Lucky Millinder (1910–1966) was not a musician but a front man and showman of the first rank. He first worked with the Mills Blue Rhythm Band from 1934 to 1938. In 1940, he formed the Lucky Millinder Orchestra, and it became an instant success. The band was initially built around a strong rhythm section with players such as pianist Bill Doggett, bassist George Duvivier, and drummer Panama Francis. Vocalist/guitarist Sister Rosetta Tharpe was a key contributor, as was alto saxophonist Tab Smith. During the war, modernist trumpet players such as Dizzy Gillespie and Freddie Webster were in and out of this band. Eddie Davis and Sam Taylor were saxophonists in the band while Sir Charles Thompson and Ellis Larkins were pianists at one time or another. Still, the Millinder band was powered by popular vocalists and hit records: Trevor Bacon, who also played guitar in the band, sang popular tunes such as "Big Fat Mama," "When the Lights Go on Again," and "Sweet Slumber" (the latter two each being #1 on the Race Records chart) while Sister Tharpe had strong vocals on "Shout Sister Shout" and "That's All." The band was coming off a #1 hit instrumental with "Apollo Flyer," which featured tenor saxophonist Stafford "Pazuzza" Simon. In 1944, Wynonie Harris, the leather-lunged blues shouter, was briefly with the band. His first recording, his only one with the band, was another #1 hit, "Who Threw the Whiskey in the Well?" His replacement was Benjamin "Bullmoose" Jackson, who also played saxophone in the band. Millinder was booked by the Gale Agency and recorded for Decca.

Even with the end of the war in the Pacific, there were shortages to overcome, rationing to be observed, and lots of very good musicians in uniform. The ability to overcome these difficulties was often what kept these bands going, but many were unable to sustain their existence in the immediate postwar era. Some bands, such as the Kansas City orchestras led by Harlan Leonard and Jay McShann, had already folded while Andy Kirk's would be a memory within just a few years.

Among swing era bandleaders, Benny Carter and Fletcher Henderson tended to concentrate on arranging in the coming years. In Carter's case, he found a way into the highly restricted world of writing music for Hollywood films and largely put his substantial jazz-playing abilities on hold until the early 1950s when he began a lengthy association with the promoter Norman Granz. Henderson fronted small groups on occasion and led orchestras for special events, but his star was clearly in decline. A noted arranger since the 1920s, he still wrote arrangements for Benny Goodman; but by the end of the decade, he had suffered serious health issues.

Louis Armstrong formed his All-Stars in 1947, and that six-piece combo provided the great man with a new focus and huge lift to a career that had been sagging under the weight of a mediocre ensemble. Earl Hines, who had led his own big band since 1929 and had been an Armstrong associate in the 1920s, was a part of the first Armstrong All-Stars before returning to leadership duties with his own combos.

The 1947 death of Jimmie Lunceford effectively put an end to his band that had suffered from major defections of key personnel since 1942. Pianist/arranger Eddie Wilcox and tenor saxophonist Joe Thomas fronted the band following Lunceford's death and continued to record into 1949, but by the middle of that year, each had gone on to other things. Wilcox began an association with Derby Records in New York that involved producing, arranging, and even recording a few big band sessions of his own while Thomas put together a sextet that recorded for King and provided backing for R&B vocalists.

Billy Eckstine's modern jazz band gave up the ghost in early 1947 after a less-than-three-year existence. Rampant drug use and the inability to maintain a constant personnel in his band had hurt his cause. His records, on De Luxe and National, excellent as they were, were pressed on inferior material, a casualty of wartime shellac rationing. He signed with MGM Records, a new label with deep pockets, and was recorded mostly in a pop format that provided him with a considerable number of hits over the next five years. Eckstine had found his fame as a stand-up singer. He continued to be the preferred balladeer of bebop fans.

Cab Calloway, the popular showman, had been hurt more than anyone else by the AFM strike of 1942. He went two and a half years without a single recording session when he was accustomed to six or seven recording sessions per year prior to WWII. His 1943–1944 band had a major soloist, Illinois Jacquet, in its personnel but went completely unrecorded; and Calloway was unable to get much mileage out of his prominent role in the 1943 film **Stormy Weather**. He cut back to a small group for touring purposes in mid-1947 although he continued to record with larger ensembles and, on occasion, recruited a big band for theater engagements. In time, he became known for his acting ability; and apart from a reprise of old hits, his repertoire remained static, signifying a slow, steady retreat from the limelight.

Cootie Williams (1911–1985) found popularity on record, but that wasn't enough. His big band was first recorded in 1942, and his recordings for the independent label HIT in 1944 found a ready audience. He also discovered Eddie "Cleanhead" Vinson who sang on several hit records with the band, but when Vinson left in late 1945, Williams never found another high-quality blues shouter to fill his shoes. The Williams big band also recorded for Capitol and Majestic from 1945 to 1947, trying to recapture the magic; but by the end of 1947, he had cut back to a small band and signed with Mercury. Williams led R&B-oriented combos, usually featuring a strong tenor sax soloist, in addition to his powerhouse trumpet, for the next fifteen years.

Beginning with Benny Goodman, in the mid-1930s, white bands had utilized black players in starring roles; and fortunate musicians such as Roy Eldridge (with Artie Shaw), Peanuts Holland—later Clark Terry (with Charlie Barnet), Willie Smith (with Harry James), and Charlie Shavers (with Tommy Dorsey) were currently holding prominent well-paid roles in white orchestras. Black arrangers creating music for white orchestras was not at all unusual. Jimmy Mundy, Andy Gibson and Fred Norman were among the most prominent free-lance arrangers.

By 1948, Lucky Millinder had two white trombonists in his band, and both the Ellington and Basie bands would employ white musicians shortly thereafter. It would be the 1960s before the idea of blacks and whites making music together would be accepted nationally, but even at this early stage, there were cracks in the barrier.

PROMINENT MUSICIANS

Small record labels were springing up all over Los Angeles. While Capitol had established itself before the ban, important new LA labels were ARA, Atomic, Black & White, Excelsior, Exclusive, Juke Box (soon to become Specialty), Modern Music (soon to become Modern), and Philo (soon to become Aladdin). Much of the new black music talent first exposed during this time was the result of the influx of new labels. There was more opportunity to be recorded. Some of the key small-group leaders in Los Angeles during 1945 included T-Bone Walker, Jay McShann, Jack McVea, Roy Milton, Nat "King" Cole, Joe Liggins, and Slim Gaillard. Local big bands were led by future stars Gerald Wilson and Johnny Otis. Singers Helen Humes and Big Joe Turner were both Los Angeles based during much of the year.

New York was home to the corporate offices of the big record labels as well as the headquarters of major music publishers. There were plenty of clubs to play. This began in the mid-1930s with the repeal of the Volstead Act and the opening of now-fabled nightspots in Harlem and on 52nd Street. Much of the jazz recorded there was the result of access to an exceptional talent pool.

Coleman Hawkins (1904-1969) was at a peak in 1945. In 1939, he had returned from an extended European stay and recorded "Body and Soul" for RCA/Bluebird and the record had sold very well. An attempt at leading a big band did not work out but Hawkins could be found regularly on 52nd Street in small combos. Ahead of his time in terms of harmonic conception, he was at home with swing stars or the growing number of modern jazz players. Hawkins was in great demand for record dates: during 1944 he led a session per month for the entire year and racked up an equally impressive number of appearances as a featured sideman.

While Hawkins was the dominant tenor sax stylist of the time his position would be challenged in years to come. But in 1945, Herschel Evans, Dick Wilson and Chu Berry were dead, Ben Webster was scuffling and Lester Young was in the Army. In January 1945, Hawkins began a long engagement in Los Angeles. During the period he recorded twelve sides for Capitol with Howard McGhee on trumpet and Sir Charles Thompson on piano. He also began working with promoter Norman Granz who would be a major employer of his in the years to come. Upon his return to New York he resumed his regular routine on 52nd Street.

Lloyd "Tiny" Grimes, the master of the four-string guitar, had completed a stint with Art Tatum's trio (bassist Slam Stewart was also involved) and was fronting combos on 52nd Street while recording for a variety of labels; Hot Lips Page, the great trumpet player and blues master, made lots of records during the year with bands large and small; Stuff Smith, Tab Smith, and Paul and Dud Bascomb were all regulars on the New York scene. Pete Brown and Ben Webster were working on 52nd Street. Sammy Price and Cozy Cole were active as much in recording studios as they were in live performance. Among the pianists, Art Tatum, Albert Ammons, and Mary Lou Williams were highly regarded veterans while Erroll Garner was a top newcomer. Ella Fitzgerald was the top female singer while Billie Holiday held on to a strong following, and Lionel Hampton's Dinah Washington was looked on as a potential star.

Of all the New York freelance musicians, the busiest was tenor saxophonist Don Byas (1912–1972) who was in demand for swing, blues, or bebop record dates, big band or small. From early 1944 through the summer of 1946, Byas recorded more than sixty selections as a leader and recorded more than twice that number as a featured sideman. Byas was a truly versatile stylist. His soulful side was displayed on "Harvard Blues" with Count Basie and his own ballads such as "Laura" or "Candy." At the same time, he was Dizzy Gillespie's first choice on tenor sax for quicksilver performances such as "Bebop" or "A Night in

Tunisia." In September of 1946, he joined Don Redman's band for a European tour. When the tour concluded, Byas stayed, living first in Paris and later in Amsterdam.

Small labels that were involved in recording black music in the New York area were Apollo, Asch, Beacon, Blue Note, Commodore, Continental, DeLuxe, Guild, HRS, Keynote, Majestic, Manor, Musicraft, National, and Savoy. Exclusivity was rarely employed with small labels, and many jazzmen made records for several of these labels. There were also many short-lived labels that recorded fine music but sometimes didn't last more than a single session. Of the big labels, Decca was dominant: Buddy Johnson, Louis Jordan, Ella Fitzgerald, Billie Holiday, Lionel Hampton, and Lucky Millinder were all exclusive Decca artists.

Trumpeter and vocalist Henry "Red" Allen with alto saxophonist Don Stovall and trombonist J. C. Higginbotham wrapped up a successful two-year stay in Chicago in the summer of 1945. Allen was an entertainer with a long track record who had recorded more than one hundred titles before the AFM ban. Yet apart from a session recorded for World Transcriptions that was manufactured for radio play, there were no recordings by the Red Allen group during its stay in Chicago.

Chicago had long been a city with ample resources for recording.

There was a large talent pool and plenty of existing studio space, but the independent recording industry had yet to develop in the Windy City. There were simply not any prominent small labels. When Mercury Records opened its doors in the fall of 1945, Chicago had its first new label of prominence. Others followed, but Mercury was the biggest and most successful. Chicago had long been a key recording center for blues artists, and that continued to be the case. Most of the independent record companies started in Chicago in the next few years were either blues labels or featured a mixture of blues and jazz artists.

THE RECORD INDUSTRY

The year 1945 was the time that the independent record labels first began to show some clout. In 1944, eight of the year's top Race Records were on either Decca or Capitol. In 1945, Decca continued to show strength; but for the first time, the #1 Race Record of the year, Exclusive's "The Honeydripper" by Joe Liggins, was on an independent label. Entries by Cootie Williams on HIT and Cecil Gant on Gilt Edge made the top 10. New York and Los Angeles were responsible for the vast majority of labels, yet newcomers such as Queen Records in Cincinnati showed considerable promise.

Adequate distribution was becoming an issue of major importance. Independent record distribution companies were popping up all over the country, and virtually all of them were local operations, serving only their immediate surrounding areas. Distributors were responsible for supplying the area jukeboxes and helping to develop what radio play was possible. Each independent distributor would, in time, represent dozens of labels. Of the established labels, Decca and Capitol had branch offices in most major cities. RCA Victor, the industry leader, had exceptional national distribution.

In black neighborhoods, records were sold in liquor stores, shoe-shine parlors, barbershops, and grocery stores among many other locations; but the major problem was keeping a steady supply of the most popular titles. It had been common practice for some time for railroad porters to deliver records from town to town. While this was still happening, legitimate wholesale distribution was the goal of each new label. As the world entered the nuclear era with the devastating attacks on Hiroshima and Nagasaki in August 1945, the black record business in America was just getting started. The musicians were already creating music of lasting value. Creating the business apparatus to bring the music to the people was a work in progress. While swing was still the dominant music in both large and small groups, bebop had announced its arrival, traditional New Orleans jazz had been revived, and rhythm and blues was still to come. The trade press thought of all black music as race music. It had been this way since the 1920s. By the end of the decade, this attitude would change; and within a remarkably short period, black music would become a driving force for musical change in America.

NORMAN GRANZ

Among the important musical events that happened in the fall of 1945 was the addition of Illinois Jacquet to the Count Basie band. Jacquet had heard the early Basie orchestra as a teenager in Houston and had based his tenor style on the best elements of both Lester Young and

Herschel Evans. To that he had added his own bag of tricks that had vaulted him to local stardom in Los Angeles. There he had appeared for almost a year at Billy Berg's Swing Club in Hollywood, the most popular jazz spot in the city.

In addition to leading his combo, Jacquet also worked as an individual for Norman Granz, the young promoter, who began by staging jam sessions at various clubs on off nights. Beginning in July 1944, Granz had branched out into monthly concert promotions dubbed Jazz at the Philharmonic (JATP).

But the economic climate in Southern California changed very quickly as summer melted into autumn 1945. Defense plants, the biggest single employer in the area, were closing left and right; and the free-spending crowds that had filled Billy Berg's or the clubs along Central Avenue began to disappear. Granz had taken a JATP tour up into Canada where, because of economic conditions and the promoter's own inexperience, it went broke, stranding the musicians. Granz had to sell almost everything he owned in order to secure first-class railroad passes for his players to return home. It was an astute move. The word spread quickly among major jazz stars that Norman Granz took care of the players he hired. Granz and Jacquet would meet up again; but for the time being, since his job at Billy Berg's had ended, a weekly paycheck and a starring role in his favorite band seemed the right thing to do for Illinois Jacquet.

Norman Granz regrouped after the failure of his West Coast tour in the fall of 1945. He came to New York in February 1946 and met with representatives from both the Gale Agency and Shaw Artists Guild about a cross-country tour for the spring of the year and to arrange for the release of the first JATP records. Each agency booked shows in half the country. Granz made contact with theater owners in each territory and soon would do all the booking himself.

The Granz method of jazz presentation involved utilizing the star soloists of the big bands in a staged jam session. This opened up new vistas for players such as Roy Eldridge, Willie Smith, and Lester Young who had been featured sidemen in big bands. The shows were also famous for combining fresh young talent such as Jacquet with established stars such as Coleman Hawkins. The repertoire played consisted of the blues and well-known jazz standards, and competition between the players in performance was encouraged. The spontaneity achieved in the first JATP concert of July 2, 1944, became the model for future concerts.

The first JATP records, from a February 1945 concert, created a sensation. For the first time, the onstage banter of the musicians and crowd reaction were very much a part of the records. The two songs, "How High the Moon" and "Lady Be Good," from a Los Angeles concert on February 12, 1945, were each edited into three parts and issued on one side of three 78 records and sold in an album on Asch Records. These were showcases for the soloists, and the only ensemble playing came during the final out chorus. Among the players on the first records were Jacquet, Willie Smith, and Gene Krupa—all of whom became key members of JATP tours in the future. The early JATP shows were recorded by the Armed Forces Recording Service and used for broadcasts to troops overseas. Granz had a deal with Moses Asch to release JATP concerts on record, but the two men were constantly at odds, and the one-year deal was over by the spring of 1947. Soon there were lawsuits, and it took Granz several years before he got his recordings back.

Granz had been producing studio dates for Philo with Lester Young and Helen Humes during 1945 and 1946. After his experience with Moses Asch, he had a desire to cement a deal with a label that would free him from the mundane aspects of the business. Since JATP was becoming a national organization, he needed a label with the ability to promote and distribute nationally. He found one in Mercury, and the deal Granz made with them in 1947 was not only the first production and distribution deal in the record industry but also one that would serve as a model for other such deals in the future. All his recording activities would appear under the same umbrella.

While the JATP concerts would, in time, present major stars on almost every instrument, this was not the case in the early years. Los Angeles–based saxophonists such as Vido Musso, Bumps Myers, Wild Bill Moore, and Maxwell Davis were occasional participants on an as-needed basis in Southern California JATP shows. This changed after Granz met with the New York agencies. His springtime tour involved a set roster of musicians, and while Dexter Gordon filled in for a few dates in the Midwest, this had become the exception rather than the rule. Rhythm section players were occasionally selected from a pool of talented local players, but the horn players could be promoted at each stop.

When the JATP troupe left Los Angeles in late April 1946, they were headed for New York to play three dates at Carnegie Hall. Granz had with him Lester Young, Buck Clayton, Coleman Hawkins, and pianist Kenny Kersey. Helen Humes was the featured vocalist. Boogie Woogie pianist Meade "Lux" Lewis had his own set while Charlie Drayton and Shadow Wilson completed the rhythm section. They were joined by special guest Illinois Jacquet for the Carnegie Hall shows.

JACKIE ROBINSON–JOE LOUIS

In October 1945, Jackie Robinson was signed to play baseball by the Brooklyn Dodgers. Robinson was a WWII veteran who had been a four-sport standout at UCLA. Robinson did not play for the Dodgers during 1946 but instead for their International League farm club in Montreal. In 1947, he joined the parent club, becoming the first black player in Major League baseball since the 1880s. His accomplishments earned him the National League Rookie of the Year Award. Although their rivals, the New York Giants, were quick to sign such black talent as Hank Thompson and Monte Irvin, the Dodgers were first and soon signed additional black stars such as Roy Campanella and Don Newcombe. They would be black America's team for many years.

Joe Louis returned to the ring in 1946. He had been in the army since 1942, and it had been more than four years since he had fought professionally. The Brown Bomber was still the heavyweight champion and had a ring record of fifty-six wins with a single loss (to Max Schmeling—whom he later dispatched in a rematch via a first-round knockout). Ten years to the day that he was knocked out by Schmeling, he returned to fight Billy Conn at Yankee Stadium in New York. Often the opponents that Louis faced were of inferior ability and were referred to, by sportswriters, collectively, as members of the "Bum of the Month Club." Billy Conn was a different story. The 1941 Louis-Conn matchup was one of the most exciting fights in Louis's career. Louis had been behind on points when he knocked out Conn in the thirteenth round.

The buildup to this fight had been tremendous, with unprecedented radio and newspaper coverage. The result was disappointing. Conn proved to be much less a challenge the second time around, and Louis knocked him out in the eighth round. King Joe was back.

Duke Ellington lost a major voice in his orchestra when trombonist Joe "Tricky Sam" Nanton died in July 1946. Shortly thereafter, Ellington overheard an RCA employee utter a racial slur at one of his record dates in the summer of 1946 and decided that it was time to leave the label. He was lured by an exceptional financial offer from Musicraft, a New York–based independent that had also signed Dizzy Gillespie and Sarah Vaughan. There were thirteen titles (including a pair of two-part performances) recorded during the fall of 1946, but that was all. Ellington drew his guaranteed money early in the relationship, and because of cash flow problems, Musicraft could not continue recording the Ellington orchestra. The deal was dissolved, and Ellington was on Columbia by August of 1947. This was a costly mistake by Ellington because one of his greatest train songs, "Happy Go Lucky Local," was among the Musicraft sides. If it had been recorded for RCA or Columbia, it would have sold in much greater quantities because of superior distribution. In time, and in the hands of tenor saxophonist Jimmy Forrest, the main strain would become better known as "Night Train." The Ellington output for Columbia from 1947 to 1950 is generally considered to be below his lofty standards, without hit songs or memorable solos. While still a hero in the black community, it would be 1951 before Duke Ellington would return to his place at the head of the pack.

In January 1947, shortly after Duke Ellington departed RCA Victor, Count Basie came aboard. Basie's RCA recordings from 1947 to 1950 were, like Ellington's of the same period, disappointing. When Illinois Jacquet left in September of 1946, Basie lost the spark plug soloist who had ignited enthusiasm for the band during the preceding months. The tenor sax chairs in the Count Basie band had proved to be a springboard to stardom in the past. Basie was unlucky in that the tenor players who came through the band in the late 1940s such as Jesse Powell, Paul Gonsalves, Wardell Gray, Weasel Parker, and Jimmy Tyler were unable to leave any lasting imprint or find any niche in the band. Gonsalves, who became a key member of the Ellington band in 1950, and Gray, who stayed briefly with Basie before joining Benny Goodman, found the right spot for themselves in time while the others toiled in relative anonymity.

The most popular black band of 1946 was that of Lionel Hampton. He was breaking attendance records all over the country. Hampton recorded a wide variety of music for Decca, big band and small. Much of it found favor with the black community, but Hampton had a white following as well, dating from his tenure with Benny Goodman.

Milt Buckner arranged several Hampton big band recordings in late 1945 and early 1946. Included were two-part treatments of "Rockin' in Rhythm" and "Air Mail Special," which featured the soloists in the band. Chief among them was Arnett Cobb on tenor sax while among the others featured were Buckner, a teenaged Johnny Griffin on tenor, Mitchell "Booty" Wood on trombone, and Joe Morris on trumpet. But the big success was "Hey! Ba-Ba-Re-Bob," the best-selling single of Hampton's career. It reached #1 during a twenty-five-week stay on the Race Charts.

Dinah Washington had departed at the end of 1945, and there was no immediate replacement for her. She had not been well served by Decca who recorded only a single vocal during her three-year stay in the band. Decca had a problem when Washington recorded "Salty Papa Blues" and "Evil Gal Blues" for the Keynote label with a small group from the Hampton band. Decca responded by deliberately limiting the recorded output by Dinah Washington with the Hampton band.

Decca faced a similar problem with Lucky Millinder. Both Annisteen Allen and Bull Moose Jackson, his two vocalists, had been recording for the Queen label with small groups out of the band. More often than not, leaders were happy to see their men pick up an extra payday, but the fact that Jackson had a hit with "I Know Who Threw the Whiskey in the Well" meant that Millinder couldn't follow up his own hit, "Who Threw the Whiskey in the Well?" from the previous year! The label followed the Dinah Washington pattern with Bull Moose Jackson. "Chittlin' Switch" was his only recorded vocal with Millinder despite being in the band for more than three years! Decca was clearly not happy about this trend. What was demonstrated in the most obvious fashion was that old way of slowly building sidemen and band singers into leaders would not work as long as all these little record companies kept cherry-picking the key talent. Star soloists had been able to command their own recording deals since the '20s and always would, but star vocalists? *That* was something else. The year 1946 was, in many ways, the peak for the Hampton big band. By the end of the year, many of the key sidemen had departed; and the replacements, by comparison, did not really measure up.

Lucky Millinder had a strong 1946 as well. Key musicians such as Sam Taylor on tenor sax and pianist Sir Charles Thompson came into the band, and most importantly, the aforementioned vocalists Allen and Jackson had become a pair of very strong stylists. The band's biggest hit of the year was "Shorty's Got to Go," a novelty that featured a Millinder vocal and strong Taylor saxophone. "(Ah-Yes) There's Good Blues Tonight" with Allen singing was paired with "Chittlin' Switch" featuring Jackson's vocal, and the coupling had sold well. One title that was held back for more than eighteen months was "Fare Thee Well, Deacon Jones," which featured a major solo from Sam Taylor, heralding the many powerhouse efforts that would appear in the next decade.

Ella Johnson, the star vocalist of the Buddy Johnson band, rarely recorded without her brother. His skills as a songwriter and arranger made certain that her position in the band was always the central focal point. Arthur Prysock (1924–1997), the band's romantic balladeer, found his first taste of success on the band's version of "They All Say I'm the Biggest Fool," the Johnson band's best-selling record of 1946. The song had been recorded in October 1944 but held back for over a year before seeing a Decca release.

Decca was obviously having problems sorting out the talents of the various band singers they were dealing with. Prysock made his own session for Haven in 1946, but those records went nowhere, and his star began to rise within the band as Buddy Johnson wrote some wonderful blue ballads tailored to his ability. In time, Prysock came to share the Johnson band vocal spotlight equally with Ella.

He recorded another twenty-two titles with the Buddy Johnson band before leaving at the end of 1951. These tended to be the most popular recordings by the band and like the other Johnson records sold almost exclusively to the black community. All subsequent male vocalists hired by Buddy Johnson were in the Prysock mold. Ironically, when Prysock left the band, it was because he had cut a hit single for Decca ("I Couldn't Sleep a Wink Last Night"), produced by Milt Gabler, the very producer who held back "They All Say I'm the Biggest Fool." Tenor saxophonist Purvis Henson joined the Johnson band in late 1946 and became the most heavily featured soloist on the band's recordings from that point forward.

The Erskine Hawkins band had three hits in 1946, but the results were a bit deceptive. "Sneakin' Out" was a composition by alto sax star Bobby Smith (who also wrote "Tippin' In") featuring solo work from the composer, tenor saxophonist Julian Dash, pianist Ace Harris, and trumpeters Bobby Johnson and Hawkins. Musically, it is a solid performance of pure swing. This sort of item appeared with much less frequency on the popularity charts in years to come.

"I've Got a Right to Cry" was a cover of the Joe Liggins hit. The tempo is ponderous, and the vocal by Laura Washington is pedestrian. The success of the record, which stayed on the Race Charts for ten weeks, seemed to owe more to the RCA distribution system and the song rather than the performance. The final item was a reissue, "After Hours," recorded in 1940 featuring pianist Avery Parrish. The record industry was finally back to something approximating full steam and was able to reissue key titles from an earlier time that had not been retained in the catalog because of the shellac rationing during the war. Late in the year, the band recorded "Hawk's Boogie" featuring pianist Harris, saxophonist Dash, guitarist Leroy Kirkland, as well as trumpeters Johnson and Hawkins. The spirited outing became the last major hit for this band. It enjoyed an eight-week run on the charts, peaking at #2, in May 1947.

The top records of 1946 showed a distinct trend. While the big bands were still scoring hits, it was becoming a small combo world very quickly. The biggest stars were the King Cole Trio with four hits (including "For Sentimental Reasons," which became a #1 pop hit) and Louis Jordan's Tympany Five with six, including "Choo Choo Ch'Boogie," the year's top single.

LOUIS JORDAN

Louis Jordan (1908–1975) came up through the sideman ranks as an alto saxophonist with Charlie Gaines and Chick Webb before forming his own small band in Harlem in 1938. The group, which came to be billed as Louis Jordan and the Tympany Five, grew steadily in popularity fueled by some important Decca recordings. The model for the Jordan group was Fats Waller. The performance mix consisted of hot instrumentals, novelty vocals, blues, and an occasional blue ballad. This little group swung like mad! Jordan's vocal personality may have sold the group to a large audience, but he was equally important as an alto saxophone player.

Until Louis Jordan, the instrument had found as its principal models the elegant sound of Benny Carter or the sensual brilliance of Johnny Hodges and Willie Smith. Jordan could play sweetly; but more often his tone was raspy, dirty, aggressive, and bluesy. He was frequently cited as an influence by alto saxophonists in the immediate postwar era.

Jordan had an experienced professional manager in Berle Adams, and it made a huge difference. Jordan became a radio star and was featured in movies. Beginning in 1942, his recordings were produced by Milt Gabler, who managed to pair Jordan in popular duets with other Decca stars such as Bing Crosby and Ella Fitzgerald. Special events such as the duets meant that Jordan's name was coming before the public in ways that most other black artists found impossible to attain.

Jordan had become a star during the war when his records began to sell in massive quantities. Between 1942 and 1945, he had five #1 Race Chart recordings. But none of that compares with 1946: in that year he had an astonishing thirteen records in the top 3 on the Race Charts with six reaching #1! While he never had another year quite like that, Louis Jordan had another seven #1 hits before things began winding down for him in 1950.

The group usually featured tenor sax and trumpet in addition to Jordan's alto, but first and foremost, Jordan managed to develop great rhythm sections. Guitarists Carl Hogan and Bill Jennings and bass players Al Morgan, Jesse "Po" Simpkins, and Dallas Bartley with drummer Joseph Morris, known professionally as Chris Columbus, formed a truly versatile unit. Pianists Wild Bill Davis and Bill Doggett were the players who achieved the greatest celebrity.

Davis began as a pianist/arranger in 1945 and was soon joined by Doggett. Because of Jordan's frequent recording sessions and radio appearances, there was a great demand for fresh material. In time, Doggett and Davis became almost interchangeable: while one was in New York working on new arrangements, the other was on the road playing the gigs. Davis became intrigued with the possibilities of the Hammond organ as a jazz instrument while still a member and left the Jordan organization in 1948 to pursue that dream although he would return for record dates from time to time. Doggett followed a similar path a few years later.

Louis Jordan was, without question, the biggest black star of the 1940s. But if his music represented the pinnacle of race music in the decade, it would not find a way to make a transition to the rhythm and blues era. Jordan stayed with Decca until 1954, but he had no hits at all over his final three years. Subsequent recording for Aladdin, RCA, and Mercury proved to be equally unsuccessful. His recordings of the 1960s and 1970s tended to be one-shot deals with small labels, several of them European.

Joe Liggins, Johnny Moore's Three Blazers, Roy Milton, Slim Gaillard, and the King Cole Trio continued to provide hits from Los Angeles, now becoming the source of more new race record hits than even New York. Much of the music was performed by three- or four-piece combos. The Cole Trio, Gaillard, and the Three Blazers each had a piano, guitar, and bass format. Female pianists/vocalists Hadda Brooks, Nellie Lutcher, and Julia Lee had substantial hits in the coming years. Lee was from Kansas City, but her popular risqué novelties were recorded for Capitol in Los Angeles. Other female pianists such as Camille Howard (with Roy Milton) and Devonia Williams (with Johnny Otis) made their mark around Los Angeles before the end of the decade.

NAT "KING" COLE

Nathaniel Adams Coles (1919–1965) was born in Montgomery, Alabama, but raised in Chicago. He led his first group as a teenager and made his recording debut with his brother Eddie in 1936. He settled in Los Angeles in 1937 and formed the first King Cole Trio with guitarist Oscar Moore and bassist Wesley Prince shortly thereafter. The trio specialized in jump tunes and novelty items, but their Decca recordings (from 1940 to 1941) featured solo vocals by Nat on tunes such as "This Will Make You Laugh," "That Ain't Right," and, especially, "Sweet Lorraine" that pointed the way to his postwar career.

Capitol Records, formed in 1942 by three very savvy music men, had gotten the jump on many of its smaller competitors when it settled with the AFM in 1943 and began recording while other labels such as RCA and Columbia were still affected by the musicians' strike. In November 1943, Capitol signed Cole and Stan Kenton, and both became closely identified with the label. Cole was a Capitol artist for the rest of his life.

Carlos Gastel, who would also handle Peggy Lee, had taken over management of Nat Cole. Gradually, over the next two or three years, Gastel transformed Cole from the leader of the King Cole Trio, where his exceptional piano playing was featured, to a preeminent balladeer and pop singer, rivaled only by Billy Eckstine. As a result, the emphasis on piano playing declined to the point that it was virtually nonexistent late in his career. While this was a loss for jazz in general, it was a natural transition in the career of the one of great performers of the era. The piano work that Cole produced on his own records, the first Norman Granz JATP concert and with Lester Young in 1942 and 1945, was enough to rank him as the finest pianist in California and one of the top players in the country.

ROY MILTON

Roy Milton (1907–1983) was born in Oklahoma but worked as a drummer, vocalist, and bandleader in Los Angeles beginning in the mid-1930s. His group was known as the Solid Senders and always had a strong, danceable beat. Milton was a capable vocalist; and the three-horn front line of trumpet, alto sax, and tenor sax was identical to that of Louis Jordan. Guitar was added to the lineup in late 1947, but that didn't change the sound of the band. Milton developed a repertoire of jump blues, novelty items, swing era standards, and blue ballads, many of which he wrote himself, that served him well throughout his career. The Milton beat was, initially, swing; but it made an easy transition to the rhythm and blues market by adding bluesier material with a bit more backbeat. Pianist Camille Howard, an exceptional blues and boogie-woogie stylist, and tenor saxophonist Buddy Floyd, with his sparsely noted, low moaning style, were the strongest soloists; but it was the ensemble sound that made the Solid Senders unique.

Ben Waller was Milton's manager, and he managed to keep the band in the limelight for more than a decade. The Milton band racked up nineteen national hits, including "RM Blues," "Information Blues," and "Best Wishes," with the Specialty label between 1946 and 1953. Later recordings for Dooto and King were not successful in the marketplace but were worthy performances in the Milton tradition. During the 1960s, Milton recorded singles for small, one-shot labels, but he gave up drums before the end of the decade. During the 1970s, he was frequently featured with Johnny Otis in a revue of fellow blues stars. He recorded two albums with Otis. His final recording was made in France in 1977 with some veterans such as saxophonist George Kelly and guitarist Roy Gaines.

A feature of the record business in the immediate postwar era was the advent of cover records. Most often the covers involved white artists recording songs that were hits in the black community. These covers were sold in white neighborhoods where the black recordings were not available. Because there were pockets of the country that independent distribution couldn't reach, it was also possible to have several hit versions of a hot song. In general, one version would be popular in a certain segment of the country while other versions staked out different territories. On occasion, a cover version of the same song could capture a portion of the audience as well as the original hit. In 1944, Cootie Williams Orchestra had respectable sales on "Is You Is or Is You Ain't (Ma' Baby)," which was a much bigger hit by Louis Jordan. Both Benny Carter and Nat Cole had hit versions with "I'm Lost": Carter's featured a big band while Cole's featured his trio. This trend continued in 1945 when Louis Armstrong (for Decca) and Roosevelt Sykes (for RCA Bluebird) both covered the big song of Private Cecil Gant, "I Wonder." Erskine Hawkins covered Louis Jordan's "Caldonia," and Woody Herman's white band recorded it as well, but that didn't stop Jordan from getting another #1 Race Record. These are only examples of instances where there were multiple hit versions of a song.

JOE LIGGINS

The number one record of 1945 was "The Honeydripper" by California pianist/vocalist Joe Liggins. Liggins first recorded the song in November 1944 for the Bronze label; but Leon Rene, the owner of

Exclusive Records, cut the song again with him in April 1945. This time the group was billed as Joe Liggins and His Honeydrippers. This version took off; and cover versions followed from Decca (Jimmie Lunceford), RCA Bluebird (Roosevelt Sykes again), and Columbia (Cab Calloway). When Liggins moved to Specialty Records in 1950, he recorded his song for the third time.

Liggins (1916–1987) was born in Oklahoma but raised in California since his late teens. He worked in various bands around Southern California before forming his own combo in 1944 to capitalize on the popularity of his song. The Honeydrippers featured a front line of alto sax and tenor sax supported by piano, guitar, bass, and drums. In its early years, their sound was more of a swing era combo with alto saxophonist Little Willie Jackson emulating Johnny Hodges while James Jackson had much in common with Buddy Tate, but over time a bit more insistent backbeat came to this group. Joe Liggins was a popular attraction around Los Angeles for many years. His record sales were modest for the most part, but he broke out nationally with three other songs: "Got a Right to Cry and "Tanya" (both 1946) and a huge #1 hit in 1950, "Pink Champagne."

INDEPENDENT PRODUCERS

The list of small record labels that appeared earlier in this chapter was, by no means, fixed. Small labels continued to arrive and, often as quickly, to fail. Many of these record labels were not run by music men. Some were run by retailers, others by jukebox operators or wholesalers, while still others were operated by owners with little or no connection to the music.

In order for the records to be made, someone had to deal with the musicians, unions, and studios to make certain the music was recorded in an orderly fashion. The title of Record Producer had not yet entered the lexicon in 1946. The men who made records for Columbia, Decca, or RCA were usually employees. Artist and Repertoire departments at the large labels contained men who chose material, supervised recording sessions, and approved the performance. Men such as Teddy Reig, Bob Shad, and Ralph Bass were employees of various labels at one time or another; but over time they became known as the first independent producers because they were not above operating on the side.

Teddy Reig was loud and boisterous and weighed about four hundred pounds at his peak. He was a record collector from his early teens and was among the swing fans, whooping it up at Benny Goodman's first New York theater dates. He got into the music business as a band boy with the Edgar Hayes band.

Savoy Records owner Herman Lubinsky was a tight, crusty dictator who wanted everything done his way. He would show up at New York clubs to do business with musicians and wouldn't order a drink. Reig introduced himself after watching Lubinsky being thrown out of a 52nd Street club. Reig had plenty of connections with musicians and club owners and had been involved in some session supervision on small labels prior to his involvement with Lubinsky. He convinced the Savoy owner that his knowledge and experience would benefit the label. He began working for Savoy in 1945 for the princely sum of $25 per week. His earliest work included artists such as Pete Brown and Herbie Fields who had already recorded for Savoy; but by the end of the year, he had recorded Ike Quebec, Charlie Ventura, Don Byas, and Erroll Garner. He also brought a pair of bright young stars to Savoy: Dexter Gordon and Charlie Parker. Reig did not produce all the Savoy sessions, but his projects were generally the most successful. In 1946, he produced sessions by Illinois Jacquet, Vido Musso, and Eddie "Lockjaw" Davis in addition to the first recordings of Allen Eager, J. J. Johnson, and Stan Getz.

Diminutive Bob (Shadrinsky) Shad was from the same Brooklyn neighborhood as Reig. He recalled a meeting with John Hammond where he was tested by having to identify soloists off records before Hammond would provide him with a recommendation. He got his start with Black & White, Continental, and Manor where he supervised the first Dizzy Gillespie date as a leader. That session produced "Salt Peanuts," "Bebop," "Good Bait," and "I Can't Get Started." When Herb Abramson departed National, Shad moved over there where he recorded many artists, including the Ravens and Charlie Ventura. The ultimate freelancer of this era, Shad produced for Savoy, Mercury, and other labels rarely with any credit.

Ralph (Rafaelo Basso) Bass was also a New Yorker, yet he started producing records in Los Angeles during WWII. He worked for Black & White, Beltone, and several others. The most memorable association in his early career was with T-Bone Walker (1910–1975). "Call It Stormy Monday" was Walker's biggest single record, but several others, during the years 1945–1947, sold well, and his entire output on Black & White is blues of the highest quality. Those recordings as well as sides recorded for the Comet label were eventually acquired by Capitol. While Walker would be considered a blues artist in the long term, at this particular time, distinctions of that sort had little meaning. Walker was the most popular black entertainer in Los Angeles during these years as well as being a guitarist of enormous influence. In his career, Bass worked with both jazz and blues artists, but most of his productions from the 1950s onward involved R&B artists.

Bass also worked with Slim Gaillard on several projects, including the wonderful "Slim's Jam" with Dizzy Gillespie and Charlie Parker. Jack McVea's recording of "Open the Door, Richard" was his biggest hit. In the years that followed, he was important to the careers of Big Jay McNeely, Johnny Otis, and Little Esther.

These three men were active in finding and developing talent throughout the years covered by this book, and they were not the only ones. Indeed, fairly quickly, there emerged men such as Henry Glover, Fred Mendelsohn, and Lew Simpkins—successful examples of producers who followed the same path. When not producing sessions for a label of their own, they were working for someone else's label, making records.

When the owners of Cosmo Records and National Records decided to open their own distributorship it led the way for dozens of similar arrangements. Such independent record distributors became a major growth factor in the record business. While distribution may seem to be a mundane business of shipping, receiving, warehousing, and inventorying, distributors were also actively involved in promoting the product of their labels and, often, the artists themselves. As this aspect of the record business grew, competition became fierce; and the temptation to change distributors was constantly being driven by favoritism, special incentives, and, in some territories, muscle. Over the span of this book, independent distribution would endure periods of growth, maturation, aging, and dissolution; but for the moment, it was the springboard toward getting national recognition for the artist and label.

The biggest song of 1947 was "Open the Door, Richard." This was a novelty with no fewer than six hit versions in the race music arena. It began as a vaudeville routine originated by comedian Dusty Fletcher. There were recordings by Count Basie (RCA), Louis Jordan (Decca), Fletcher's own version (National), and two for Columbia (the Three Flames and the Charioteers). The song was written and recorded first by Jack McVea. McVea was with the Lionel Hampton band when they backed Dusty Fletcher on a theater tour. He knew Fletcher's act cold and wrote the song to reflect what was being seen onstage. His record gained steam through a national appearance on Bing Crosby's radio show and in the film **Sarge Goes to Washington**. McVea's and Fletcher's recordings both crossed over to the pop charts; but the recordings by Basie and the Three Flames, because of superior distribution, each hit #1.

JACK MCVEA

A versatile reedman, Jack McVea (1914–2000) had worked with a variety of bands around Los Angeles before joining the Lionel Hampton band in 1940. Though he was best known for his work on both alto and tenor, he played baritone in the Hampton band. After leaving Hampton in 1943, McVea returned to Los Angeles. In time, he formed his own group often featured at the Downbeat Club on Central Avenue. He recorded for Rhythm, Melodisc, and Apollo before Ralph Bass signed him to Black & White in the fall of 1945. McVea recorded thirty-six sides for Black & White in the next eighteen months. While none of these sold to the level of "Open the Door, Richard," McVea's recordings were consistent sellers in the Los Angeles area.

McVea's records from this period are exemplary in their swing, paced by the leader's own alto and tenor sax work and the drums and vocals of Rabon Tarrant. The group usually consisted of trumpet, saxophone, and rhythm section, although there were additional players on some sessions. The model was clearly that of Louis Jordan's Tympany Five. McVea had been accustomed to working in Los Angeles and thus being available for JATP appearances or studio work, but the success of his hit record put him on the road, and he played all forty-eight states in 1947! Late in that year, he recorded fourteen titles for Exclusive and returned to his regular local routine.

Jack McVea was involved in Jake Porter's Combo label in the mid-1950s. He made some single records of his own and provided arrangements and backing for several vocal groups. While this work was clearly in the R&B vein, Jack McVea was never a rock 'n' roller. His only album, a jazz date cut in 1962 for the English 77 label, shows him in splendid form backed by a rhythm section of veteran Los Angeles players.

In 1966, Jack McVea began playing clarinet in the New Orleans pavilion of the Southern California theme park Disneyland. He was a part of a strolling trio with guitar and bass that would play in different locations within the area. He stayed there until he retired, with a pension, in 1991.

Louis Jordan continued to be the top race records artist in 1947 by a wide margin. He had two carryover hits from 1946 in the double-sided smash "Ain't Nobody Here but Us Chickens"/"Let the Good Times Roll." His #1 Race hits of the year were "Texas and Pacific," "Jack, You're Dead," and "Boogie Woogie Blue Plate." He had several others in the top 5.

The Jordan band had some personnel changes during 1947. Joseph "Chris Columbus" Morris joined the Tympany Five on drums; Chicagoan Eddie Johnson took over the tenor sax chair; and Bill Doggett, as pianist and arranger, began to assume a larger role. Doggett recorded with the group for the first time in November and took over the piano chair from Wild Bill Davis early the following year.

Lionel Hampton had two hits during 1947, both vocals. "I Want to Be Loved" was a cover of Savannah Churchill's big one; and "Blow Top Blues," which was recorded in 1945, featured a vocal by Dinah Washington. The Hampton band numbered as many as twenty-one pieces plus vocalists at one point during 1947, but several key members of the band had departed early in the year. Arnett Cobb took trumpeter Dave Page and trombonist Mitchell "Booty" Wood to form his first combo while Joe Morris recruited Johnny Griffin to join him in a similar venture. On the other hand, vocalist Wini Brown, drummer Earl Walker, high-note trumpeter Leo "the Whistler" Shepherd, and bassist-arranger Charles Mingus made significant contributions to the new band.

The band continued to be the top draw among the black orchestras; but those hard-charging instrumentals, such as "Flyin' Home" and "Air Mail Special," weren't selling as many records during 1947. There were several superb recordings by the band during the year. The two-sided Decca single "Mingus Fingers"/"Muchacho Azul" utilized the emerging talent of Charles Mingus. Wini Brown sang the classic blue ballad "Gone Again" while Hampton himself was in the spotlight for the low-flame favorite "Midnight Sun." "Red Top," written by Hampton saxophonist Ben Kynard, had a hit version by Gene Ammons on Mercury long before the Hampton band even recorded it! Those new labels were playing hardball.

Still, the great Lionel Hampton recording of 1947 was the concert version of "Stardust." The performance was paced by a spectacular opening solo by Willie Smith and included solos by Corky Corcoran, Charlie Shavers, and Hampton. It was issued by Decca in four parts on two 78s. The concert was part of a series presented in Los Angeles by local disc jockey Gene Norman and dubbed Just Jazz. These concerts were clearly modeled on JATP and continued into the early 1950s. Not to be outdone, Norman Granz rolled into Carnegie Hall on September 27 and had put on the most successful recorded concert in the lengthy history of JATP. This show featured Flip Phillips and Illinois Jacquet battling away on several tunes, most notably "Perdido." The records were issued on Mercury the following year in a three–78 rpm album and subsequently on 45 rpm, 10" LP, and, finally, 12" LP. Mercury always promoted heavily through the jukebox community, and it was possible to find "Perdido" on jukeboxes well into the 1960s.

Another significant development of 1947 was the debut of pianist Paul Gayten (1920–1991) on the De Luxe label. Gayten had minor hits with "True" and "Since I Fell for You," the latter featuring a vocal by Annie Laurie. As a result of this, he recorded more than sixty titles during the year. Gayten had one of the best working bands in New

Orleans for several years; and he and his label mate, Roy Brown, served notice that there was some major talent to be heard in New Orleans. He also recorded for Regal, Okeh, and various Chess labels over the next decade or so.

EDDIE HEYWOOD

At the end of 1947, Eddie Heywood signed with RCA Victor and recorded ten sides in a trio setting. This, by itself, would not be especially newsworthy except that it signaled the end of the Heywood sextets. Eddie Heywood Jr. (1915–1989) was a second-generation jazzman whose father was active in his hometown, Atlanta, Georgia, and had recorded for Okeh in 1923. Heywood worked with Benny Carter and Don Redman around New York beginning in 1938 and appeared with Billie Holiday on her "Fine and Mellow"/"Strange Fruit" session for Commodore.

Heywood led one of the last pure swing combos, beginning in 1943, and made some fine recordings for Commodore, Signature, and Decca. An accomplished pianist and arranger, his group sound was more attuned to John Kirby than Louis Jordan or Dizzy Gillespie. In Doc Cheatham, Vic Dickenson, and Lem Davis, the Heywood group employed some first-rate jazzmen; and for a time, with the addition of Henry Coker, the group included two trombones. Heywood, whose 1944 version of "Begin the Beguine" was a strong seller, found even more fame as a songwriter, composing such hits as "Canadian Sunset" and "Soft Summer Breeze" in the 1950s.

Other pianists were heard during the year: Nellie Lutcher on Capitol scored with "Hurry on Down" and "He's a Real Gone Guy" while Johnny Moore's Three Blazers featured Charles Brown on hits such as "New Orleans Blues" and "Merry Christmas, Baby." Hadda Brooks ("That's My Desire") and Julia Lee ("Snatch and Grab It") scored big hits. Albert Ammons, the great boogie-woogie stylist, not to be outdone by his son Gene, created an influential performance with "Swanee

River Boogie." Veterans such as Roosevelt Sykes, Memphis Slim, and Ivory Joe Hunter continued to be popular on record, while the recently arrived Amos Milburn had several Aladdin singles that demonstrated the potential of future stardom.

Dwight "Gatemouth" Moore recorded "I Ain't Mad at You" in 1943 for a tiny Kansas City label and rerecorded it for National in 1945. While it was only a modest success for Moore, it was recorded by Kansas City drummer Jesse Price in the fall of 1946, and both versions were still selling when Count Basie recorded it during the fall of 1947.

EDDIE "CLEANHEAD" VINSON

Eddie "Cleanhead" Vinson (1917–1988) had the biggest hit of his lengthy career with "Old Maid Boogie." Vinson was an unusual combination of bebop saxophonist and blues singer. Originally from Houston, Texas, Vinson was a part of the Milton Larkin Orchestra reed section in the late 1930s alongside Tom Archia, Arnett Cobb, and Illinois Jacquet. He left Texas with a blues show out of Chicago featuring Lil Green and Big Bill Broonzy. Vinson credited Broonzy with providing tips that influenced his own vocal style. In 1942, he joined the newly formed Cootie Williams Orchestra and stayed until 1945 when he formed his own group. Vinson's vocals sparked the Williams 1944 recordings of "Cherry Red Blues" and "Somebody's Got to Go" that were so successful. It was during his time with Williams that he came in touch with pianist Bud Powell, also a band member, and Charlie Parker, who occasionally subbed for Vinson in the Williams band. Vinson's conception on alto saxophone that combined a full tone (with considerable blues emphasis) and bebop phrasing was highly influential on the alto players of the next generation, including Cannonball Adderley, Sonny Criss, Hank Crawford, and Lou Donaldson.

Vinson himself recorded for Mercury from 1945 to 1947, King from 1949 to 1952, and Mercury again during 1954 and 1955. While Vinson was involved in R&B, his blues more accurately reflects the race music of the 1940s. He was never involved in rock 'n' roll and went through some very tough periods from the mid-1950s until the late 1960s. It was during one such slow period that he gave his compositions "Four" and "Tune Up" to Miles Davis who recorded them and kept the composer credit. His own groups, headquartered in Philadelphia, featured a mixture of old friends such as trombonist Milton Larkin and younger players such as Slide Hampton and John Coltrane. When the European market opened up for tours and recording in the 1960s, Vinson was a major beneficiary. By that time, he had settled in Los Angeles where he played locally with his own group but toured as a single, picking up rhythm sections at each new location. His recording activity picked up in 1967, and for the next twenty years, he made albums regularly in countries all over the world.

Labels that began in 1947 included MGM, which signed Billy Eckstine; Atlantic, which began with jump blues artists such as Joe Morris and Tiny Grimes; and Aristocrat and Miracle, new Chicago labels, which concentrated on blues as much as jazz. Sensation, Detroit-based, was another new entry and the first to exploit black talent in the Motor City.

LESTER YOUNG

Lester Young (1909–1959) became a major influence during this time. He had been living in California both before and after his army service in 1944 and 1945, but when JATP came to New York in 1946, Lester stayed. His work with Count Basie and Billie Holiday was known to tenor players, black and white. It was Holiday who gave him the nickname the President, soon shortened to Pres or Prez. If Stan Getz, Zoot Sims, Al Cohn, Brew Moore, Allen Eager, and others would be termed the Four Brothers School, then Gene Ammons, Dexter Gordon, Wardell Gray, and Paul Quinichette could be considered charter members of the Soul Brothers School. Each of these players, among dozens of others, was profoundly affected by Lester Young. His 1940s recordings for Keynote, Savoy, and Aladdin were strong sellers. Young benefited from the first-class management of Charlie Carpenter and the representation of the Gale Agency.

In the 1950s, Young was a strong nightclub attraction in New York City where he worked uptown at Small's Paradise and downtown at Birdland for lengthy periods on an annual basis. He played the national tours of JATP, but he was a part of shows promoted by the Birdland organization as well. He signed with Norman Granz for recording in late 1949; and his records appeared first on Mercury, then Clef, Norgran, and, finally, Verve. By 1956, his popularity had begun to wane, and the quality of his recorded performances began to vary. He was slowed by ill health in his last years, and that was compounded by his alcoholism.

The importance of Lester Young cannot be overstated. In the postwar era, his was the first new conception to gain a great following among musicians on different instruments. While the influence of Charlie Parker on modern jazz was all-encompassing and Illinois Jacquet became a powerful model for rhythm and blues saxophonists, each of their styles contained elements originated by Lester Young. It was not until the 1960s that the residual influence of Young's ideas began to disappear.

DIZZY GILLESPIE–CHARLIE PARKER

1945 was the year that Dizzy Gillespie (1917-1993) and Charlie Parker (1920-1955) consummated a musical relationship that had begun with their first meeting in 1940. Gillespie had been nursing plans for a big band. He had put those plans on the side during 1945.

During 1943 and 1944, they had played together in the orchestras of Earl Hines and Billy Eckstine. Reed players in the Eckstine band tended to absorb much of what Parker was doing while the trumpet players were fascinated by Gillespie. They had appeared together as sidemen on several record dates during 1945; but the two sessions they made under Gillespie's leadership in February and May 1945, for Guild, had turned the jazz audience on to something brand new: bebop.

This group appeared in New York concerts during May and June of 1945 and at the Three Deuces on Fifty-second Street but had not traveled. Parker was still an unknown to all but the most aware jazz fans. His first record date as a leader was made for Savoy in November 1945 and was released as Charley Parker's Ree Boppers. Dizzy Gillespie's

Rebop Six, including Parker, opened in Los Angeles, at Billy Berg's, for their first extended out-of-town appearance within a few days of the recording and well in advance of its release.

In California, Parker's heroin addiction, a part of his life since his midteens, got completely out of control. His professional demeanor disappeared, and Gillespie hired Lucky Thompson as an addition to the group to ensure that there would be six people on the bandstand at all times. On off nights, both Parker and Gillespie jammed with the local musicians, appeared on Jazz at the Philharmonic concerts, and made record dates. Without question, the gig at Billy Berg's spread bebop throughout the Los Angeles area.

While the gig was considered musically successful, there have been conflicting reports as to how strong the turnout was for this eight-week engagement. The Gillespie group was actually an *opening act* for Harry "The Hipster" Gibson, a pianist who specialized in boogie-woogie and novelty vocals ("Who Put the Benzedrine in Mrs. Murphy's Ovaltine," among others). The intermission group was headed up by Slim Gaillard who had hit novelty items ("Flat Foot Floogie" and "Cement Mixer," among others) of his own, so it was an unusual booking, to say the least. Southern California was in the midst of an economic downturn what with the closing of defense plants and the resulting high unemployment, so that may have provided a drag on attendance. Pianist Russ Freeman, who heard the group over the radio, reported that while the crowds were decent, especially in the first couple of weeks, the people were clearly not getting the Gillespie message. Yet Berg had worked with New York agencies before, and if business fell off as badly as some have suggested, he surely could have cut the date short. When the job was over, Gillespie and the remainder of the group (Ray Brown, Al Haig, Milt Jackson, and Stan Levey) returned to New York. Charlie Parker cashed in his ticket and stayed in California.

This marked the end of a significant aspect of the Parker-Gillespie relationship. From that point forward, Charlie Parker would be his own man. He was always welcome on Dizzy Gillespie's stage, and the old, combined brilliance was quickly recaptured whenever they appeared together, but Dizzy Gillespie would never again be responsible for him.

Gillespie returned from California in February 1946 and made an important record date for RCA Victor. The session involved several of the players who had traveled to California with him but with Don Byas on tenor sax instead of Charlie Parker. The music, which included "52nd Street Theme" and "Night in Tunisia," was coupled with four sides by Coleman Hawkins, recorded the same week, in a 78 rpm album titled *New 52nd Street Jazz*. RCA would not permit the use of the word *bebop*. The album sold well, and there was a considerable amount of publicity building around Dizzy Gillespie.

He formed his big band, signed with Musicraft, and made some significant recordings during the second half of 1946. However, the label could not sustain itself, and the band had not recorded for almost ten months when it made its first session for RCA Victor in August 1947. "Oo PaPa Da" from the session gained considerable airplay and got the band off to a good start. But what came the following month created something entirely different.

On September 29, the Gillespie Orchestra played Carnegie Hall in a big show featuring a reunion with Charlie Parker, a guest vocalist in Ella Fitzgerald, and the introduction of the master Cuban percussionist Chano Pozo. The new pieces introduced that night included works by John Lewis, Tadd Dameron, and Gil Fuller; but it was "Cubana Be, Cubana Bop" by George Russell, featuring Pozo, that stole the show. The dynamic Pozo opened the door to a new direction for Gillespie. From that point forward, Gillespie was at least as interested in pursuing Afro-Cuban projects as he was bebop. The evening was recorded, and portions were later issued on a variety of labels. The first sessions for RCA Victor with Gillespie and Pozo were completed on December 22 and 29. They proved to be the only ones. Pozo was murdered in a Harlem bar in December 1948.

DRUGS

Record distribution was not the only distribution business making rapid strides in 1947. The wholesale and retail business of illegal drug sales began to mushroom during this time. Within a few months of the end of WWII, illicit drug sales were common in every big city black neighborhood. American organized crime, which was behind the expansion of the drug trade, worked to establish the import and distribution on a national basis and dealt with middlemen and retailers on a local level. The sale of illegal drugs proved to be the single most successful American business enterprise of all time.

Despite billions of dollars in government spending attempting to stanch the drug trade, nothing has been able to stop it. It began with the distribution of heroin and cocaine while marijuana sales were added when that substance was banned in 1937. In time, sophisticated new designer drugs and pills were added to the mix, and each new product line found a ready clientele. Organized crime looked to the drug business to replace the income lost in illegal liquor sales when Prohibition was repealed. It succeeded beyond anyone's expectations. By the time the period covered in this book concludes, entire neighborhoods, indeed some cities, were completely decimated by the drug trade. The toll on the lives of musicians was considerable.

In April 1947, trumpet player Freddie Webster died of a heroin "hotshot." Webster had an especially lovely tone and was highly influential on the conception of Miles Davis. Never a star, Webster worked with a variety of musical organizations large and small and made just one obscure record date under his own name. He is featured on some Sarah Vaughan titles such as "You're Not the Kind" and "If You Could See Me Now." Webster's death was the first of many similar tragedies.

THE 1948 RECORDING BAN

With the recording ban of January 1, 1948, it was clear that things would be a bit different from the first ban of 1942–1944. The earlier ban affected just a couple of dozen labels, but the 1948 ban involved hundreds. With the ban on the horizon, all labels ramped up the amount of recording they did during 1947, stockpiling masters to release for an undetermined amount of time. Prior to the effective date of the settlement on December 13, 1948, the ban was observed by all the major labels: Columbia, RCA Victor, Decca, and Capitol. Some small labels observed the decree as well, and many did not survive into 1949. Other small labels, however, violated or generally ignored the recording ban.

For Bob Shad and Ralph Bass, the ban presented a problem. Each man solved his problem the same way. Bass, being based in Los Angeles, where the concert recordings of Norman Granz had created such a sensation, had recorded his own concert at the Auditorium Theater during 1946. It featured Lucky Thompson, Howard McGhee, Jack McVea, and others who were regular participants on his record dates. In July 1947, he recorded a marathon evening at the Elks Hall on Central Avenue featuring Dexter Gordon, Wardell Gray, McGhee, Trummy Young, Sonny Criss, and others. They were first issued during 1948 on a label called BOP and, usually, featured one extended solo for an entire 78 rpm side. By the end of 1948, Bass had joined the Savoy label as director of West Coast operations; and the BOP masters had been sold to Savoy where they appeared over time, in multiple volumes in all configurations, under the banner of Hollywood Jam Session.

Shad managed to start his own Sittin' in With label with a pair of titles, "Dream Girl"/"Get Lost," recorded by Charlie Ventura and Chu Berry, in a Philadelphia music store shortly before Berry's 1941 death. The label, along with sister labels Harlem, Jax, Jade, and Dale, were operated by Shad and his brother Morty intermittently while he pursued roles with Mercury and Decca. During the ban, Shad recorded up-and-coming jazz stars such as Allen Eager, Wardell Gray, and Stan Getz before concentrating more on country blues, especially Lightnin' Hopkins.

Teddy Reig was once described by Arnett Cobb as the man "who broke the recording ban." While that wasn't exactly true, it was a reasonable description of Reig's activities during 1948. Reig continued producing sessions because he realized that if he wasn't making records, Lubinsky wouldn't pay him. Reig recorded double sessions with Paul Williams and Leo Parker as well as a single session with Brownie McGhee in March; Hal Singer, Earl Coleman, and Morris Lane in June; Milt Buckner, Ralph Willis, and Brownie McGhee (again) in July; Hal Singer (again), Sir Charles Thompson, and Charlie Parker (twice) in September; and Brownie McGhee (a third time!) and Brew Moore in October. And then there was the Black Deuce.

The September 29, 1947, concert of Dizzy Gillespie at Carnegie Hall had been recorded on sixteen-inch acetate discs by the in-house recording service. During 1948, selections of the Gillespie–Charlie Parker portion of that evening were issued on three unnumbered 78s on the Black Deuce label. The songs were "A Night in Tunisia Parts 1 and 2," "Groovin' High Parts 1 and 2," and "Confirmation"/"Dizzy Atmosphere." They were issued as the Dizzy Gillespie–Charlie Parker Quintet.

There was a considerable amount of confusion regarding the recording contract of Charlie Parker. While he was in California, Ross Russell of Dial Records had signed Parker to an exclusive contract in 1946. While Parker was at Camarillo State Hospital recovering from a breakdown, Russell issued "Lover Man," a performance recorded the night of Parker's breakdown, which the artist considered demonstrably inferior. Upon his return to New York in the spring of 1947, Parker renewed acquaintances with Teddy Reig. Within days, an agreement surfaced, in Reig's handwriting, backdated to 1945, stating that Parker owed Savoy more recording.

Herman Lubinsky considered Charlie Parker to be *his* artist. Reig recorded him in May and again in December 1947; and when, years later, the Carnegie Hall acetates were discovered in the Savoy vault, it clinched the theory that the Black Deuce had been a Savoy operation. Reig and Lubinsky were constantly fighting, and when Reig left Lubinsky's employ, he took the Black Deuce masters with him. They subsequently appeared on Birdland and Roost LPs. Roost was originally Royal Roost, named after a Broadway nightclub, and founded by Teddy Reig and his partners in the fall of 1948.

The activities of Reig during 1948 might suggest that business as usual was the rule at Savoy, recording ban or no recording ban. Lubinsky routinely screamed bloody murder when another label, such as Blue Note, was discovered doing a session during the ban. But while all this devious behavior was going on, something else was happening: Savoy had a hit.

HAL SINGER

On one of his surreptitious sessions, Reig recorded Hal Singer. Singer (1919–) was born in Tulsa, Oklahoma, and had worked in Midwestern territory bands such as those of T. Holder, Ernie Fields, Nat Towles, and Jay McShann before coming to New York in 1943. Reig had been touted on Singer's abilities by Don Byas, a fellow Oklahoman, and had first used Singer on a Savoy date with alto saxophonist Lem Davis in early 1946. More recently, in March 1948, Singer had played behind Brownie McGhee on "My Fault," which would be a #2 Race hit for Savoy. Another good reason for recording Singer in 1948 was his opening break and solo on "Good Rockin' Tonight" by Wynonie Harris, a huge hit for King Records, recorded in December 1947.

"Cornbread" was a hard-driving tenor solo from start to finish with a boogie-woogie piano underpinning (played by sixteen-year-old Wynton Kelly, making his recording debut) and riffing horns in the background. As a performance, it was exciting but not nearly as exciting as the reception in the black community. "Cornbread" became a #1 Race Records hit, the first honking-tenor sax instrumental to attain that position. It launched Singer on a career as a bandleader. He was signed to Shaw Artists Guild and was soon a regular attraction on theater tours and in nightclubs. Subsequent Savoy recordings went nowhere, and Singer recorded for a variety of labels throughout the next decade. Reig recorded him in three sessions for Coral during 1951 and 1952. He returned to Savoy for sessions directed by Lee Magid in 1952 and 1953. Fred Mendelsohn, another producer for Savoy, recorded "Hot Rod," perhaps his best post-"Cornbread" solo in 1955. When Mendelsohn moved to King/DeLuxe in 1956, he recorded Singer again but more frequently spotlighted his saxophone in the accompaniment to singers as diverse as Little Willie John, Titus Turner, Annie Laurie, and Little Jimmy Scott.

Singer had done this work for other labels as well, becoming one of the first tenor sax specialists in the highly competitive world of studio sidemen. As this work dried up in the late 1950s, Singer made his first LP, the exceptional *Blue Stompin'*, for Prestige. By 1964, Singer had moved to Paris where he resides to this day, still active.

Largely forgotten by American listeners, Singer has recorded a considerable number of LPs for various European labels in a jazz context. He has one other distinction. His signature song was so associated with him that he became the first in a long line of saxophonists to have the song title integrated into his professional moniker. For many years, he has been known as Hal "Cornbread" Singer.

JOHNNY OTIS

Johnny Otis (1921–2012) was born John Veliotes, of Greek-American extraction. He was raised in a black neighborhood of Oakland, California, and worked as a drummer in several all-black orchestras beginning in his late teens. He was a regular in the Central

Avenue entertainment district in Los Angeles and was working with the Harlan Leonard band when it folded. He was encouraged to form his own big band by the owners of the Club Alabam and was resident there for much of 1945. His first record date in September 1945 produced a hit with "Harlem Nocturne"/"Round the Clock Blues," the latter featuring a vocal by Count Basie's singer, Jimmy Rushing. The date was recorded for the local Excelsior label, which recorded several other fine sessions with the band. "Harlem Nocturne" sold well enough to get the Otis Orchestra on the road, and much of 1946 was spent traveling across the country, including an appearance at New York's Apollo Theater. Upon his return, Otis opened a nightclub called the Barrelhouse where he appeared with a small combo.

Until this time, Otis had been a drummer and was good enough to have recorded with Lester Young and Illinois Jacquet. In time, he gave up drums in favor of vibes. As his experience with the Barrelhouse grew, he began to discover and nurture young talent such as saxophonist Cecil McNeely and singer Esther Mae Jones. These artists were more oriented toward blues and black popular music than jazz, and as Big Jay McNeely and Little Esther, each was about to burst forth with a big hit record.

Lionel Hampton, Erskine Hawkins, Buddy Johnson, and Lucky Millinder were all signed to major labels and thus had no new recording sessions in 1948. They also, between them, had no hits. While Hawkins and Hampton were recorded very quickly after the settlement, it was fifteen months for Millinder and eighteen months for Buddy Johnson between recording sessions. While this period of enforced inactivity was not the final nail in the coffin for black big bands, it certainly contributed to their downfall.

Louis Jordan had one #1 Race hit in "Run Joe" and a #2 Race hit in "Barnyard Boogie," but in general, this was the slowest year for Jordan since 1941 since several of his records barely grazed the bottom of the charts. The sound of the Jordan group remained the same during the year, and the only major personnel change was the fact that Bill Doggett was now the permanent pianist.

Small combo instrumentals were very successful during 1948, but these were not bebop tunes or swing songs: they were, more often than not, blues or ballads. Newly arrived labels such as Sensation in Detroit and Miracle in Chicago were often the source of these new hits. Established labels such as Savoy and King were growing more prominent with a similar sound.

KING RECORDS

King had begun life in 1943, as a country and western label, owned by Syd Nathan, based in Cincinnati, Ohio. King's first black music was recorded in the summer of 1945 on the subsidiary Queen label. Queen continued until 1947 when it was folded into King. Because King recorded both country and race music, songs from their in-house publishing catalog would often be recorded by artists in both fields. In 1948, among those featured on the King roster was Bull Moose Jackson, who had huge hits with ballads such as "I Love You, Yes, I Do," a holdover from 1947, and "I Can't Go on Without You," a second #1 hit. The two-sided smash "All My Love Belongs to You"/"I Want a Bow-Legged Woman" coupled a ballad with a typical blues novelty. Jackson had formed his own touring band, the Buffalo Bearcats, which featured three horns and a four-piece rhythm section. Similar-size combos were appearing with regularity; and among those using similar instrumentations were saxophonists such as Arnett Cobb, Earl Bostic, and Illinois Jacquet.

Also on King was Wynonie Harris, a shouter in the Big Joe Turner mold, who had a big record with the aforementioned "Good Rockin' Tonight" and its follow-up "Lollypop Mama." Harris (1912–1969) had recorded for Aladdin, Apollo, Bullet, and Hamp-Tone before arriving at King in late 1947. Harris did not record with a working group, and his sessions were always produced with specially assembled groups of accompanists.

King had recording facilities in Cincinnati, and the Harris sessions recorded there featured players from the local area who would also back other King artists in similar fashion. At other times, these accompanying units would be made up of touring Midwestern groups such as those led by Todd Rhodes or Sonny Thompson. When Harris was recorded in New York, the players were most often current or former members of the Lucky Millinder band. Harris had strong years from 1948 to 1952, the year of his last hit record. His style would seem to be one that would easily translate into rock 'n' roll in the mid-1950s. In fact, it did not. With a few scattered exceptions, his recording career was over by the end of 1954, and he himself was out of the business by 1964.

LONNIE JOHNSON

Perhaps the most astonishing success story of 1948 was that of Lonnie Johnson (1894–1970). He was born in New Orleans and was possessed of a singular guitar style. That style, at once both jazzy and bluesy, was highly influential on players of the next generation such as B. B. King. He played with Louis Armstrong, Eddie Lang, and Duke Ellington, among dozens of others, as a studio sideman beginning in the mid-1920s. He recorded over one hundred thirty titles under his own leadership for Okeh from 1925 to 1932. Johnson's output ranged back and forth across blues and jazz but always at the highest level. After a hiatus during the Depression, he returned to recording in 1937 first with Decca and then, from 1938 to 1944, with RCA Bluebird. He came to King in December 1947.

Like so many black recording artists, Johnson was billed as a blues singer. Without question, Johnson could and did sing blues; but in his case, the label "blues singer" didn't begin to tell the story. The term was code for black vocalist so much so that Billie Holiday was also billed as a blues singer during this time. At the end of Johnson's first King session, he recorded a ballad, "Tomorrow Night," written in 1939. Johnson's recording utilized a guitar introduction not far removed from the trademark introductions of the Ink Spots and featured an impassioned vocal. The performance created a sensation. It became a #1 hit and stayed on the Race charts for thirty-three weeks. It even cracked the top 20 on the pop charts. King managed to sneak in an under-the-table date with Johnson in August of 1948 when he recorded another ballad, "Pleasing You." Using a similar formula, Johnson and King scored a #2 Race hit.

Lonnie Johnson remained at King through 1952. Apart from some sides for Rama in 1956, Johnson's recording career seemed over when it was revived by Prestige/Bluesville where he was recorded for LP release. He made four fine LPs during 1960–1962. He continued to record for a variety of labels through 1967.

All King recording was done under the direction of Henry Glover. This pioneering black producer is rarely mentioned in the history books. Glover was involved with King for almost fifteen years, and he produced important country artists as well. He deserves mention as a jazz producer of organ combos: the Bill Doggett and Eddie "Lockjaw" Davis–Shirley Scott groups first recorded for King. Glover later produced for Roulette.

The full impact of Dinah Washington was first felt in 1948. Her version of "It's Too Soon to Know" reached #2 and had an eleven-week run, but "Am I Asking Too Much" was her first #1. Significantly, this woman who had been thought to be a pure blues singer while in the employ of Lionel Hampton had turned out to be able to sing (and sell) love songs. She proved, over time, to be able to sing (and sell) almost anything.

Nellie Lutcher and Julia Lee had more piano/vocal novelty hits for Capitol during 1948. The former had several minor hits and one #2 smash, "Fine Brown Frame," while Lee connected for the second consecutive year with a huge #1, "King Size Papa," which lasted for twenty-eight weeks on the Race charts. Other substantial successes by female singers/pianists during the year included Paula Watson ("A Little Bird Told Me" on Supreme) and Rose Murphy ("I Can't Give You Anything but Love" on Majestic). Memphis Slim ("Messin' Around" on Miracle) and Ivory Joe Hunter ("Pretty Mama Blues" on Pacific) each had #1 hits among the male singers/pianists.

Three new blues stars emerged in Roy Brown, Pee Wee Crayton, and Arbee Stidham. Crayton was a California guitarist very much inspired by T-Bone Walker. He had a huge record with "Blues After Hours" on Modern. The tune is a slow instrumental featuring Crayton's guitar throughout. Stidham, originally from Arkansas, recorded "My Heart

Belongs to You" in Chicago with two saxes and Tampa Red on guitar. Each of these songs hit #1 on the Race charts with Stidham's staying for twenty-four weeks and in the process becoming RCA's biggest Race hit of the decade. Stidham never had another hit, but Crayton scored in 1949 with "Texas Hop" and "I Love You So."

Roy Brown scored the first #1 record by a New Orleans–based Race artist with "'Long about Midnight," the first of his "Midnight trilogy." "Rockin' at Midnight" and "Boogie at Midnight" were strong performers in 1949. And more hits would follow.

Blues shouters and guitar players were not new to the Race charts. But the number of bluesy instrumentals was a new phenomenon. Aside from "Cornbread," "Deacon's Hop," and "Blues After Hours," Detroit bandleader Todd Rhodes had a big hit with "Blues for the Red Boy." This slow grinder was a stripper's favorite for years and was used as a theme song by Alan Freed during his Ohio period. Sensation, the Detroit label that recorded Rhodes, recognized its inability to spread the song nationally; so they entered into a deal with Chicago-based Vitacoustic Records. A bit later, the masters were licensed by King.

SONNY THOMPSON

Yet the biggest instrumental was the two-part "Long Gone" by Sonny Thompson on Miracle. Born Alfonso Thompson (1916–1989) in Mississippi, his family moved to Chicago when he was very young, and he studied piano privately and at Wendell Phillips High School. His first recordings on the Sultan label in 1946 showed him to be a technically proficient player with a strong left hand. Despite the fact that the music recorded was boogie-woogie, one can hear the inherent talent in his playing. He had been working around Chicago, as a soloist for several years, when he came into the Miracle Records orbit. He was initially a session player with Gladys Bentley and Dick Davis until he began doing his own dates in late 1947. Producer Lew Simpkins recorded him as Sonny Thompson with the Sharps and Flats. On the third session, Simpkins and Thompson collaborated on a slow two-part blues, "Long Gone." Part 1 featured a Thompson piano solo and a guitar solo by Alvin Garrett. Part 2 featured a tenor solo by Eddie Chamblee. The record entered the Billboard Race Charts in May, hit #1 in July, and stayed on the charts for almost eight months! Thompson followed up with "Late Freight," another slow blues that hit #1. The success of these recordings launched Thompson as a national touring attraction, who often composed hit material for himself and others. In time, he signed with King and teamed with vocalist Lula Reed. He always kept a tenor sax in his recording groups. After 1950, it was usually David "Bubba" Brooks.

Meanwhile, Eddie Chamblee, who had billing on part 2 of "Long Gone," had his Chicago gigs billed as Eddie "Long Gone" Chamblee. The record launched Chamblee's career as a prominent Chicago session man and ultimately as a recording artist and touring bandleader in his own right.

That is not the end of "Long Gone." The theme is a statement virtually identical to Meade Lux Lewis's tune "Yancey Special," and in January 1950, a lawsuit claiming plagiarism was launched by Lewis's publisher. To the astonishment of almost everyone, the judge ruled for the defendant, and the tune was placed in the public domain!

Sonny Thompson recorded for King Records through 1956. He was also heard backing other groups, without credit, notably the Charms on De Luxe. He cut several sides for the Chart label around this time but from this point forward devoted most of his time as a music director and producer of recording sessions for Chess and King, where he was a part of Freddie King's early successes. His final recording was an album for the Black and Blue label during a 1972 tour of France.

One of the great ballads of 1948 was "It's Too Soon to Know." There were hit versions of the song by Ella Fitzgerald and Dinah Washington, but the original version and the #1 hit was by the Orioles. This group was originally from Baltimore and featured the romantic lead singing of Earlington Tilghman, known professionally as Sonny Til. The Orioles had a huge impact on the scene and scored two more #1 hits with "Tell Me So" (1949) and "Crying in the Chapel" (1953) for the Jubilee label. In tandem with the Ravens, an older and more established group, they set the example for many black vocal groups, often with the names of birds, who became an exploding part of the business in the coming years.

Music wasn't the only area where newly important arrivals would affect the scene. In 1948, Larry Doby and Satchel Paige became the first black players on a World Series–winning baseball team. Doby had joined the Cleveland Indians in 1947 but had played sparingly. In 1948, playing center field, he had come into his own and, like Jackie Robinson of the Brooklyn Dodgers, went on to a Hall of Fame career. Teddy Reig recorded Brownie McGhee celebrating the new era on "Robbie Doby Boogie" on Savoy. Buddy Johnson followed a few months later with "Did You See Jackie Robinson Hit That Ball?"

Later in the 1948 season, Leroy "Satchel" Paige was signed by the Indians and won six of seven decisions. Paige was forty-two years old and a legendary talent from the Negro Leagues. The remainder of the American League was slow to integrate: segregation was still the law in Washington, D.C., and St. Louis; and the owners of teams such as the Boston Red Sox, Philadelphia Athletics, and New York Yankees were a long way from becoming enlightened. New York did not add a black player until 1954, and Boston waited until 1959. As a result, when Cleveland came to Detroit to play the Tigers, the park was sold out with Detroit-area black people coming to root for Larry Doby of the Indians!

Until 1948, commercial records were manufactured to play at 78 rpm. All that changed when Columbia introduced the long-playing record at a New York press conference on June 21, 1948. Long-playing records at Columbia were pressed on vinyl, a quieter surface when compared to shellac 78s. The actual grooves were smaller (microgroove), and a special stylus was needed to play them. There were few phonographs available to play the new, 33 1/3 rpm speed, but Columbia had made a deal to package a player with three LPs for a special price. Less than two weeks later, the label had one hundred titles on sale in the new format. The most popular form of LP would be 10" with the longer, more expensive 12" LP initially used for classical recordings. Over time, the 10" LP would disappear, and the 12" would become standard. There was no patent on the LP since Columbia wanted other labels to participate in order to ensure the success of the format. Decca and Mercury were aboard almost immediately.

Until this point, virtually all innovation regarding phonograph records had come from RCA. It seemed unlikely that Columbia's main rival would embrace the new idea, and indeed, it was two full years before RCA issued its own line of LPs. But RCA was not about to concede first place in phonograph technology to Columbia. They would surely come up with something.

By 1948, tape was beginning to replace acetate as the primary mode of recording. Decca was the first label to begin tape recording full-time. Bing Crosby, the biggest star on Decca, was an early investor in the Ampex Corporation, the manufacturer of tape machines. While the changeover was implemented at independent recording studios as the opportunity presented itself, by 1950 the conversion was virtually complete. Acetate would still be utilized, but now it was used for cutting individual demo records that had been recorded on tape. It would continue to be used for that purpose until the advent of the cassette.

Long-playing records. Bird groups. Bebop. Dozens of new record labels. Jazz at the Philharmonic. Heroin. These were just some of the things that contributed to the changes in race music in the few short years following the end of WWII. There had been little in the way of recording during 1948, but with the end of the AFM ban, there would be much more to come. There would be more technical innovation, there would be more heroin, there would even be more war. And the music? That would surely continue to change, to evolve, to embrace new rhythms, new labels, and new stars. But it would be called something other than race music.

Illinois Jacquet, 1992 by Joe Rosen

ILLINOIS JACQUET

MIDSUMMER NIGHT'S SWING IS A series of dance-oriented concerts presented out of doors during June and July by Lincoln Center in New York City. Founded in 1989, each concert in the series contains a different style of music; the final concert of the season for the first sixteen years had been by the big band of Illinois Jacquet. This band was the last link to the venerable New York institution, the Savoy Ballroom. The Savoy, known uptown as "the Track" and to the general public as "the home of happy feet" was the great dancehall of Harlem.

The Jacquet band had a solid beat, one that attracted Broadway dancers on a night off as well as swing dancers of all shapes and sizes. It did not directly reflect the music of Lionel Hampton, Cab Calloway, or Count Basie, in whose orchestras Illinois Jacquet starred back in the 1940s. Yet it did conjure up images of those bands and others who reflected the black swing tradition. It was a tradition Illinois Jacquet knew well.

Although Jacquet was born in Broussard, Louisiana, in 1919, he was raised in Houston, Texas. His father worked for the Southern Pacific Railroad. His father, two sisters, and three brothers were all musicians. He attended Phyllis Wheatley High School in Houston and was taught music by Percy McDavid, an educator often cited by his students as a major influence on their lives. In 1937, he joined the Milt Larkin band in Houston on alto saxophone. His fellow alto saxophonist was Eddie Vinson, not yet Cleanhead. The tenor chairs were occupied by Tom Archia, a high school classmate of Jacquet's, and Arnett Cobb, he of the big sound and commanding presence. While Jacquet would become known as a "Texas tenor," the truth is that while he was living in Texas, he played alto saxophone. And for someone who has been honored by the states of Louisiana and Texas, the city of Los Angeles played an important, if generally uncredited, role in his development.

In September 1939, he was sent by his family to study with Lloyd Reese at Los Angeles City College. A brother and sister accompanied him. Reese had a number of pupils, including Dexter Gordon, who went on to achieve professional stardom. While his formal study lasted only a semester, Jacquet participated in the local jam session scene and became well known around the city. He struck up a friendship with Nat Cole, the leader of the King Cole Trio. Cole was a pianist whose influence on the local scene was enormous. In time, it would be his singing that made him a household name. Another friendship was developed with Aaron "T-Bone" Walker, the great guitarist and blues singer. Walker, at the time, was the most popular black entertainer in Los Angeles.

In May and July 1940, Nat Cole recorded with Lionel Hampton for RCA. In October of that year, Hampton left Benny Goodman and formed his own big band. He offered the piano chair to Nat Cole. Cole declined but recommended his young friend Illinois Jacquet. Hampton already had Marshall Royal and Ray Perry booked to play alto sax, so Jacquet joined the Hampton band on tenor saxophone.

Jacquet became a star soloist in the first Lionel Hampton band with his solo on "Flyin' Home" in 1942. A short bit on "In the Bag," the B side of "Flyin' Home," was his only other solo with Hampton. There have been rumors of other features and even a tenor battle with Dexter Gordon, but no recorded evidence has ever surfaced. The influence of Illinois Jacquet on the Hampton band continued long after his departure since his replacements were invariably called on to produce the same level of excitement.

In 1943, he left Hampton for the band of Cab Calloway. On the surface, the move looks unusual. Hampton's band was playing great jazz nightly while Calloway's band was fronted by a vocalist more interested in entertaining the audience with novelty songs. Yet the status was different. Calloway had been on the scene more than a decade while Hampton's crew was new. The chair Jacquet was moving into had once been occupied by Chu Berry, one of his heroes. Jacquet inherited several of Berry's features. The Calloway job also paid substantially more money.

The Calloway tenure proved to be a source of frustration for Jacquet. Because of the AFM recording ban, no commercial recordings were made during his time in the band. Calloway would not perform "Flyin' Home" because of its association with Hampton. There are a few airchecks that demonstrate the evolution of the Jacquet style, and he can be seen on-screen as a member of the Calloway band in the feature film **Stormy Weather**.

Back in Los Angeles in the spring of 1944, with the help of his brother trumpeter Russell Jacquet, Illinois formed a band that had an extended stay at Billy Berg's Swing Club in Hollywood. During this period, he began an association with promoter Norman Granz. Granz ran jam sessions at local clubs on off nights; but on July 2, 1944, he promoted a benefit concert to aid in the defense of some Chicano youngsters who had run afoul of the law. The concert was billed as Jazz at the Philharmonic because the event was held at the Philharmonic Auditorium. The success of that first concert sparked additional Granz-promoted shows, all featuring Jacquet. The first concert was recorded by the Armed Forces Radio Service for broadcast to American troops overseas. That same summer, Jacquet was a part of a Granz-assembled cast in the award-winning film short **Jammin' the Blues**. In August 1945, the Jacquet band made its first recordings. The band recorded for Aladdin, Apollo, and ARA all in the same month! Yet the band broke up the following month so that Illinois could join Count Basie.

The Basie period was a very good one for Illinois Jacquet. He was featured on the band's new recordings of "Mutton Leg" and "The King," and his playing drew rave notices wherever the band appeared. It looked as though he would settle in for a good long run as a star soloist in one of the greatest jazz bands of all time. Then in early 1946 came the first Jazz at the Philharmonic records.

Recognizing the potential in the live recordings, Granz arranged to record his concerts whenever possible. A concert of February 12, 1945, had "How High the Moon" and "Lady Be Good" recorded. The nine-piece group featured Jacquet in the company of Willie Smith, Charlie Ventura, Howard McGhee, and Gene Krupa, among others. Those were the first JATP sides released on record. Shortly thereafter, "Blues" and "Lester Leaps In" from the July 2, 1944, concert were issued.

Those recordings created a sensation. The lengthy performances would often take four 78 rpm sides to complete. For the first time, the

Jacquet style, featuring incredible energy and climactic, screaming high notes, was on display in multichorus solos taking up a full side of a 78 record. This was a brand-new, innovative style for the tenor saxophone.

The critical reception given the recordings was varied: there was universal praise for the work of pianist Nat Cole and guitarist Les Paul, but the work of Illinois Jacquet was given short shrift by white critics. He was viewed as someone who relied on tricks to stir the audience to pandemonium. While this view has modified with the passing of time, a white musician/critic recently referred to those solos as "silly."

There were more JATP performances and more recording for Savoy and Apollo in 1946. Jacquet starred with Coleman Hawkins and Lester Young in the first New York concerts of JATP and left the Basie band in August. By early 1947, his touring band had been formed.

The basic instrumentation was two trumpets, tenor sax, baritone sax, piano, bass, and drums. A trombone was added a few months later. For recording sessions, a rhythm guitar or alto sax was sometimes added. The band served as a model for many other "little big bands" that would appear on the scene over the next decade. During 1947, recording was done for Apollo, Aladdin, and RCA Victor. The RCA Victor deal, which began in December, was an exclusive contract and a big step-up for the saxophonist. The band was all-star caliber with trumpeter Joe Newman, trombonists J. J. Johnson and Henry Coker, baritone saxophonist Leo Parker, pianists Sir Charles Thompson and John Lewis, as well as drummers such as Shadow Wilson and Jo Jones on board at one time or another.

Yet the JATP experience continued. In the late 1940s, JATP toured in the spring and fall of the year. Beginning in 1950, the tours were done in the fall only. As international touring became possible, that was done in the spring while the domestic tours, averaging about six weeks in length, would begin in early September. A live recording of a Carnegie Hall concert on September 27, 1947, which teamed Jacquet and Flip Phillips on tenor saxophones, helped put JATP on the permanent map.

The key item of the four tunes recorded that night was "Perdido," written by trombonist Juan Tizol and well known in its recording by the Duke Ellington Orchestra. The lengthy solos, first by Phillips, then trumpeter Howard McGhee, Jacquet, and trombonist Bill Harris, created enormous audience response. The arrangement worked out by

Phillips and Jacquet on the closing bridge served to increase the tension of the performance.

The new configurations of records, 45 rpm and 33 1/3 rpm, permitted "Perdido" to be issued on 78 and 45 singles or LP. In the latter case, the complete performance could be heard over the two sides of a ten-inch LP. The 45 rpm version was a big jukebox item for many years. In time, everything recorded that evening (including "Mordido" and "Endido") came to be released on twelve-inch LP, but "Perdido" was the biggest selling of all JATP recordings.

The emphasis on the tenor sax competition in "Perdido" created the anticipation of excitement in the JATP shows that was nearly always delivered. It created a permanent spot for Phillips in a continually changing roster of star talent recruited for each tour. Jacquet rejoined JATP in 1951, but for the moment, he was hot all by himself.

Jacquet recordings on Aladdin ("Flyin' Home Parts 1 and 2" and "Jivin' with Jack the Bellboy") and Apollo ("Bottoms Up" and, especially, "Robbins' Nest") were big sellers, and the RCA contract produced a hit song in 1949 with "Black Velvet" (known as "Don'cha Go Away Mad" when a lyric was added). Jacquet was a very hot attraction on the club circuit and was frequently teamed with Ella Fitzgerald for concert appearances. He appeared on the Ed Sullivan–hosted **Toast of the Town** TV show in 1948.

When Jacquet's RCA contract had been completed, he turned to Norman Granz for recording. Granz had a production and distribution deal with Mercury.

Granz and Jacquet struck pay dirt in 1952 when one of his recordings, "Port of Rico," became the first organ and tenor sax hit. The organist was his old boss Count Basie; and the tune was titled to honor Buffalo, New York, DJ Joe Rico, although some insist it was intended to honor the MC of the Apollo Theater Amateur Night. The record had an eleven-week run on the R&B charts, peaking at #3. The performance itself was relaxed and laid back—a far cry from the honking and squealing style he introduced in the 1940s.

The last recordings with the group were cut at the end of 1954, and the group disbanded shortly thereafter. The cost of fronting a band that size became prohibitive. In 1955, Jacquet rejoined JATP after a three-year absence and was also featured on the tours of 1956 and 1957. His own recordings were albums by this time, all-star affairs with guests such as Sweets Edison and Roy Eldridge. His final session for Granz was with organist Wild Bill Davis. Clearly, this was an attempt to recapture some "Port of Rico" magic, but it didn't happen.

With the dissolution of JATP, club work for Jacquet slowed in the late 1950s. He worked frequently as a single, picking up rhythm sections at each new venue. One-shot recordings were made for Roulette (1959) and Epic (1962), which attempted to recapture the band sound. When Esmond Edwards signed him to Argo in 1963, there was a genuine attempt to bring him back to prominence.

The Argo period found him in excellent settings with new material prepared for him, but he was undergoing some dental problems at the time, and results don't quite reach the heights they might have under different circumstances. The period did produce three excellent combo albums, his only recording with a string orchestra and his first live album featuring organist Milt Buckner.

By the mid-1960s, Buckner would be a frequent companion in a joyous little trio that often found Jo Jones or Alan Dawson in the drum chair. This group lasted until Buckner's death in 1977. During the same period, Jacquet often used guitarist Tiny Grimes or bassist Slam Stewart as featured stars in piano-based units. He made four LPs for Prestige during 1968 and 1969. The music was superb, but sales were disappointing.

The 1970s found Jacquet working regularly in Europe and Japan. The opening of international markets was beneficial to many other musicians of his era. Jacquet had been to Europe for the first time in 1954 but would be a regular world traveler for much of the decade. He was recorded frequently during the 1970s for labels in England, Holland, Sweden, and Japan; but his most rewarding work was done for the French label, Black & Blue. From 1972 to 1978, he made six LPs for Black & Blue and appeared on projects by other artists as well. There was a studio date for an English label, and his participation in an all-star jam recorded in Tokyo in 1980.

In 1983, Jacquet formed a big band. This seems impossible. By their midsixties, most jazzmen are content to do what works best for them in performance and to seek a comfort zone in terms of travel. Jacquet plunged into the tasks of orchestra leader and assembled a unique and distinctive band that recalled the very best of the black swing ensembles. An interesting mixture of eager youngsters and seasoned veterans formed the unit, and while the turnover in personnel was considerable, there were always quality players on board. In dealing with the music, Jacquet was a perfectionist and rehearsed the band like a drill sergeant. He insisted on the proper dynamics, intonation, and feeling for each piece. He attracted arrangements from the likes of Neal Hefti, Phil Wilson, and Wild Bill Davis. Eddie Barefield, who played with the band for several seasons, wrote some of the more popular arrangements. As a front man, Illinois Jacquet featured a dapper, elegant appearance and a penchant for talking to his audience. The only recording of the band is *Jacquet's Got It*, a 1987 Atlantic album, although there is music by the band from a European tour included in his film biography, **Texas Tenor**, by Arthur Elgort. Two CDs of live performances in Europe were issued after his death.

Illinois Jacquet was an important figure in jazz for a number of reasons. He was an innovator as well as an immensely popular stylist. That combination is most unusual since even the greatest jazz players are generally one or the other. Chu Berry was an influence on the young Jacquet while Ben Webster's influence revealed itself over time. Certain aspects of Lester Young's playing were incorporated into his style while others, gleaned from Herschel Evans, were also apparent. Yet the synthesis was complete early in his career. He had formed a unique, original saxophone style. His playing was instantly recognizable, and it led directly to his stardom. The more extrovert aspects of his style gradually diminished over time, yet it is precisely those components that were so influential on rhythm and blues saxophonists. Jacquet was also a showman capable of some outrageous onstage antics, yet he never adopted the well-scripted gymnastics of the R&B stylists. He was simply the last great black swing tenor saxophonist.

As a major star of the Jazz at the Philharmonic era, he was concerned with the creation of the solo. The essence of the JATP Jam Session, set when two or more players on the same instrument were involved, was competition. To gain an edge, Jacquet paid special attention to entrances and climaxes. There is a finely sculpted quality to many of his best efforts.

"Flyin' Home," recorded by Lionel Hampton in 1942, included Jacquet's first recorded solo. The tune had been written by Hampton when he was a part of Benny Goodman's combo; and he had recorded it under his own name, first, for RCA in 1940 with a pickup group of mostly white musicians from the Goodman band. On that recording, Budd Johnson had the tenor solo.

In the fall of 1940, when Hampton formed his first big band, it was clear that "Flyin' Home" would be a big number for the band. One early arrangement featured solos by trumpet, trombone, tenor, and baritone saxophones. When it came time to record for Decca, producer Milt Gabler knew it would be too long, so he shortened the performance. Hampton's own work on his signature song ended up being an intro and a bridge. The two-chorus tenor sax solo by Illinois Jacquet was the centerpiece of the performance.

Jacquet's "Flyin' Home" solo suggests the influence of Herschel Evans, the original Texas tenor saxophonist, especially in the tonal quality. The other aspect of the solo is the incorporation of diverse yet recognizable fragments from other songs. Much has been made of the entrance with its quotation of "Martha," yet there is also a quote from Evans's "Texas Shuffle" solo with Count Basie, and it is also clear that he was familiar with Paul Bascomb's work on the 1940 Erskine Hawkins recording of "Nona." The Jacquet solo was so memorable that it soon became important to have it included as part of the tune.

Hampton recorded a second version for Decca, featuring a tenor solo by Arnett Cobb, in 1944. Despite the excellence of that solo, Cobb, in time, integrated the Jacquet solo into his own presentation. Indeed, in the dozens of recorded versions of "Flyin' Home" by Lionel Hampton throughout his career, the Jacquet solo is always a key element.

July 16 was the final concert of the 2004 Midsummer Night's Swing series. Loyal fans appeared in large numbers, although the expectations were somewhat muted. With Jacquet's advancing age, the band had reduced its amount of touring. Appearances in the United States, outside of the New York area, became infrequent, although the band still rehearsed and occasionally played international concerts and festivals. In his 2003 Midsummer Night's Swing appearance, Jacquet had appeared quite frail, used a cane to walk onstage, and played while sitting down.

For 2004, he still needed help to get onstage, and those around him appeared a bit apprehensive, but once the music started, he found new life. For the first time in several years, he stretched out: taking an exceptional solo on "Tickle-toe" and an extra chorus on "Doggin' Around." His theme statement of "On the Sunny Side of the Street" was exquisite. The band was in top form as well, clearly inspired by the leader. The final selection of the evening, as it was every night, was "Flyin' Home." Six nights later, he died of heart failure.

In evaluating the career of Illinois Jacquet, it is important to remember that he was a star: the first new jazz star of the post-WWII era. He dressed like a star, carried himself like a star, and performed like a star. He was featured in films, on television, on radio, and on hit records. His name was known in all countries where jazz is popular.

His career suffered the inevitable ups and downs, but at no time was his playing less than compelling. His decision to form a big band relatively late in life and focus all his energy on that project is unprecedented. He could have made much more money and had many fewer headaches doing something else. That he accomplished this so well for so long is not surprising. He called upon the wisdom of his teachers such as Percy McDavid, Lloyd Reese, Lionel Hampton, and Count Basie. He imparted the lessons he had learned to his younger band members. He began by playing in a big band, and he went out leading one. The last song he played reprised the first solo he recorded. He truly went out in the great jazz tradition: with his boots on.

RECOMMENDED RECORDS:

The Complete Illinois Jacquet Sessions, 1945–1950 (Mosaic 4CD); *Flying Home: Best of the Verve Years*, 1951–1958 (Verve CD); *Swing's the Thing with Roy Eldridge*, 1956 (Verve ICD-J); *Bottoms Up*, 1967 (Prestige OJC-CD); *Jacquet's Got It*, Big Band, 1987 (Atlantic CD)

RHYTHM AND BLUES

"I should have called it blues and rhythm."—Jerry Wexler

"I should have called it rhythm and gospel."—Jerry Wexler, on another occasion

JERRY WEXLER DID INDEED COIN the term *rhythm and blues* in a 1949 piece for *Billboard* magazine. He also admitted that others contributed to the origin of that phrase. At any rate, the magazine began to utilize rhythm and blues (R&B) as a term to describe black music. The magazine's popularity charts reflecting both jukebox play and record sales were officially changed from race music to rhythm and blues on June 25, 1949. This is where the first great divide of black music takes place. Prior to this, everything was race music. Now, if your music wasn't R&B, it had to be something else. In time, all black secular music would be termed R&B; but for the moment, if R&B was what was hot and you weren't R&B . . .

Jazz had been suffering under similar divisions. The rediscovery of New Orleans jazz had been going on for a decade. Elderly musicians were being rediscovered and praised, sometimes deservedly. At other times they were celebrated largely for being alive. Bebop was a more recent development. The music of Dizzy Gillespie and Charlie Parker had garnered substantial press and controversy. Each style had their partisans. Those who favored the older style proclaimed it "the real jazz" while the boppers referred to them as "moldy figs." This sort of infighting did neither side any good and continued to plague jazz for years to come.

Changes in the way music was perceived tended to affect musicians in different ways. For some, it meant more opportunities. For others, it meant confusion. Bebop was a different method of playing from the jazz that had been forged in the 1930s. R&B would be different in yet another way. Great jazz musicians such as Roy Eldridge and Terry Gibbs sought psychiatric advice in the 1940s when confronted with bebop while others simply adopted the most obvious qualities of the new style and used it as an adjunct to what worked in their individual presentation. The musicians who had graduated from the big bands were generally better prepared to find a way in the middle of all this change.

For one thing, many had benefited from the music training in the public schools they attended. While they are rarely mentioned in history books, music teachers made lasting impressions on many great jazz players. Captain Walter Dyett at Du Sable High School in Chicago and Percy McDavid at Phyllis Wheatley High School in Houston are two who are cited most often. Yet men such as Samuel Browne and Lloyd Reese in Los Angeles, Louis Cabrera and Harry Begian in Detroit, and Major N. Clark Smith who taught in both Chicago and Kansas City are examples of others who should be celebrated more frequently. Graduates from these and other programs became the professional musicians of their era. Equipped with these acquired skills, they had a chance to cope with the racist attitudes of the nation. They had the tools with which to earn a living.

Musically, much had happened since the record industry resumed activity after the second recording ban that lasted most of 1948. Labels without enough masters to last out the recording cessation folded left and right. King and Savoy acquired labels in distress and would continue to do so throughout the coming years, as would Specialty, Imperial, and Mercury.

Sometime after the fact, Duke Ellington referred to this period as "the era of the tenor sax." In the years following the recording ban, tenor saxophonists did indeed come to the fore. And they did so in record numbers! In the big band era, few tenor saxophonists had name recognition. Fans knew Coleman Hawkins first. Later they came to be aware of Chu Berry, Lester Young, and Ben Webster. Yet Budd Johnson, Buddy Tate, and Joe Thomas produced their excellent work in relative anonymity.

While some of the new talent was developed in big bands, an increasing number of tenor sax stars arrived with little or no orchestral experience. As big bands became less of a force in the music business, the number of celebrity sidemen continued to decrease. Small combos of four to seven pieces fronted by a tenor saxophonist would become the order of the day. If the first recording ban had provided singers with an opportunity, the reedmen gained most of the ground after the second AFM recording ban.

Because he was not a union musician, bluesman John Lee Hooker was not only discovered but also recorded extensively during 1948; and his first recording, "Boogie Chillun," became a big hit. Hooker was an example of a performer who benefited from the ban. There were several other bluesmen with similar stories, and though it was never advertised as such, this country blues activity would pave the way for its inclusion into the folk music revival toward the end of the 1950s.

45 RPM SINGLES

In terms of the technology relating to the record business, the changes and advances were led by the major companies.

RCA introduced the 45 rpm single in the spring of 1949. Initially reissues were emphasized, but in a very short time, a series of simultaneous 78/45 releases were announced. RCA also introduced a record player that would play only 45s. The original releases were pressed on color-coded vinyl. For example, pop releases were black while "blues and rhythm" were orange. (The first was "Bring Another Half a Pint" by Sonny Boy Williamson.) But this approach was short lived.

In retaliation, Columbia promoted a line of 7" 33s, which did not catch on. The other big labels were making decisions as well: Mercury and Decca were on board with LPs very quickly while Capitol and MGM were issuing 45 releases, mostly back catalog, in 1950. Yet there were anomalies such as the R&B line started by MGM in 1952, which was 78 rpm only.

In the eighteen months following its announcement, RCA would spend more than five million dollars promoting the 45. The public, which had been introduced to the LP less than a year prior to the arrival of the 45, was confused. Record sales actually fell in 1949. It became obvious that standardization and compatibility were what was needed. The three-speed record player was an answer, but it was the jukebox industry that assured the survival of the 45.

Until 1950, jukeboxes played 78s and had a capacity of forty-eight titles. That year, the Seeburg Company introduced a new model, the M100B, which effectively doubled the number of selections possible by utilizing 45 rpms. It was an instant hit, and all jukebox manufacturers embraced the new configuration. While some record labels were slow to adopt 45 rpm, others fell quickly into line.

Savoy and Modern began production on 45s in early 1950. It would be a full year before King, Specialty, and Atlantic came aboard. Major labels continued to use 78s for their promotional copies until the middle of 1954. In August 1954, RCA announced that 45 rpm sales accounted for 56 percent of their dollar volume and that the LP now outpaced 78 by 23 percent to 21 percent. In many white locations, R&B records were accounting for 20 percent or more slots on jukeboxes. Earl Bostic was among the top 10 jukebox artists nationally in 1954.

RCA, Columbia, and Decca were the three largest record companies in 1950. Each of them had wholly owned distribution and was a full-service label with classical departments, pop divisions, and kiddie records. Each was slower to adapt to changing trends in black music than a specialist, independent label would be. But in the coming years, each reacted to the R&B explosion in similar ways.

During this period, RCA would form Groove Records, Decca would form Coral, and Columbia would revive its Okeh imprint to focus on R&B. At one point in the next few years, each of these new labels would be distributed by independents and not through the house system. RCA had a long and honorable association with black music throughout the Race Records era. At the start of 1949, the label still had Count Basie, Erskine Hawkins, Lucky Millinder, and Illinois Jacquet on their roster. The following year, they were all dropped as the label pulled back to find the next direction. The Bluebird label that had yielded so many prominent blues stars was phased out, and label "X" was formed to deal with jazz and blues reissues for both the 45 and LP markets.

Illinois Jacquet signed with Norman Granz while both Erskine Hawkins and Lucky Millinder went to King. Count Basie recorded for Columbia during 1950 and 1951 but was featured on the parent label and not on Okeh. Columbia, through Okeh, managed to be more successful in R&B than would Groove or Coral and was home to artists such as Big Maybelle, Johnny Ray, and Chuck Willis before the operation was folded into Epic Records in 1954. Epic pursued a more general direction and had a hit artist almost immediately with Roy Hamilton.

In January 1950, Louis Jordan announced that he was taking several months off to recuperate from a throat condition and general exhaustion. His longtime manager, Berle Adams, decided to retire at this point. Adams had health issues of his own and wanted to settle in California and return to the agency business. Jordan returned to record "Blue Light Boogie Parts 1 and 2," which became a #1 R&B hit. It was his last hit of any consequence. Against all advice, Jordan formed a big band in 1951 that would cost him lots of money and produce no hit records. He had been the top black recording artist of the 1940s and continued to record for Decca for three more years, but there were no hits, and as a recording artist, Louis Jordan quickly became yesterday's news. The decline in Jordan's sales seemed to affect the entire label, and the only black music hit of any consequence during this period was a ballad by Arthur Prysock, "I Couldn't Sleep a Wink Last Night."

By 1953, record sales were booming once again with LPs accounting for about 20 percent of total sales, and the 78-to-45 ratio had fallen to about two to one. The 78 would continue to fade as the 45 became more popular with younger record buyers, and while some ethnic and gospel labels would press 78s into the early '60s, the emphasis at most labels had shifted exclusively to 45 long before that. By 1953, it was generally considered that, in R&B, a sale of 40,000 was considered a "hit" and anything that sold 100,000 was acknowledged to be a "big hit." Sales on some titles had reached 300,000. These figures are rough approximations, and the actual profitability would include the calculation of overhead costs. Some labels, Modern, King, and Duke/Peacock, invested in their own pressing facilities and plants to handle printing and fabricating. Others, such as Jubilee, had a distribution component.

The 10" LP was standard for most labels. Columbia had a 12" line, Masterworks, which was devoted to classical music; but there was no line of 12" LPs for new pop releases. This resulted in odd success stories such as Duke Ellington's 1952 Masterworks album, *Ellington Uptown*, which became a big seller, powered by Louie Bellson's drum work on "Skin Deep." It would be 1955 before the 12" LP became the standard.

R&B RADIO

If the record industry was shaking itself out in the early years of R&B, radio was innovating as well. In 1949, WDIA in Memphis went to an all-black music format. This was an astonishing, instant success. That success brought out similar shifts in other territories. WLAC in Nashville switched to a black music format, but the difference was that the station could be heard in about two-thirds of the country!

Radio licenses during this time were often allocated to stations that operated dawn to dusk. They tended to be low-power stations, but when they went off the air in the evening, the frequency that they utilized became vacant. Thus, a distant signal utilizing the same frequency became audible when during the daytime it was not. Other licenses, such as that held by WLAC, were clear channel, a frequency with no obstructing stations at that spot on the dial. In 1951, WERD in Atlanta became the first black-owned station in the country.

The black audience in the South, which had always bought records in quantity, now became a major force in the industry. That R&B could be a winning music formula for more general music formats was obvious; and independent stations not affiliated with the NBC, CBS, or Mutual networks were quick to add an R&B show, usually at night, to a block-programmed format. For many white teenagers across the country, the nightly R&B show became a destination. In some cities, you could find an R&B disc jockey broadcasting from the window of an all-night record store. Other DJs broadcast live from nightclubs. The man who started this was 'Symphony" Sid Torin (1909–1984).

SYMPHONY SID

Torin was born Sidney Tarnopol. He was playing records on New York radio in the 1930s before the term *disc jockey* was invented. He had appeared on WBNX, WHOM, and WWRL before landing at WJZ, a clear-channel station. He billed himself as the "all-night, all-frantic one" and began late-night remotes from the Royal Roost club in 1948. Many of these broadcasts were recorded off the air and showed up decades later on LPs. Sid was an early champion of bebop, and many New York area fans credit him with introducing Charlie Parker and Dizzy Gillespie to listeners of his show. Sid had his own theme song, "Jumpin' with Symphony Sid," a dedication from Lester Young, which was covered by many different artists. In 1949, the remotes moved to Birdland, which built a broadcast booth on the premises for Sid.

Sid was no purist, however, and was quite capable of featuring nonbebop players and R&B vocal groups such as the Ravens and the Orioles. His was a black music mix that predated R&B. As a jazz DJ, he is well remembered along with men such as Gene Norman in Los Angeles, Dave Garroway in Chicago, and Bill Randle in Detroit and Cleveland as pioneering jazz radio men. He moved to Boston in 1952, where he worked days at WBMS and nights at WCOP, before returning to New York in 1957. Upon his return, he got more involved in the exploding Latin music scene, but he always maintained his jazz credentials. He was a part of the New York radio scene well into the 1970s.

During the heyday of Symphony Sid in the late 1940s and early 1950s, there were other jazz shows in New York, but the advent of R&B began to change things, and many of the late-night radio shows tended to have less of a jazz focus. They were more expressly tailored to an increasingly younger black audience to whom bebop and subsequent modern jazz experiments were relatively meaningless. It was not unusual to find jazz as a part of the mix, but it was jazz of a specific sort. Little Walter broke through with a blues harmonica instrumental ("Juke") on Chess, the first of a number of hits for this artist. There were piano hits for Lloyd Glenn ("Chica Boo" and "Old Time Shuffle Blues") on Swing Time and Ivory Joe Hunter on King and MGM, although Hunter's vocal balladry would soon leave his fine blues piano work in the background. Apart from these items, the key jazz instrumentals that found play on R&B radio (and were thus considered R&B records) featured saxophones. Some of the producers associated with the race music era were involved.

BIG JAY MCNEELY

On November 15, 1948, Ralph Bass, newly installed as Savoy's man in Los Angeles, recorded saxophonist Cecil McNeely. McNeely (1927–), who would become known professionally as Big Jay McNeely, was a twenty-one-year-old tenor player who had grasped the essentials of Illinois Jacquet's style and had heard records such as "Cornbread." He had attended high school with bebop saxophonist Sonny Criss and was becoming well known in Los Angeles through his appearances in the house band at Johnny Otis's club, the Barrelhouse. McNeely had no experience with big bands but was one of the first musicians to have an impact as an R&B soloist.

The first McNeely session was followed shortly by a second Savoy date on December 13 that produced "Deacon's Hop." Propelled by hand claps, the performance was a medium tempo tour de force for the tenor player who trotted out a menu of smears, screams, farts, and squeals to produce a huge record. "Deacon's Hop" entered the Billboard Race chart on January 24, 1949, and achieved #1 status in a twelve-week stay on the chart. The hit launched McNeely as a combo leader, and he toured nationally for over a decade.

The Savoy sessions were nonexclusive, and McNeely was quickly recorded by a variety of local labels, including Exclusive, Aladdin, and Imperial. He was reunited with Ralph Bass at Federal from 1952 to 1954 and after that made sessions for Vee Jay, Atlantic, and Swingin', where he scored his second major hit recording with "There Is Something on Your Mind" (with a vocal by Little Sonny Warner) in 1959. McNeely worked around Southern California for much of the 1960s, recording an album for Warner Brothers and a session for Modern in 1965. Before the end of the decade, he was out of music on a full-time basis. His career resurrection in the early 1980s was caused by his re-discovery during an R&B revival in London.

McNeely's importance to R&B is based on his extra musical gyrations as much as it is on what he played and recorded. He lay on his back; he walked the bar and even did walks outside the nightclub, blowing all the while. This extracurricular activity was instantly absorbed by the younger R&B instrumentalists.

LITTLE ESTHER–ETTA JAMES

The combination of bandleader Johnny Otis and vocalist Little Esther (1935–1984) was another of the Ralph Bass projects that struck pay dirt. Otis recorded in the neighborhood of seventy sides for Savoy in less than eighteen months. The vocals of Little Esther, soon to be fourteen years old, were in the fashionable Dinah Washington mold and were featured in duets with Mel Walker and with the Robins, a vocal group including some members who would later form the Coasters. The earliest of these recordings from November 1949 were closer to the race music model than R&B, but by the time Otis's Savoy tenure came to an end, they were solid R&B. Otis had four major hits during 1950 and 1951: one was a solo vocal for Esther, one was a solo vocal for Walker, and two were duets. The Johnny Otis show, firing on all cylinders, hit the road in the spring of 1950 and crisscrossed the country for most of the year. The show also featured band instrumentals and a blues singer so that Otis had the first self-contained R&B revue to achieve major success. Future package shows would use the Johnny Otis show as a model.

By the end of the year, it was all over. Ralph Bass left Savoy and joined the King organization where he founded the Federal label, taking Little Esther with him. Johnny Otis replaced Little Esther with Linda Hopkins, but the hits on Savoy stopped coming. Otis signed with Mercury in 1951. Both Johnny Otis and Little Esther would have new life down the road: Otis, whose hits dried up in 1952, would return with a hit single, "Willie and the Hand Jive" in 1958 while Esther, now Esther Phillips, had a chart topper with "Release Me" in 1962 and a disco era smash with a version of "What a Difference a Day Makes" in 1975. After Linda Hopkins's departure, Big Mama Thornton came aboard; and shortly thereafter, Otis came up with another discovery.

Etta James (1938–2012) had several things in common with Esther Phillips. She was discovered by Johnny Otis and had a hit while still a teenager. "The Wallflower" from 1955 was a number one R&B hit better known in the cover version as "Dance with Me, Henry." Her earliest work was on Modern, and that was followed by a lengthy stay with Chess, usually on the Argo label. This relationship produced a number of best sellers, beginning in 1960 and lasting until the middle of the next decade. She did it with vocal duets, blues, and even string-laden, jazz-oriented ballads such as "At Last," a number 2 R&B hit in 1961. After a hiatus, she emerged as an album artist in the 1980s and continued to make excellent, award-winning jazz and blues albums regularly until her death.

PAUL WILLIAMS

While Ralph Bass was breaking new artists in Los Angeles, Teddy Reig was seemingly possessed of a magic touch in New York. Reig recorded right through the 1948 ban, and as normalcy resumed in the record industry, Reig went back into the studio with Paul Williams. Williams (1915–2002) was recruited from King Porter's band in 1947. Herman Lubinsky had been alerted to the Porter band by his Detroit distributor and had sent Reig to check it out. What he found was a thoroughly professional, reasonably conventional band led by trumpet player Porter that featured a handsome, sweet-toned alto sax player, who doubled baritone, named Paul Williams. Williams was, in Reig's term, the "glamour-puss." In signing Williams to Savoy, Reig made it clear that he didn't want sweet-toned alto sax; he wanted honking baritone sax! Williams was resistant at first, and they agreed to try some recording on each horn.

Williams was initially recorded with pianist T. J. Fowler's band, and from that first session came "Thirty-Five Thirty." The tune was named for the address of a Detroit record shop and was a race chart item for eight weeks in 1947. It was the only baritone sax feature of the six tunes recorded.

Williams then formed a fine band featuring trumpeter Phillip Guilbeau, tenor saxophonist Wild Bill Moore, and pianist Floyd Taylor, Williams's cousin. This group was recorded extensively between October 1947 and March 1948, sometimes under Moore's name. There had been some minor success with several instrumentals, but nothing approaching "Thirty-Five Thirty."

In early 1948, saxophonist Arnett Cobb underwent serious spinal surgery and had to cancel a series of theater engagements. The Williams band was pressed into service to cover the dates. It was the group's first road experience.

Reig went to Baltimore in order to help the band with its first appearance at the Royal Theater. During rehearsal, they discovered that the microphone on the stage used for soloists was operated mechanically from under the stage. Reig positioned himself under the stage, and during a frantic number (later recorded as "The Twister"), Williams blew at the microphone while Reig gradually lowered it to the floor. The audience left raving about the saxophone player who "blew the microphone right into the floor." From that point forward, Baltimore was Paul Williams's town!

In the fall of 1948 prior to his second appearance at the Royal, Williams and his band were in the audience at a Lucky Millinder band rehearsal when the band tried out an especially attractive instrumental. Williams thought that he might use it for an upcoming record date, but the tune at that time had no title. While working on the tune during a club engagement in Pennsylvania, he noticed patrons doing an unusual dance to this new tune. When he inquired about the dance, he was told it was the Hucklebuck. That was the tune title he gave when the band recorded on December 15, 1948.

While "The Hucklebuck" recording took off like a rocket, some backstage manipulations were going on. The tune was written by well-known composer/arranger Andy Gibson, who was Lucky Millinder's cousin. Because Millinder had yet to record the tune, it hadn't been copy-written. When Millinder recorded his version on January 3, 1949, it was titled "D Natural Blues"; and when it was determined that the two songs were identical, all hell broke loose. Ultimately, it took a court case to decide the fate of the tune. Millinder stated he didn't want any piece of "The Hucklebuck"; he only wanted "D Natural Blues," so the copyright of that song stayed with him. Millinder and King Records' producer Henry Glover, a former trumpet player in the Millinder orchestra, are credited as the writers. The Millinder performance, featuring a strong tenor sax solo by Harold "Babe" Clarke, was a hit record, reaching #4 on the R&B charts during a twelve-week stay.

"D Natural Blues" may have been a hit, but "The Hucklebuck" was a phenomenon. It was the first major dance to emerge from the black community since the end of WWII. As a record, it was the biggest R&B record of 1949. It stayed on the R&B charts for thirty-two weeks, including a fourteen-week run as #1! A lyric was written by veteran songwriter Roy Alfred, and the song had dozens of pop covers. Among the R&B covers was a #5 hit version by Roy Milton, the first with a vocal. The dance never caught on to the extent that the twist would a few years later, but it spawned all manner of imitations, notably "The Applejack" by Joe Morris on Atlantic. Herman Lubinsky, Savoy owner, maintained that "The Hucklebuck" would have been an even bigger record if there had been a tenor sax solo instead of the jazzy trumpet played by Guilbeau.

Savoy, like so many of the independent labels of the era, expected to be the publisher of any original material recorded for the label. The publishing on "The Hucklebuck" was credited to United Music, a BMI firm. United Music was Teddy Reig and his friend, promotion man Juggy Gayles, who fronted the company. When Lubinsky got wind of this, he fired Reig. Although Reig returned to Savoy, briefly, in 1951, the bloom was off; and he produced no more R&B hits. He continued to record key jazz artists for his Royal Roost label and would be heard from again.

Because Paul Williams did not write or publish "The Hucklebuck," his monetary reward was considerably less than that of Andy Gibson or Teddy Reig. Williams did write "Hoppin' John," the B side of "The Hucklebuck," so he derived some mechanical income from the sale of his hit record. But later couplings of the song did not include another Williams performance. Record industry contracts were all cross-collateralized in those days, and the earnings from one record date were applied to the cost of the next one. Paul Williams was recorded by Savoy until the end of 1951. He had no more hits.

Along the way, Williams developed a reputation as an excellent bandleader. His groups were always tight and well rehearsed. His band headlined the Moondog Coronation Ball for Alan Freed, March 21, 1952, in Cleveland. This event is often credited with being the first rock-'n'-roll concert. Williams was in demand for theater tours because his group, in addition to playing its own set, was capable of backing the vocal groups who were so popular at the time. Paul Williams and his band were a key component of countless R&B tours throughout the 1950s. Because the band was a touring attraction, it did not do much studio recording, notable exceptions being those backing Ruth Brown on some Atlantic sessions. Williams helped start the careers of several outstanding musicians through the years, among them singers Joan Shaw and Little Willie John, saxophonist Noble "Thin Man" Watts, and blues guitarist Bobby Parker. After leaving Savoy, he recorded for several labels with the best results coming on Mercury (1952), Jax (1954), and his final session, for Vee Jay, in 1956.

Williams had developed a network of contacts throughout the music business, so when he got tired of enduring the antics of the increasingly younger singers he had to accompany on tours, he gave it all up. He formed a booking agency, the Entertainment Bureau, which he operated for many years.

The year 1949 found "D Natural Blues" by Lucky Millinder to be the only hit by a black big band. The year 1950 was no better with Lionel Hampton's "Everybody's Somebody's Fool," with a vocal by Little Jimmy Scott, the only hit of any substance.

DUKE ELLINGTON

Duke Ellington had been at Columbia since 1947 and had been concentrating on longer works for his concert performances. He recorded a 12" LP for Columbia Masterworks in 1950 with extended versions of four songs: "The Tattooed Bride," "Solitude," "Mood Indigo," and "Sophisticated Lady." He was the first black bandleader to record an LP. He was still recording singles for the label, but from this point forward, he would also record LPs on a regular basis. In early 1951, the Ellington band underwent major personnel changes.

Johnny Hodges (1906–1970) had been a part of the Ellington organization since 1928. The elegant glissandos of his ballads and the deep-rooted feeling of his blues were the major components of his alto saxophone style. With the departure of Cootie Williams (1940) and Ben Webster (for the last time in 1949), he had become *the* star soloist in the band.

He signed a recording contract with Norman Granz in 1951 and left the Ellington band, taking trombonist Lawrence Brown and drummer Sonny Greer with him. Another former Ellington star, Al Sears, joined the new Hodges group to play tenor sax and handle the business. On March 3, the Hodges band recorded the Sears composition "Castle Rock," and the group was off to a great start with an R&B hit! At the time of the signing, Granz's productions were being released on Mercury; but Johnny Hodges remained with

Granz and his Clef, Norgran, and Verve labels for the next seventeen years.

Ellington brought in three replacements, all from the Harry James band: alto saxophonist Willie Smith, trombonist Juan Tizol, and drummer Louie Bellson. Tizol had been with Ellington from 1929 to 1944. He had written for the band, and his compositions "Caravan" and "Perdido" had become not only popular favorites within the band but also jazz standards on their own. Tizol had left Ellington to join James and was asked by Ellington to rejoin for one year and to bring Smith and Bellson along on the same terms. Smith had been a featured soloist with Jimmie Lunceford from 1930 to 1942 and joined James shortly after Tizol. Smith, whose alto style had a lot in common with Hodges, did not stay beyond the one year. He worked with JATP during 1952 and 1953 before returning, as did Tizol, to James in 1954.

Louie Bellson (1924–2009) was not a long-term member of the Ellington band, but his influence was enormous. Not only was Bellson a dynamic drummer with a style much more modern than that of Greer, he was a legitimate innovator whose double bass-drum setup remained mandatory for all Ellington drummers after his departure. Bellson was also a composer-arranger who brought tunes such as "The Hawk Talks" and "Ting-a-Ling" into the band. His major feature with the band, "Skin Deep," sparked the second Ellington LP, *Ellington Uptown*, making it a major hit. The exceptional recording quality of "Skin Deep" was used to demonstrate high-fidelity equipment for many years.

Bellson married singer Pearl Bailey in 1953 and began a career in tandem with hers. He toured with JATP in 1954, an experience that he credited with bringing his name before the public. Once he had settled in Los Angeles, Bellson became the first-call drummer for Norman Granz's Verve recording sessions. A prolific composer and arranger, Bellson led his own big band for many years and recorded dozens of albums for a variety of labels.

Bellson was a part of the band for less than two years, but he was often recalled by Ellington for roles in special productions such as **My People** or recording or television work. Drum features would be an integral part of Ellington performances from this point forward. When Bellson departed in January 1953, Ellington had to figure out how to keep that sound. Butch Ballard and Dave Black were tried, but neither proved to be what Ellington needed for the long term.

COUNT BASIE

If Duke Ellington had discovered new inspiration, Count Basie was scuffling. He had been forced to break up his orchestra and was working nightclubs with a small combo. He had returned to Columbia for recording, and while the small-group recordings were of top quality and featured great jazzmen such as Wardell Gray, Buddy DeFranco, and Clark Terry, sales were minimal. It would be twenty-one months before Count Basie would reform his big band. When he did reform, he had a new label and a hit record to help him along.

Basie had signed with Norman Granz early in 1952. His initial recordings were big band singles and small-group albums. It was the big band single "Paradise Squat" that featured Basie on organ and Eddie "Lockjaw" Davis on tenor that put the band back on the road to recovery. Davis and his sectionmate Paul Quinichette had kept up the two tenor soloist tradition that Basie had featured since the beginning.

Davis left Basie in the spring of 1953 to form his first organ group. Paul Quinichette left the band around the same time and recorded three sessions with different organists for Mercury during 1953. Quinichette made several LPs in the company of former Basie sidemen throughout the 1950s, but he never again worked with the band. Davis, on the other hand, returned to the band on many different occasions. In time, the Count Basie band replacements for Davis and Quinichette, Frank Wess, and Frank Foster proved more than adequate and maintained a long-term identity with the band.

Basie first recorded a big band album in December 1953 and did two more in August 1954. These were 12" LPs on the Clef label, and Granz continued to lead all jazz producers in issuing the larger albums. The three albums were volumes 1 and 2 of *Dance Session* and one titled *Basie Jazz*.

Arrangers, now more than ever, were an important part of the band. Charts from band members such as Ernie Wilkins and Frank Foster were having a major impact on the band, but outside writers Neal Hefti and Manny Albam were also regular contributors.

If the 1952 band had been a new beginning for the Count Basie Orchestra, then the 1953–1954 band showed how well the band was coalescing as a unit. There had been one change among the brass players while the reeds and rhythm remained intact. The band that plays together plays *together*.

In the case of the Ellington and Basie bands, the years 1953 and 1954 can be viewed as transitional years. The music performed and recorded during those years was well within the tradition of quality established by each organization, but it did not quite reach the heights delivered by their predecessors. Ellington spent those years with Capitol. He was still recording for single release although those dates frequently featured the singers in the band. Concept albums were a part of the mix as well as with the first Ellington trio album and an album of swing standards among those recorded. While the personnel of the band remained largely intact, there was something missing; a spark was lacking.

BUDDY JOHNSON

Buddy Johnson managed to keep most of his key players together for many years. From the time the band signed with Mercury in 1953, it was on a continually rising tide. While Johnson had never been able to find another balladeer of Arthur Prysock's caliber, Prysock's departure in 1952 had forced the band to get stronger in other ways. The Johnson band, like that of Lionel Hampton, emphasized a hard-rocking bluesy style as opposed to the swing approach of other bands. The Mercury recordings were often arranged by Slide Hampton or Gil Askey, and Mercury was not afraid to add specialist solo players such as Mickey Baker or Sil Austin to the band on record dates. Recordings such as "Hittin' on Me" and "I'm Just Your Fool" were top 10 R&B records, something no other black big band could achieve at this time. The Johnson band toured constantly, always playing black venues.

LIONEL HAMPTON

Lionel Hampton had made no records in 1952, and much of what he did in 1953 was recorded in Europe. This was a major loss for the music since the 1953 Hampton band contained a mix of players that was truly unique. The sensational young trumpet player Clifford Brown was on that band, as was Clifford Scott, the tenor saxophonist, who would create the famous solo on Bill Doggett's "Honky Tonk Part 2" a few years later. The pioneering electric bassist Monk Montgomery and exceptional drummer Alan Dawson were in the same rhythm section. Other key members of the band were trumpet players Quincy Jones and Art Farmer, trombonists Jimmy Cleveland and Buster Cooper, as well as saxophonists Gigi Gryce, Anthony Ortega, and Clifford Solomon. Jones and Gryce each arranged for the band. Based on the broadcast recordings of this band, its potential was met only in part. The band broke up upon its return to the United States, and Hampton began a new recording arrangement with Norman Granz.

It was Granz's idea to feature Hampton in the company of JATP regulars: Oscar Peterson, Ray Brown, and Buddy Rich. The first recording was in September 1953, and there would be many similar sessions involving Hampton as a soloist in a small group over the next two years. The recordings, issued on 10" and 12" LPs and simultaneously on 45 rpm and 45EP, were among the finest of Hampton's career. His big band, with entirely new personnel, continued to be a strong touring attraction both in the United States and Europe, but it was no longer a force on records.

MILT BUCKNER

Milt Buckner left the Hampton band for the final time in 1952. Buckner (1915–1977) had joined Hampton in 1941 on piano. He was soon providing many of Hampton's arrangements as well. It was his arrangement and piano work on "Hamp's Boogie Woogie" that provided Hampton with his first #1 Race Records hit. Buckner left Hampton in 1949, in order to lead his own big band. Despite some excellent recordings for MGM and a solid schedule of bookings, the big band failed. Upon his return to Hampton in mid-1950, he found that he would have to double. Doug Duke, his replacement, had brought organ into the band. Buckner took to the instrument with great enthusiasm. In this instance, as an arranger as well as a player, he heard the same potential that his friends Bill Doggett and Wild Bill Davis had discovered. When he departed Hampton, he settled in Philadelphia, which had an unusually large number of clubs featuring organists. It was also home to Doc Bagby, Jackie Davis, and Doggett who were already well-known practitioners. Philadelphia was not the only city with a growing number of organ rooms; it was noted in 1954 that there were five different organists working in Harlem at the same time!

For the next ten years, Buckner concentrated on organ recording for Capitol, Argo, and Bethlehem. Buckner, short and stout, had trouble reaching the foot pedals of the instrument; and he employed a bass player on his records. His touring trios featured saxophone and drums. Buckner was a popular entertainer who worked constantly. He was immensely popular in Europe and was an annual visitor to France and Germany beginning in the mid-1960s. He recorded more than thirty albums in Europe over the next decade often playing piano. In the United States, he was frequently found in the employ of his old Lionel Hampton bandmate Illinois Jacquet; and that fun-loving trio, often with drummer Jo Jones as the third member, was a popular attraction throughout much of the 1970s. Buckner died in 1977 while on a job with Jacquet in Chicago.

In terms of influence, Buckner was much more influential as a pianist. His "locked hands" style was adopted by George Shearing, Red Garland, and other players; and the piano records that he made in Europe are superb. His organ style is reflected in the playing of Shirley Scott, another Philadelphian, who shared many of Buckner's characteristics in her work.

The line between jazz and R&B was blurred during the early 1950s. Following the lead of Gene Ammons's ballad hit "My Foolish Heart," tenor saxophone players routinely recorded ballad versions of pop songs, often with an echo chamber as part of the mix. The success of "My Foolish Heart" and Tab Smith's "Because of You" was noticed and emulated by almost all the indie labels at the time. Thus, Buddy Lucas was recording ballads for Jubilee and Lynn Hope first for Premium, with his hit treatment of "Tenderly," and then Aladdin; Hal Singer was doing the same for Coral and Savoy while Claude McLin and Eddie Johnson were waxing ballads for Chess. Prestige formed a separate numerical catalog dubbed the Tenor Sax Series to feature tenor stars such as Gene Ammons, Sonny Stitt, and Wardell Gray, although ballads were just a portion of the recorded repertoire.

EARL BOSTIC

In terms of instrumentalists who broke through during the R&B era, Earl Bostic stood out. Bostic (1913–1965) was born in Tulsa, Oklahoma, and had worked with a variety of bandleaders since coming to New York in 1939. He was a talented arranger who wrote charts for several big bands, and although most of his own groups were small combos, he worked with Lionel Hampton during WWII and had even made a big band session of his own for Majestic in 1945.

Bostic began to record for Gotham in 1946 and did a considerable amount of work for that label through the end of 1947. He signed with King in 1949, and his Gotham masters were acquired by King. Bostic's first two King sessions featured six-piece combos in the same manner as his Gotham sides, but when Ralph Bass joined the King organization, things changed. Bass joined King in order to launch the Federal label in the fall of 1950. The only King artist he produced on a regular basis was Bostic, and this was largely because of what happened on January 10, 1951.

A typical Bostic session until then would consist of a jump-blues item for his vocalist, something fast to feature his spectacular alto saxophone technique, perhaps a blues-oriented original or two, and sometimes a classical piece such as Schubert's "Serenade" or "The Merry Widow Waltz." Rarely was a standard from the great American songbook on display. What Bass did was to emphasize Bostic's gift for interpreting melody and exploit his rasping, wide-vibrato attack in unique arrangements of well-known songs. On his first date with Bostic, after the obligatory jump blues, a vocal ballad, and an instrumental version of "I Can't Give You Anything but Love," Bass called the old Duke Ellington favorite, "Flamingo," which featured prominent vibes and a strong backbeat in the accompaniment. Bostic delivered an unforgettable treatment, and the record was a huge #1 R&B hit remaining on the charts for twenty weeks. "Sleep," recorded at his next session, was actually issued first and created some noise in advance of "Flamingo" with a similar formula. That formula would appear with near certainty on every Bostic session for the rest of the decade, and while he never had another hit the size of "Flamingo," his records were routinely featured on R&B radio and on jukeboxes even in white neighborhoods. By 1954, Bostic was making LPs in addition to singles, and his albums were among the most popular in the King catalog. A heart attack in 1956 curtailed his traveling, but he continued to record albums for King. In 1959, King took the extraordinary step of having Bostic rerecord eight of his monaural albums in stereo, something that confused record collectors for years. During the soul jazz era, in 1963, Bostic recorded two fine LPs with Groove Holmes on organ and Joe Pass on guitar. Earl Bostic suffered a second fatal heart attack in 1965; he was only fifty-two years old.

JIMMY FORREST

Jimmy Forrest (1920–1980) was from St. Louis and was raised in a musical family. He played tenor sax in bands led by Don Albert, Jay McShann, and Andy Kirk prior to joining Duke Ellington in August 1949, replacing Ben Webster. Ordinarily this would have meant a major opportunity since both Webster and Al Sears had cemented reputations during their time with Ellington, but Ellington was undergoing a difficult time, and there were even suggestions in the press that he should disband.

While his stay with Ellington was only about one year, Forrest took two things with him upon his departure. His own treatment of Ellington's "Carnegie Blues" became "Bolo Blues" when Forrest recorded it for United Records in November 1951. The other side of "Bolo Blues" was "Night Train," the main strain of which came straight out of "Happy-Go-Lucky Local," some vintage 1946 Ellington and a song that was originally part of the "Deep South Suite."

"Night Train" became a huge hit, reaching #1 on the R&B charts, inspiring dozens of covers (some of which also became hits) and becoming the theme song of many late-night R&B radio shows across the country. It also became an overwhelming favorite of stripteasers. Forrest had a minor hit with "Hey, Mrs. Jones" also on United, but after 1952, he had no more. He encountered some drug problems and did some jail time. When he emerged from prison, he came to New York and established himself as a first-rate jazz soloist, working for the most part with Harry "Sweets" Edison from 1958 to 1962. He made several exceptional recordings for Prestige, as leader and sideman, during the same period. After a period of less productive activity in California from 1963 to 1973, he joined the Count Basie band and sparked that band for several years. His last major association was in a band co-led with trombonist Al Grey.

ATLANTIC RECORDS

Of the R&B labels, Atlantic seemed the one most poised to challenge Aladdin, King, and Savoy, the leaders in the field. But Ahmet Ertegun had a different sort of problem. He was hearing music in his head that he was not hearing in the recording studio. He was hearing the vocal quality he wanted in his singers, but he couldn't find the type of accompaniment that made him confident in the finished product. He was afraid that his records would not gain acceptance in the black community. They sounded old fashioned, not competitive, not contemporary. He was afraid that the new sounds coming from New Orleans or Los Angeles would make Atlantic obsolete in short order.

Ertegun (1923–2006) was a partner in Atlantic Records. The label had opened its doors in January 1948, after doing a considerable amount of recording during the last few months of 1947. But now, with the ban over and new recording under way, the music was changing. Ertegun and his Atlantic partner, Herb Abramson, spent a lot of time listening to the records of their competitors. What made the successful records successful? Was it the song? Was it the singer or group? Or was it the groove?

In the summer of 1948, while the recording ban was still in force, Atlantic had recorded one of its bands, the Tiny Grimes Quintet, in Cleveland. Grimes (1916–1989) was a popular four-string guitarist who had appeared with the Cats and the Fiddle as well as the Art Tatum Trio before forming his own group. Earlier editions of the Grimes band had featured saxophonists Charlie Parker, Paul Bascomb, and John Hardee. His latest discovery was Wilbert "Red" Prysock (1926–1993), a powerhouse tenor sax man in the tradition of Arnett Cobb and Illinois Jacquet, who was routinely able to blow the house down all by himself. Of the Atlantic recordings by the group, "Annie Laurie" is a standout while "Flyin' High" gives Prysock a chance to shine.

Upon leaving Grimes, Prysock joined the Tiny Bradshaw band where he created a memorable solo on Bradshaw's recording of "Soft." After brief stays with Roy Milton and Cootie Williams, Prysock formed his own group and was signed to Mercury by Bob Shad. Screaming tenor sax instrumentals were Prysock's specialty, and he recorded dozens of them throughout the 1950s, notably "Hand Clappin'." Red Prysock was involved in some of the earliest New York stage shows of Alan Freed but did little in the way of studio work because of a heavy touring schedule. When things slowed down for him in the early 1970s, he took over the bandleading chores for his brother Arthur Prysock, and the two toured together into the 1990s.

Red Prysock was also a singer with a rich baritone much like that of his brother. He sang on two issued titles with the Grimes unit. Ahmet Ertegun was less enthusiastic about the singing but very interested in the saxophone playing. The year 1949 was the time that the tenor saxophone became the dominant instrument in black music. Hal Singer and Big Jay McNeely had #1 R&B hits. Illinois Jacquet had been recording for the industry leader, RCA Victor, while Arnett Cobb would be signed to Columbia in 1950.

Herb Abramson had worked at National Records, where he had produced Billy Eckstine, Big Joe Turner, and the Ravens prior to joining forces with Ertegun to form Atlantic. He was later described by Ertegun as a great idea man, someone capable of hearing music before it was recorded. Not all his ideas were successful, but Abramson came up with his share of hits. Finding hot sidemen was not one of his strengths.

The first Fats Domino records for Imperial had made a big impression on Ahmet Ertegun. Ertegun was exceptionally knowledgeable on the subject of blues piano; and he felt that the piano style of Fats Domino, or something similar, would be part of the next wave of popular black music. The piano players in New York were jazz players. He needed someone who could play blues first and foremost. To that end, he asked saxophonist Frank "Floorshow" Culley, one of his artists, to look for a pianist who could play in that style. Culley returned from a gig in Columbus Ohio with Van "Piano Man" Walls.

Van Walls (1918–1999), born in Kentucky but raised in Charleston, West Virginia, was recorded as a leader several times for Atlantic; but most of the music was not issued. He was also employed as a sideman beginning in 1950, and in that capacity, he became a key member of the Atlantic house band. Along with bassist Lloyd Trotman and drummer Connie Kay, Van Walls would play on dozens of Atlantic R&B hits in the coming years.

The sound of honking tenor sax and bluesy piano would be the foundation on most R&B records in the 1950s. Ertegun had used Budd Johnson as his first musical director, but as a saxophonist, he was not the answer. Certain musicians such as Culley, whom Ertegun had used on the Clovers' first record and Red Prysock, were not always available for studio dates because of their constant traveling.

Freddie Mitchell (1918–2010) was employed on some dates. Mitchell had been recording with some small success for the Derby label. One of his records had been "Moondog Boogie" in honor of Alan Freed. The title was later changed to "Rock-'n'-Roll Boogie" and was recorded on the first Freed big band album. Mitchell was also involved in the Freed stage shows and also wrote some original material for the record dates, but by the end of the 1950s, things had slowed down considerably for him.

Ruth Brown's boyfriend, Willis Jackson, had showed some real promise. He was another high-energy honker whose work was present on parts 1 and 2 of Cootie Williams's "Gator Tail" in 1949. He also had the solo on Brown's first big hit, "Teardrops from My Eyes." Jackson would be recorded regularly between 1951 and 1953 and provide useful support on records by the Clovers and Brown, but it wasn't until Sam Taylor came off the road to settle in New York that Atlantic found its main tenor sax soloist.

SAM "THE MAN" TAYLOR

Sam Taylor (1916–1990) was born in Tennessee. His family including father, mother, and brother Paul were all musical. He began professionally with Scatman Crothers in 1937 before joining Doc Wheeler's Sunset Royal Orchestra. Wheeler's was another of the almost forgotten black big bands of the pre-WWII era. The leader was Indiana-born trombonist Wheeler Morin (1910–2005). This band featured such other future stars as alto saxophonist Bobby Smith, trumpeter Cat Anderson, and guitarist/arranger Leroy Kirkland. The Sunset Royals cut twelve titles in three separate sessions for RCA Bluebird in 1941 and 1942, and it was on those recordings that we first hear Sam Taylor.

Taylor went on to spend time with both Cootie Williams and Lucky Millinder during the war, but in 1947, he replaced Ike Quebec in the Cab Calloway band. He stayed with Calloway into 1952 when he settled in New York and worked his way into the recording studio scene. It was there that he was welcomed by the small group of arrangers such as Kirkland, Jesse Stone (who had also arranged for the Sunset Royals), Sy Oliver, and Howard Biggs who provided the arrangements for many New York R&B recordings. Alan Freed dubbed him Sam "the Man" Taylor.

He was important not only to Atlantic but also to virtually all the New York R&B labels. At Atlantic, he was especially prominent on sides by Clyde McPhatter and the Drifters, LaVern Baker, and Big Joe Turner. Among his best-known solos are "Mess Around" by Ray Charles (Atlantic), "Don't Be Angry" by Nappy Brown (Savoy), and "When You Dance" by the Turbans (Herald).

Taylor continued to be a mainstay throughout the New York scene until the end of the decade. By the early 1960s, the honking and screaming solos that had made him a key man in New York studio circles had been replaced, on his own recordings, by a lush, big–toned approach to ballads. He recorded more than a dozen albums of standards, often with string-section accompaniment, for MGM, Prestige/Moodsville, and Decca. These LPs were very popular in Japan, and Taylor recorded LPs exclusively for the Japanese market, the first American jazzman to do so. He continued to do this into the early 1970s. During Atlantic's greatest period, the only other saxophonist used regularly on New York R&B sessions was Al Sears.

BIG AL SEARS

Sears (1910–1990) was a complete musician in the sense that at various times in his career, he was a sideman, a bandleader, a recording-session player, and a leader of his own record dates. He also worked as a music publisher, label manager, and business manager for different groups he played with. He was born in Illinois and was a professional musician by his late teens. He worked out of Buffalo and the Cincinnati area for many years before landing in the name bands of Andy Kirk, Lionel Hampton, and, from 1944 to 1948, the Duke Ellington Orchestra. Sears established himself as a soloist with the Ellington band. He termed himself a "salesman" when he worked with Ellington, suggesting, modestly, that after Johnny Hodges, Harry Carney, and other Ellingtonians, there was little left to play.

Sears was a honker to be sure, but his style emphasized a deep moaning sound that was especially effective on slow blues material. Among his features with Ellington was "Carnegie Blues," later adapted by Jimmy Forrest into "Bolo Blues." After leaving Ellington, he joined the Johnny Hodges band that recorded his composition "Castle Rock." The tune that featured an unbilled Sears throughout became a top 5 R&B hit in 1951. Although he was of average height, Alan Freed nicknamed him "Big Al Sears." Among his celebrated solos are Big Joe Turner's "Flip, Flop, and Fly" (Atlantic), "Saved" by Lavern Baker (Atlantic), and "It Hurts Me to My Heart" by Faye Adams (Herald).

KING CURTIS

King Curtis Ousley (1934–1971) came to the attention of Atlantic in 1958 through his appearance on records by the Coasters produced by Leiber and Stoller. Until 1958, most Coasters recording was done in Los Angeles; but once the producers moved to New York, King Curtis was on almost everything. If he was new to Atlantic, Curtis had been active around New York, playing sessions and even recording dates of his own for several years. Once he began recording for Atlantic, he shifted into high gear. The numbers of calls for Sam Taylor and Al Sears began to decline, although they never completely disappeared.

Curtis recorded his own projects for Atco and then went to Prestige where he made jazz albums and played behind a number of older blues singers on Bluesville in addition to making his own R&B LPs for Tru-Sound. Upon exiting Prestige, he immediately hit the jackpot with "Soul Twist," a #1 R&B hit on Enjoy in 1962. Later hits came with "Soul Serenade" on Capitol in 1964 and "Memphis Soul Stew" and "Ode to Billie Joe" on Atco. Upon his return to Atco in 1965, Curtis became more than just a bandleader and session player; he was active as a producer and became very much a part of the Atlantic inner circle. He assembled one of the last great R&B ensembles, the Kingpins, which featured pianist Richard Tee, guitarist Cornell Dupree, bassist Chuck Rainey, and drummer Bernard Purdie. In addition to their own jobs, the Kingpins backed Aretha Franklin in her greatest period. Curtis's only rival for rock-'n'-roll saxophone supremacy in the 1960s was Motown's Junior Walker.

If Sears and Taylor were the top 2 session saxophonists in New York before King Curtis, Jesse Powell, Hal Singer, and Jimmy Wright were also present on lots of record dates. Being the house tenor player for Rama, Gee, End, Gone, and other George Goldner labels meant that Wright (1907–1987) was heard on all the Frankie Lymon and the Teenagers, Cleftones, and Valentines hits. He also appeared on several Freed New York concerts.

Jesse Powell (1924–1982) from Fort Worth, Texas, replaced Illinois Jacquet in the 1946 Count Basie band. He played bebop with Howard McGhee at the 1948 Paris Jazz Festival and played in the same reed section as Jimmy Heath, John Coltrane, and Paul Gonsalves in the 1949–1950 Dizzy Gillespie big band. He had recorded a couple of dates for Federal in the early 1950s before hooking up with the Jubilee/Josie combine in 1954. There he played most of the tenor solos on the Cadillacs' hits and made a few isolated items of his own. In the 1960s, he made albums for Tru-Sound and Kapp. A big-sounding Texas tenor, Powell had a tonal quality very close to that of Herschel Evans. For much of the 1960s and 1970s, he played in Harlem operating beneath the radar.

Bob Porter
by Susan Kaprov

Al Sears, Courtesy of Billy Vera

Sam "the Man" Taylor, 1945, Courtesy of Mark Cantor

Alan Freed Rehearsal 1956. From left: Alan Freed, Morris Levy, Teddy Reig, Chuck Berry, Lillian Briggs (trombone), Leroy Kirkland (in suit), Lloyd Trottman (bass). Remainder unknown. Courtesy of Billy Vera.

Ralph Bass 1991
by Joe Rosen

Paul Williams 1992
by Joe Rosen

Cootie Williams 1966
by Ed Berger

Jack McDuff 1961 by Frank Wolff

Lou Donaldson 1961 by Frank Wolff

Jack McDuff, Jimmy McGriff, Gloria Coleman, Charles Earland. 1992 by Bill May

The chapters on Gene Ammons, Hank Crawford, Grant Green and Grover Washington, Jr originally appeared as much shorter pieces in Radio Free Jazz. Thanks to Ira Sabin.

Photo credits:
Esmond Edwards photographs are (c) Esmond Edwards/CTS Images.
Frank Wolff photographs are (c) Francis Wolff/ Mosaic Images LLC.
Joe Rosen photographs are (c) Joseph A. Rosen. Bill May photograph (c) Bill May.
Cootie Williams photograph (c) Ed Berger.

Photographers unknown on the following: Al Sears and Alan Freed rehearsal courtesy of the Billy Vera collection. Sam "the Man" Taylor photograph courtesy of the Mark Cantor collection. Houston Person-Grant Green photograph courtesy of the Bob Porter collection.

Cover Photo:
The group is the Jimmy Smith Trio; Jimmy Smith, organ; Eddie McFadden, guitar and Donald Bailey, drums. The photo is by Frank Wolff. The photo is (c) Francis Wolff/Mosaic Images LLC.

R&B SAXOPHONE STARS

There were similar specialists in other recording centers such as Chicago, New Orleans, and Los Angeles.

In Chicago, both Eddie Chamblee (1920–1999) and Red Holloway (1927–2012) were active in the 1950s. Chamblee did lots of session work for Chess, United, and other smaller labels. He ultimately left Chicago with the Lionel Hampton band in 1955 and became music director for Dinah Washington the following year. He married Dinah in 1957, and that led to a pair of his LPs recorded for Emarcy. The marriage didn't last, and Chamblee moved to New York where he made one album for Prestige and played with a variety of leaders. He occasionally reunited with Hampton and toured Europe with him during the 1980s.

Holloway worked at Chance and Vee Jay records as a tenor man of all trades throughout the decade before joining Lloyd Price and then Jack McDuff. He settled in Los Angeles in 1967 where he played with everyone as leader of the house band at the Parisian Room for fifteen years. During that time, he also managed to tour with British bluesman John Mayall in 1974 and 1975 and co-lead a two-tenor group with Sonny Stitt on occasion. With the move to a touring schedule with Price and McDuff, much of Holloway's work fell to Gene Barge.

Barge (1926–) settled into blues work in Chicago after working in Norfolk, Virginia, with Gary "US" Bonds. He was heard on the Bonds hits "Quarter to Three" and "New Orleans." His duties at Chess included producing and arranging as well. Among his most famous solos are "CC Rider" by Chuck Willis (Atlantic), "Wang Dang Doodle" by Koko Taylor (Checker), and "Don't Mess Up a Good Thing" by Fontella Bass and Bobby McClure (Checker).

Red Holloway did his share of studio work in Los Angeles, but by the time he arrived, the demand was considerably reduced. And most of what was left was the property of Plas Johnson (1931–). Johnson was originally from New Orleans and made a few records with his pianist brother Ray before being drafted. Originally inspired by Lee Allen, he settled in Los Angeles after his discharge from the military in 1954.

Johnson became a protégé of Maxwell Davis. Davis (1916–1970) played a vast percentage of R&B saxophone solos on LA record dates from the mid-'40s to mid-'50s. By the time Plas Johnson arrived in town, Davis was growing less interested in playing and more interested in arranging and producing, which he did for Aladdin, Modern, and many other labels. Plas leaped immediately into the scene and never looked back. His distinctive sound graced hundreds of recordings of all kinds. Among his finest sideman work is with Sam Cooke ("Twistin' the Night Away") on RCA, King Pleasure ("DB Blues") on Aladdin, and the Drifters ("Your Promise to Be Mine") on Atlantic.

He made his own albums for Tampa, Capitol, Charter (under the name Johnny Beecher), and Concord and, intermittently since the 1980s, his own Carell Music label. He and Red Holloway teamed for a 2001 session, *Keep That Groove Going*, for Milestone.

If most of the Los Angeles R&B work was done by Plas Johnson, virtually *all* the tenor solos on New Orleans sessions were handled by Lee Allen. Allen (1927–1994) began playing professionally with Paul Gayten and worked on sessions for Gayten and Dave Bartholomew, the two major R&B producers in New Orleans. It didn't much matter whether it was done for Imperial, Chess, Specialty, or Ace; if it was recorded in New Orleans, it was Lee Allen on tenor sax. The only major exception was the recordings of Fats Domino where Allen's work was shared with others, notably Herb Hardesty. His signature song "Walkin' with Mr. Lee" was a minor hit for Ember in 1958. The heyday of New Orleans R&B recording was over by 1960, and Allen moved to Los Angeles. He left music about this time but returned in the '80s as a part of the roots/rock band the Blasters. He was also a part of Fats Domino's touring band on many occasions. Included among his many memorable solos are "Let the Good Times Roll" by Shirley and Lee (Aladdin), "I Didn't Want to Do It" by the Spiders (Imperial), and "Long Tall Sally" by Little Richard (Specialty).

While baritone sax was featured on many R&B recordings in most cases, it was exclusively an ensemble instrument. The one player who was used as a soloist on New York sessions was Haywood Henry (1913–1994). Henry was a member of the Erskine Hawkins band until the mid-1950s. In the Hawkins band, he doubled clarinet and occasionally tenor sax, but he was the key baritone sax man on many of arranger Jesse Stone's sessions and Alan Freed stage shows. His famous solos include "Shake, Rattle, and Roll" by Big Joe Turner (Atlantic), "Speedo" by the Cadillacs (Josie), and "Hey, Bartender" on Cat by Floyd Dixon.

MICKEY "GUITAR" BAKER

The quintessential guitarist of the era was McHouston "Mickey" Baker. Baker (1925–2012), born in Louisville, was discovered and promoted by Leroy Kirkland. He was first heard on Savoy with Varetta Dillard in 1952 but more importantly for Atlantic on "Mama, He Treats Your Daughter Mean" by Ruth Brown. His playing changed the entire era, and it didn't matter whether it was his bluesy intros and fills, his strong backbeat, or a solo style that brought something new to the blues. There is no guitarist playing R&B in the 1950s who didn't get something from Mickey Baker. In Jerry Wexler's words, he was "the Man."

Baker had a huge record of his own with "Love Is Strange," a duet with Sylvia Vanderpool, which became one of the most memorable records of the early rock-'n'-roll era. It was sparked by a guitar line that Baker copped from a Billy Stewart record where it was played by Chicago bluesman Jody Williams. The success of "Love Is Strange" took Baker out of the recording studios as Mickey and Sylvia became a mainstay on the touring shows of the time. When he returned to the studios, his magic was no longer special. The music had changed and moved on. Baker moved to Paris in the mid-1960s and became very much a part of that city's musical landscape, as a player, a recording artist, and an author of guitar instructional books.

In the early 1950s, singers and vocal groups were coming into the music on an almost daily basis. The raw talent of many of these performers needed to be shaped and molded by arrangers who knew what they were doing. Kirkland, Stone, and Biggs were among the key arrangers involved in the early years of rhythm and blues in New York.

In other parts of the country, important arrangers included Willie Dixon, the key organizer at Chess; Lloyd Glenn, the music director for Swingtime and Aladdin at various times; Maxwell Davis, who would be in charge of sessions in Los Angeles for Aladdin, Specialty, and Modern; Joe Scott, an important part of Duke/Peacock in Houston; and Dave Bartholomew, Imperial's man in New Orleans. Pianist Allen Toussaint worked as a producer with a variety of New Orleans labels in the early 1960s. In some cases, these men would be arrangers only; at other times they might be used as players as well, but in all cases, their opinions were frequently solicited and always valued. In some cases, they were de facto producers.

For Atlantic, the choice of sidemen on a recording session was an important part of the preparation. Unlike other labels where those choices were left to the arrangers, Atlantic would specify who would be the tenor sax man, guitarist, and rhythm players. Ertegun's partner, beginning in 1953, Jerry Wexler (1917–2008), suggested that these decisions were not the product of deep philosophical discussions but more of a question of using the very best, hottest players available. And when they were hot, everyone wanted them. Sidemen were never credited in those years, and in many instances, their identity was a closely guarded secret. The golden years for this group of Atlantic studio players were 1953–1955. Ertegun and Wexler created masterpieces of R&B during that time. They were the classic examples of New York City R&B just as Chess captured the best in Chicago blues, and the Dave Bartholomew–produced Imperial sessions were the quintessential New Orleans R&B recordings. Oddly enough, all hit creative peaks during the same years.

MORE R&B RADIO

Radio in the 1950s was on the AM band. Many stations specialized in block programming: a set amount of time, usually sponsored, devoted to a specific topic.

That format, as well as the network programming of CBS, Mutual, and NBC, was being challenged. The assault was coming not from stations but from personalities. Radio fans were developing an affinity with DJs rather than formats, even stations. For R&B radio, the nighttime was the right time. By the mid-'50s, there was at least one R&B show in every big city. And the hosts of those shows were some of the legendary voices in radio.

The disc jockeys are an essential ingredient in the history of the music. Hunter Hancock in Los Angeles, Poppa Stoppa in New Orleans, Bill Cooke in Newark, Al Benson in Chicago, Tommy "Doctor Jive" Smalls in New York, Zenas Sears in Atlanta, Bill Marlowe in Boston, and George "the Hound" Lorenz in Buffalo were some of them. Most but not all were white. Alan Freed was white, and more than any man, he brought R&B into the homes of white America.

ALAN FREED

Freed (1921–1965) was a jazz lover first. He played trombone and was an enthusiastic fan of swing music in his youth. At one point, his dream was to lead his own big band. During a brief stay in college, he became interested in broadcasting. He chose it as a profession, and after working at several Ohio stations, he landed at WJW in Cleveland in the fall of 1951. It was here that he created the persona of Moondog. Once he latched on to the gimmick, he described his audience as Moondoggers and billed himself as King of the Moondoggers. In time, he would give up the name, but from late 1951–1954, Alan Freed was Moondog. And on March 21, 1952, working with a local promoter and record store owner, he rented the Cleveland Arena for a live show touted as the Moondog Coronation Ball. Although the Dominos, Danny Cobb, and Varetta Dillard were on the show, top billing went to Tiny Grimes and his Rockin' Highlanders and Paul Williams's Hucklebuckers.

Williams played the only song that night as the arena was stormed by somewhere, depending on the estimates, between six and ten thousand gate-crashers; and chaos ensued. Many years later, *LIFE* magazine referred to the event as the first rock-'n'-roll concert. It was hardly that, but significantly, the overwhelmingly black audience did not think to ask for their money back, so the promoters actually made a tidy profit!

LEW SIMPKINS

Of the new R&B labels, United Records, a Chicago-based independent owned by Leonard Allen and Lew Simpkins, showed the most promise. Simpkins had started at the Miracle label where he produced the Sonny Thompson smash "Long Gone." He then joined Miracle owner Lee Egalnick when he formed Premium; but when Premium folded, he convinced his friend Allen, a Chicago policeman, to put up the money to start United.

Simpkins's first hit for United was by alto saxophonist Tab Smith whose silky ballad reading of "Because of You" hit #1 on the R&B charts. Smith (1909–1971) had played and arranged for Count Basie and Lucky Millinder before forming his own combo during WWII. Stylistically he had more in common with Johnny Hodges than he did with Earl Bostic or James Moody, other hit-making alto saxophonists of the time. Although he had no other hits, Smith recorded for United into 1957 and also recorded sessions for Chess and King before the end of his recording career in 1960.

Simpkins used Universal studios in Chicago for his sessions and benefited from the superior audio quality rendered by engineer Bill Putnam. United proved to be a major competitor for Chess during the early 1950s as Simpkins brought major blues artists such as Roosevelt Sykes, Memphis Slim, and Robert Nighthawk to the label in addition to jazz stars such as Paul Bascomb, Gene Ammons, and Leo Parker. When Simpkins died in 1953 at the age of thirty-five, the music lost one of the great producers of the era. United would continue for a time, but it was never the same again.

TINY BRADSHAW

Myron "Tiny" Bradshaw (1905–1958) had emerged as one of the most exciting combo leaders. He had fronted a big band during the 1930s and 1940s that was headquartered in Ohio. Originally inspired by Cab Calloway, Bradshaw could croon smoky ballads or jump the blues with the best of them. He trimmed down to combo size in the late 1940s and found a niche where others could not. His first King label hits "Well, Oh Well" and "I'm Going to Have Myself a Ball," both from 1950, were classic jump blues featuring strong tenor sax work from Rufus Gore. In 1952, Red Prysock joined the band and created a hit with his tenor sax work on "Soft." A follow-up, "Heavy Juice," also scored with black record buyers. From this point forward, virtually all Bradshaw recordings would be instrumentals. This wasn't so good for an uncredited sideman like Prysock, but after Bradshaw suffered a stroke in 1954, his band was able make records despite the fact that the leader was disabled! The instrumentals featured Prysock or replacements such as Sil Austin, Noble Watts, and Gore. They continued through 1955, and a final session was cut in 1958 shortly before Bradshaw's death.

This was just about the end of the road for the Erskine Hawkins and Lucky Millinder big bands. Hawkins had contributed much to the music and would continue in diminished form. Like his Gale Agency stablemate Buddy Johnson, Hawkins had long been identified with Harlem's Savoy Ballroom, but ballrooms were closing left and right. The full Hawkins band worked on Alan Freed shows, but his final two record dates of the 1950s (King in 1953, Decca in 1956) were made with a trimmed-down nine-piece band. He would record again in a small-group jazz context during the early 1960s.

Millinder, whose final King date, with a pickup band, was cut in early 1955, did some disc jockey work in New York for a period before leaving the business entirely. He had one more recording date, for Warwick, in 1960. He died in 1966.

Alan Freed continued to promote live shows throughout Ohio.

He used the black big bands as part of his stage shows that were being promoted all over Ohio. Count Basie, Buddy Johnson, and Erskine Hawkins all worked side by side with the Moonglows, Flamingos, Tiny Bradshaw, Big Joe Turner, and other R&B hit makers not only in Freed-promoted shows but also on package tours put together by Shaw, Gale, or other top agencies. Tenor sax stars Arnett Cobb, Sam Butera (signed by RCA), and Rusty Bryant, who had strong-selling Dot singles, were on display as well.

In September 1952, plans to syndicate his radio program were announced. WNJR in Newark, New Jersey, was the first station in the east to carry the show. The following year, he produced his first stage show in Newark. It attracted more than ten thousand fans, and the audience was predominantly fifteen to twenty years old and about 20 percent white. Beginning in September 1954, Alan Freed was heard on WINS, New York. Syndication to as many as sixty markets was sought.

NORMAN GRANZ

Norman Granz was rolling like a juggernaut through the jazz business of the early 1950s. Jazz at the Philharmonic had become an international touring organization. The troupe played Europe for the first time in the spring of 1952 where they were a huge success. The fall tour of the United States began September 12 and played sixty-four cities and four universities. In 1953, JATP undertook an expanded European schedule; and after a lengthy fall tour, it continued on to Hawaii and Japan, where the musicians were treated like visiting royalty.

Beginning in 1949, Granz had become Charlie Parker's major patron. After signing Parker to Mercury, Granz recorded him in a variety of settings in addition to straight-ahead bebop: big bands, voices, Latin jazz, and, most successfully, with strings.

Parker was not a JATP regular but was presented with JATP on special Carnegie Hall occasions that were recorded and ultimately issued under the JATP banner. Parker was also a participant in the earliest of Granz's studio Jam Session made for 12" LP. While the concept of some of these projects could be questioned, Parker's own work was beyond reproach. He was consistently brilliant. By 1954, Charlie Parker's work was losing some of its luster. He died in March 1955.

His sidekick Dizzy Gillespie had fallen on hard times. His big band broke up in 1950, and his Capitol Records deal was not renewed. He recorded a small-group date for Prestige and a 10" LP with strings for Discovery before forming Dee Gee Records with Detroit businessman Dave Usher in April 1951. He continued to operate Dee Gee until its 1953 bankruptcy but also recorded for French Vogue while in Europe and did a one-shot for Atlantic, who also licensed some of the French material for US release. In December 1953, Granz signed him to his new Norgran label, and they began a period of rewarding collaborations that presented Gillespie in a number of challenging settings.

In 1953, Granz left Mercury at the conclusion of his production and distribution deal and formed his labels: Clef, Norgran, and Down Home. Because the stars of his JATP shows also recorded for his labels, Granz had a unique ability to cross-promote. He made licensing deals for his records in different European countries so that when JATP toured Europe in the spring, he was able to again use promotional tie-ins to benefit record sales and concert tickets. Regulars on the JATP circuit in the early 1950s were tenor saxophonists Flip Phillips, Ben Webster, and Lester Young; trumpet stars Roy Eldridge and Charlie Shavers (collectively known as the Midgets); trombonist Bill Harris; alto saxophonist Willie Smith; and drummers Gene Krupa and Buddy Rich. Anchoring everything was the Oscar Peterson Trio with Barney Kessel or Herb Ellis on guitar and bassist Ray Brown. Yet Ella Fitzgerald had become the most important part of the show, and her closing set was usually the most popular moment of the evening.

Some of the showcase numbers devised by Granz for his concerts included items such as the Challenges, featuring tenors and trumpets going at each other, the Ballad Medley with each of the players doing a chorus of a favorite standard, and the Drum Battle, usually featuring Krupa and Rich. Granz stated that 1954 was a banner year for JATP, with a $360,000 domestic gross for thirty-seven dates, an increase of 20 percent over 1953.

MORRIS LEVY

Other promoters were very much aware of Granz and his success. While Shaw Artists and the Gale Agency each took big losses on 1954 jazz tours, the Birdland organization of Morris Levy had the benefit of its own radio show (which continued after the departure of Symphony Sid) and its own theme song ("Lullaby of Birdland"). It had opened a second Birdland, in Miami, earlier in the year. In August, the organization promoted events at Carnegie Hall in New York as well as Symphony Hall in Boston with the likes of Count Basie, Billie Holiday, and Lester Young that were so successful that plans were laid for a full-scale tour. Levy was also promoting R&B shows, having worked on Alan Freed's first ventures in New York in December.

Morris Levy (1927–1990) came up through the nightclub business as a photo and hatcheck concessionaire. His first major club was Birdland, which he opened in 1949. The basement club on Broadway just north of Fifty-second Street played the best jazz groups in the country for the next fifteen years. The emcee was diminutive Pee Wee Marquette, who would introduce each member of the band and identify celebrities in the house. The club also had a section for underage patrons. Levy would later have a piece of other clubs, notably the Roundtable and the Embers.

Levy got into publishing with Patricia Music whose first copyright was "Lullaby of Birdland," written by George Shearing. He was a powerful force in the publishing business for many years. In 1950, Levy had been partners with Bob Weinstock in Birdland Records. Within months of the start, Levy got into a financial jam and was bailed out by Weinstock. In return, Weinstock got the Birdland masters including exceptional sessions by Stan Getz and Gene Ammons. It took a few years, but Levy returned to the record business with a greater commitment and greater success.

In 1956, Levy formed Roulette Records that started with rockabilly hits by Buddy Knox and Jimmy Bowen. Roulette built a strong jazz LP catalog, much of it produced by Teddy Reig, with artists such as Count Basie, Maynard Ferguson, Joe Williams, and Sarah Vaughan. Roulette was a powerful label in the pop and R&B fields for the next twenty years.

Tiny Bradshaw instrumentals and Earl Bostic records were minor success stories in 1954, but Arnett Cobb and Sil Austin contributed solos to hit records by the Midnighters, the top R&B group of the year. David "Bubba" Brooks played behind the Charms while Sam Taylor was blowing on hit records by the Chords ("Sh'Boom") and the Drifters.

Lee Allen was on seemingly *every* R&B record that came out of New Orleans whether it was by the Spiders or Fats Domino or Smiley Lewis. Al Sears was moaning behind Faye Adams or the Hearts. Clearly, the high-water year for rhythm and blues was 1954; but consider the diversity: New Orleans R&B, Chicago blues, great vocal groups from almost everywhere, the Memphis music of B. B. King and Johnny Ace, and even a hit from Buddy Johnson and his band ("I'm Just Your Fool"). All this would change but the reasons for this change are equally diverse.

While the Korean War was winding down in July of 1953, much of the jazz record business was on vacation. Within a month, Blue Note would be recording Bud Powell, Sidney Bechet, and Clifford Brown; Art Farmer made his leader debut, and Teddy Charles produced some West Coast jazz for Prestige; Doug Duke was recording an organ trio for Savoy while Stan Getz with Bob Brookmeyer, Louie Bellson, Buddy Rich, and the second Jam Session featuring Count Basie were Norman Granz productions of the time. Johnny Ace, B. B. King, and the Orioles were hot on the R&B charts while Nat "King" Cole had a top-selling 10" LP: *Two in Love*.

BOB SHAD

After Bob Shad had spent a few months with Decca, he returned to Mercury where he headed up the new Emarcy label. This was an LP line that concentrated on jazz and jazz-related projects. None of the other large labels followed this lead, but Emarcy became an important factor in the jazz LP business for the rest of the decade. The major signings at Emarcy were Cannonball Adderley and the Clifford Brown–Max Roach group. Brown (1930–1956) had appeared on Prestige and Blue Note prior to Emarcy, but it is his 1954–1956 recordings for which he is best remembered. Brown was unquestionably a great trumpet player and the natural heir to Fats Navarro (1926–1950) as a master of modern, melodic, improvisational flow. His 1956 death in an automobile accident was a major blow to the music.

Emarcy also recorded singers signed to the parent company such as Patti Page, Sarah Vaughan, and Dinah Washington in a jazz context.

KING PLEASURE-JAMES MOODY

There had been one new musical development in jazz that had shown some commercial potential. It was not actually all that new, but it came directly from the culture. Scat singing had developed by using wordless syllables to emulate instrumental solos, but vocalese involved creating a lyric for a solo that had already been recorded. The first and most important solo to receive that treatment was Coleman Hawkins's "Body and Soul," but Illinois Jacquet's "Flyin' Home" solo from Lionel

Hampton's Decca recording was another. At social functions, young adults would display their abilities at what was originally referred to as "blowin'" by improvising a lyric to a solo from a well-known record. Teenagers, around a jukebox, had been doing the same thing for quite a while. While vocalese didn't have that great an impact, it should be pointed out that doo-wop harmonies and the poetry of rap developed in similar circumstances.

It was King Pleasure (born Clarence Beeks, 1922–1981) who first brought vocalese to prominence. Pleasure produced hit recordings of solos by James Moody ("Moody's Mood for Love") and Gene Ammons ("Red Top") for Prestige. The hit status was the result of heavy airplay on black radio. Yet these records were aired only in big northern cities and held almost no appeal for Southern markets. The acceptance of vocalese demonstrated that the right jazz record could be a factor on R&B radio shows in the years to come. Pleasure found additional material in solos by Charlie Parker, Stan Getz, and Lester Young. While not achieving the sales success of his hits, they were a staple of jazz radio long after they were first issued.

Given Pleasure's success, it is a bit surprising that more vocalese wasn't attempted at the time; but the Annie Ross recordings of Wardell Gray's "Twisted" and "Farmer's Market" were the only other, even modest, hits. After Pleasure left Prestige, he had no hits on other labels. Vocalese receded into the background, but the methodology had been established, and it would be back.

The source of "Moody's Mood for Love" was an alto solo played by James Moody, on a borrowed instrument, for the Swedish label, Metronome, in 1949. The instrumental was licensed to Prestige for US distribution. Jazz radio started the record, and Symphony Sid was a key disc jockey in creating the hit because of his clear channel on WJZ.

When Moody (1925–2010) returned to the United States after a three-year European stay, he was a star with a hit record. He was quickly signed by Bob Shad for Mercury and was recorded from 1951 to 1953 with a seven-piece band similar to those of other saxophonists such as Arnett Cobb and Earl Bostic. Babs Gonzales contributed vocalese to two of the Mercury sides, but once Moody moved to Prestige in 1954, he hired Eddie Jefferson to sing.

It was Jefferson (1918–1979) who had written the lyric to "Moody's Mood for Love." This was objected to strenuously by the original writers of "I'm in the Mood for Love" who forced Prestige to withdraw the single.

White label bootleg 45s of "Moody's Mood for Love" were sold under the counter by record stores in black neighborhoods for years to come. Jefferson would create more vocalese with the Moody band, notably "Disappointed," based on a Charlie Parker solo, which was a jukebox favorite.

The Moody band walked a fine line between jazz and R&B. It was part of R&B package tours and even did studio accompaniment for the Moonglows on one occasion. Yet the band featured arrangements by young writers such as Quincy Jones and Benny Golson as well as some extended blowing on items such as "Jammin' with James" and "Wail Moody Wail." Moody moved to the Argo label in 1956 and continued to record there even after the band broke up in 1961.

RALPH WEINBERG

Ralph Weinberg died in 1953. Little known outside the agency business, Weinberg was an example of an important component in the black music business that went back to the prewar era. Weinberg would buy four to six weeks of dates from Gale, Shaw, or ABC in order to promote shows through Virginia, West Virginia, the Carolinas, and North Georgia. He knew every theater, ballroom, nightclub, ballpark, arena, auditorium, and tobacco warehouse in his territory. He kept black artists working when nobody else in his area could have. Other Southern promoters included Frank Painia in New Orleans, Don Robey in Houston, and Howard Lewis in Dallas. These men were some of the leading suppliers of talent to what was referred to as the "Chittlin' Circuit."

Joe Louis had lost his heavyweight title, had retired from the ring, and had been the subject of relentless harassment by his government regarding income taxes. It would continue for the rest of his life. Doubtless, better advice and better decision making by the Champ would have saved him considerable grief, but the attitude of the United States toward one of its legitimate heroes was unforgivable. The next wave of highly visible athletes such as Jim Brown and Bill Russell would not make those mistakes and would be more in line with the Jackie Robinson model.

Brown v. Board of Education was decided in 1954, and the legal basis for segregation was overturned. In the unanimous Supreme Court ruling, Chief Justice Earl Warren stated, "In the field of public education, the doctrine of separate but equal has no place." The attitudes of Americans would be slow to change, but the first move toward equality had been made. It would take well over two decades to see tangible results in many parts of the country.

The United States had concluded another war, this time on the Korean Peninsula. The Korean War was not given that status by the politicians who termed it a "police action." Despite the fact that thousands of American soldiers had died in that "police action," it ended not with a formal surrender aboard a battleship but a truce. The United States still has thousands of troops in Korea, and the edgy relationship between North and South Korea still exists, as does the truce.

Plans for the demolition of the Savoy Ballroom were announced. The property had been sold to the city of New York, and the formal closure of Harlem's legendary dance hall would signify the end of another era. It would take until 1958 for the official closing, but the die had been cast.

The sidemen of the black big bands were now faced with handwriting on the walls in very bold print. Many of them, who had been employed in the same unit for many years, would now have to find new ways to make a living. Erskine Hawkins's sidemen such as Leroy Kirkland, Sammy Lowe, and Heywood Henry would find work plentiful in the recording studios. Others would have to scuffle, and many left music altogether. Black music had changed in six years from a specialty business for a few independent record labels to a major factor in the entertainment world. Record manufacturing and distribution, radio, jukeboxes, and touring had all undergone significant changes during that period; but those organizations that survived the pitfalls had been able to grow and prosper.

For jazz, things had also changed. The music was becoming increasingly segregated. Bebop, soon to be known as hard bop, couldn't exist on the same stages with New Orleans revivalists; and the attitudes of fans tended to suggest that one could appreciate one *or* the other. It would take the arrival of the Jazz Festival, a new concept in 1954, to permit the different styles to come together under the same banner.

In 1945, there were few studio jobs open for black musicians, but rhythm and blues had changed all that. In 1949, most recording was done by working groups; but by the end of 1954, that was no longer the case. The need for tenor sax soloists and rhythm section players who specialized became the rule following the lead of Atlantic Records. In time, music fans would come to know the identity of the players in the recording orchestras hired by Dave Bartholomew in New Orleans, the Funk Brothers of Motown fame, and the Stax Records house band; but in the mid-1950s, the identity of recording session sidemen was still privileged information.

It was still very much an "us" (black acts, black records, independent labels, BMI) vs. "them" (white acts, white records, major labels, ASCAP) adversarial situation. The difference was that there were now over one hundred labels working the jazz and R&B territories. If the big labels ever figured out how to do what the indies were doing, things could change very quickly. The major labels had superior financial, promotional, and distributional resources; and it would be possible for them to co-opt the whole scene.

Gene Ammons 1958 by Frank Wolff

GENE AMMONS

FUNERALS ARE FOR THE LIVING; and to soloist Floyd Overall, who sang "Precious Lord," or Rev. Marion H. Hall, who read scripture and a prayer, it was business as usual. For some people, funerals are a livelihood. For the one hundred fifty odd souls who gathered at the Tabernacle Missionary Baptist Church in Chicago on Saturday, August 10, 1974, it was a distinctly gloomy day. Rain started at 9:30 AM and would last until late afternoon.

The Reverend Edsel Ammons gave a brief tribute to his brother; Reverend Gatemouth Moore spoke; and the eulogy was delivered by the pastor, Dr. Louis Rawls, father of the singer Lou Rawls. The front pews were arranged in a unique fashion: the left front was occupied by the de facto family, including longtime companion Geraldine Marshall, while the right front contained the family de jure headed by wife Mildred Ammons. Front row center was empty-functioning as a kind of DMZ.

There was music: Chicago tenor man Prince James played "The Lord's Prayer" while Sonny Stitt, on tenor, did "My Buddy." The recessional was, appropriately, "Red Top," the longtime Ammons theme, with James joining Stitt and the rhythm section of Amina Claudine Myers, Pete Cosey, and Ajaramu Joseph Shelton.

If press releases are the publicity for personal appearances, obituaries serve the same function for funerals. The *New York Times* obit was incredibly bungled and contained a good deal of wrong information.

The date of birth was incorrect on the funeral program, and two of the pallbearers were not present. There were floral bouquets from Ray Charles and Miles Davis, among many others, but the size of the crowd seemed slim for such a favorite son of the Windy City. No doubt it was still the middle of the night for his professional associates, but if there is to be an epitaph for Gene Ammons, it would surely be the old blues refrain: "If it wasn't for bad luck, he wouldn't have no luck at all."

Gene Ammons was born in Chicago on April 14, 1925. His father, Albert Ammons, was the finest of all the boogie-woogie pianists; and his mother was also a pianist. Gene began on C-melody saxophone and took up tenor at Du Sable High School where he studied under Captain Walter Dyett, the legendary educator who helped so many Chicago musicians during this time. Prior to graduation, he left school to join the band of another Chicago legend, trumpeter King Kolax.

In 1944, he joined the big band of Billy Eckstine. The Eckstine band was an incubator for the burgeoning bebop movement; and stars such as Dizzy Gillespie, Fats Navarro, and Art Blakey were a part of it. Charlie Parker was with the band briefly while Wardell Gray recorded with it. During the time Ammons was with the band, he sat in the same reed section with future associates Leo Parker, Dexter Gordon, and Sonny Stitt. This was a band filled with "tempestuous youth," in Gordon's phrase, and there are dozens of stories involving the personal excesses of its members. It was also about this time that he acquired a nickname that would stay with him throughout his life. Some members of the band had visited a store in order to check out new hats. When Eckstine discovered what Ammons's hat size was, he blurted out, "You jug-head motherfucker!" It wasn't long before the nickname became, simply, Jug.

Ammons was one of the few who stayed straight during this period. Perhaps because of this, Eckstine rewarded him with the lion's share of the saxophone solos on the band's recordings. Among the earliest Eckstine jazz favorites was "Blowin' the Blues Away," a tenor sax battle involving Ammons and Gordon. Ammons, always a listener, had battled Gordon by throwing some of Dexter's phrases back at him. When Lester Young heard the record, he told Gordon that "Lady Jug copped your shit."

Ammons stayed with the band until its early 1947 breakup. Returning to Chicago, he made his first records, for Mercury, and had an immediate hit with "Red Top." The performance, in which Ammons begins his solo with an audacious quotation of "Alice Blue Gown," is a memorable one; and the saxophone solo was given words (by King Pleasure) that resulted in a rebirth of popularity six years later. The theme is still a popular one among jazz and blues groups, and it is not uncommon for a blues pianist or guitarist to remember Ammons's solo when performing the song. He recorded for Mercury from 1947 to 1949 with time-out for the recording ban imposed by the American Federation of Musicians during 1948. He also recorded for Chess during this period. During much of 1948, he was involved in the tenor battles that had become a growing part of Chicago nightlife. He took on Tom Archia, Dick Davis, Eddie Chamblee, and Eddie Johnson, among others, in local contests (often run by DJ Al Benson) and never lost a match. The late 1940s was the era when the legend of Gene Ammons grew in his own hometown.

He spent six months with Woody Herman beginning in the spring of 1949. This was an unusual step since the only other black musicians were trumpeter Ernie Royal and bassist Oscar Pettiford—who didn't stay very long. The band was a good one with lots of talent but also lots of heroin addicts. Ammons wasn't used to a great extent on Herman's Capitol recordings. He had a short bit on "Not Really the Blues," but his work on "More Moon" contained another memorable solo. During his stay, the band had a lengthy tour with the Nat "King" Cole Trio that generated several radio broadcasts. Hearing Ammons play solos that were once given to Stan Getz shows how much influence he had on players in the band in a very short time.

Listening to the early recordings of Gene Ammons is instructive since his style seems fully formed. While he was very conversant with the harmonic intricacies of bebop, that was not the only music he played. Illinois Jacquet played a part in his conception. The hard-driving honking of Jacquet was absorbed and filtered through his own persona to be used in his way when needed. Possessor of an enormous tone, Ammons would use it to full advantage on ballads ("My Foolish Heart," the first hit of Chess Records, is a standout from this period). At other times, especially in these early years, he would modify his sound to emulate the style of Lester Young. Yet the single most important quality of a jazz soloist is evident in Ammons's work from the beginning: he is a master storyteller. His solos have a beginning, a middle, and an end. He was a deft interpreter and a great communicator.

In 1950, Ammons began an association with Sonny Stitt. The Ammons group, which also featured pianist Junior Mance, was assembled and managed by Richard Carpenter throughout its entire existence. The unit featured the tenor sax battle as a part of the act. In some arrangements, Ammons would play baritone sax in the seven-piece band; and on others, Stitt would play it. At the time of the group's formation, each man had a recording deal with Prestige, so the billing was equal on the records. Ammons, because of his popularity, was a bit more than a senior partner when the group first got started; but in time, it became more balanced, and the group was a successful one at a time when there were not a lot of popular jazz groups. From their earliest session came "Blues Up and Down," a staple in Ammons's repertoire for the rest of his life. It was first recorded for Birdland, a label co-owned by Morris Levy and Bob Weinstock. Within a few short months, Weinstock bought out Levy; and the music was reissued on Prestige, the label that Ammons would call home for most of his career.

About the time of the 1952 breakup of the Ammons-Stitt group, Ammons began his long battle with heroin addiction. This coincided with recording done for Decca and United that still featured the seven-piece group. By the end of 1954, he was living in Washington, D.C., and would work as a single, picking up local rhythm sections in his travels. He rejoined Prestige Records that year, and for the next five years, he would be recorded in a context best described as the Hi-Fi Jam Session.

Prestige would hire six or seven players to make an album. With liberal allowances for solos, most of the albums would have only four very long songs. The playing on these Jam Sessions was variable. When good, as on "The Happy Blues," a tune from the album of the same name, it was quite good and featured a fine, relaxed groove; yet just as often it missed the mark. One thing for certain: being one of four or five horns in a blowing session context was not the best way to showcase Gene Ammons as Gene Ammons.

Ammons's first major brush with narcotics violations happened in 1958. A conviction for possession resulted in a two- to three-year sentence. Released on parole in June 1960, Ammons immediately came east to record for Prestige. In the two albums recorded on that occasion, we meet the mature Gene Ammons at his very best.

Boss Tenor, the album recorded by Ammons on June 16, 1960, is generally considered to be his masterpiece. For the first time in an album setting, Ammons is the only horn; and his gifts for bluesy, melodic playing are on full display. "Canadian Sunset" from this session was a jukebox favorite, and the album was a best seller. The rhythm section assembled for this album was made up of Prestige regulars:

pianist Tommy Flanagan, bassist Doug Watkins, and drummer Art Taylor. Some additional spice was added with the presence of conguero Ray Barretto. Apart from Flanagan, the other players had been a part of the last Ammons album, *Blue Gene*, done two years earlier.

The album that was recorded on the following day yielded *Angel Eyes*, another enormous hit, even though it wasn't released until four years later! This would be the first Ammons album with organ accompaniment. Frank Wess, an old colleague from the Billy Eckstine band, was on hand playing tenor sax and flute; Johnny "Hammond" Smith was the organist while Watkins and Taylor reprised their roles of the day before.

Shortly after the recording sessions, Ammons was returned to prison for a parole violation. It wasn't until January of 1961 that he was able to resume playing full-time. By then, based on the success of *Boss Tenor*, he was a certified star.

It is during the period 1961–1962 that the Ammons legend begins to build nationally. A listen to almost any of his recordings from that time will find him in top form. Outstanding among them were *Jug*, which was similar in concept to *Boss Tenor* and contained another jukebox favorite, "Exactly Like You." The album also produced two other 45 singles. The day before recording *Jug*, Ammons recorded *Nice 'N' Cool*, the first of his three all-ballad albums for the Prestige subsidiary, Moodsville.

There were reunions with Sonny Stitt as well: *Boss Tenors* and *Boss Tenors in Orbit* for Verve, *Dig Him* for Argo, and *Soul Summit* for Prestige. In addition to these albums, he had developed a fine rapport with organist Jack McDuff, and they appeared on record together on three occasions during this time.

Throughout this 1961–1962 period, Gene Ammons was dealing with an out-of-control heroin habit, yet his playing is invariably satisfying. Classics seemed to roll out of the Prestige pressing plant with regularity, and much of the sub-rosa recording done for Pacific Jazz and Chess was also of top quality. Black people began to plan their vacation schedules around his personal appearances.

Ammons recorded an album, *Bad Bossa Nova*, in September 1962 that became an important musical landmark. This is the first example of some great funk grooves that would prove so enticing to the next generation of musicians. On tunes such as "Ca'purange" and "Moito

Mato Grosso," the group would show the way for artists such as James Brown who would provide the next development in funk. It was also the last Gene Ammons album for many years. His addiction problem had caught up with him again.

The arrest warrant charge, this time, was possession with intent to sell. The case against Ammons was built with all the subtlety of an inquisition. In today's judicial climate, the case would clearly be one of entrapment, but that didn't help Ammons in the Illinois of 1962. He spent more than seven years behind bars.

In another aspect of the Gene Ammons–Prestige Records relationship, the company had sued Chess for recording Ammons while Prestige had an exclusive contract for his services. Prestige was awarded ownership of the Chess Ammons recordings in addition to a hefty financial settlement.

Some of the sessions acquired from Chess were unreleased. Bob Weinstock would carefully parcel these albums out. Combined with his own sessions and reissues, there would be a steady flow of Ammons albums until the end of the decade. When the *Bad Bossa Nova* album was reissued as *Jungle Soul* with a new cover, sales took off once again. Upon his release from prison, Ammons praised Weinstock for keeping his name alive all those years.

Summing up this period of Ammons's recording career, it seems clear that producer Esmond Edwards knew exactly how to get the best out of Ammons. No other period in Ammons's career is quite as creative. Edwards used to talk about a "light groove" feeling for tenor sax soloists that might bring out some of the players' best work. He recorded a number of tenor players for Prestige: Willis Jackson, Arnett Cobb, Eddie "Lockjaw" Davis, Buddy Tate, and Jimmy Forrest, among others. Ozzie Cadena produced *Bad Bossa Nova*, and there is no telling what that combination might have delivered long term under different circumstances.

When Ammons emerged from prison in 1969, he was not a well man. An enlarged heart and emphysema were two problems he carried with him as he returned to the jazz scene. But the old fire was still there. He had his horn with him in prison and composed a number of original tunes that were used on his first new recordings. His return gave a new lift to jazz in general; and his first new Prestige album, *The Boss Is Back*, leaped immediately onto the *Billboard* magazine popularity charts.

He formed a new band, his first since the '50s, including guitarist George Freeman, which quickly became one of the most popular attractions on the road. Ammons, the bandleader, was something to watch. He was a master at making his audience feel relaxed. A typical set might start with something very fast in order to get the players properly warmed up. He would then take the microphone and begin talking to the audience and introducing his sidemen. He might comment on something in the news or perhaps the weather, but all the time he was talking, his organist would be playing soft chords behind him that would gradually swell to the point that he'd introduce one of his hit ballads, and the club would go wild. Saxophonists as diverse as Houston Person and Pharoah Sanders would appear at his gigs, watching all this very closely.

More hit albums followed: *The Boss Is* Back featured a reunion with Junior Mance while *Brother Jug* contained the jukebox hit "Didn't We." *The Black Cat* featured strings for the first time, and *My Way* had a full orchestra. Reunions with Dexter Gordon and Sonny Stitt were also recorded. He toured Europe for the first time and found eager listeners all over the world. Despite doctors' orders to stop smoking, he smoked heavily. His recordings from 1972 onward began to show a diminishing of his talent. The tone had lost some of its fullness, and his improvisational flow became more fragmented. He had lost a considerable amount of weight and looked old beyond his years. What ultimately claimed him was diagnosed as bone cancer compounded by pneumonia. He was forty-nine years old.

In terms of popularity as a jazz saxophonist, Gene Ammons was second to none in his era. He had chart records in four different decades. He sold 78s, 45s, LPs, tape, and, eventually, CDs. He did it with ballads, blues, bebop, and funk. He had hits with big bands, small groups, Latin bands, organ combos, or straight-ahead rhythm sections.

This final period of Gene Ammons's life should be looked on as a "last hurrah." Writers who previously had paid little attention to him or his work were falling all over themselves to say kind things, pop stars were trying to get close to him, and international celebrity would surely have been his had he lived longer. But he ran out of time. If it wasn't for the bad luck, he wouldn't have no luck at all.

As an addendum, the story of Howard Cohen should be included. Cohen was a CD retailer in Atlanta, the owner of International Records.

When two of Ammons's Moodsville albums (*Nice an' Cool* and *The Soulful Moods*) were packaged on a single CD (*Gentle Jug*) in 1992, he took to playing it in-store and over time had sold more than five thousand copies—from one location! And there was no press to celebrate this, no personal appearance, no special record label promotion. The communicative power of Gene Ammons had simply survived his death eighteen years earlier.

RECOMMENDED RECORDS:

1947–1949 (Classics ICD-F); *Boss Tenor*, 1960 (Prestige RVG-CD); *Gentle Jug*, 1961–1962 (Prestige OJC-CD); *Bad Bossa Nova*, 1962 (Prestige OJC-CD); *Boss Tenors in Orbit*, with Sonny Stitt, 1961 (Verve VD)

THE BIG BEAT

"THE BIG BEAT HAS ARRIVED! The New Swing Era for the new Teen Age generation has finally burst loose on the popular music horizon. Just as with 'The Swing Era' of 1936—so has this new musical thrill been 'panned' and 'knocked' by those in the music industry who don't like it . . .

And, as in the past, the shrill outraged cries of those same critics will gurgle gasp and be lost beneath the new birth of the dance business—the new excitement of a new generation seeking to 'let off steam' the happy way—to the new 'Big Beat in American Popular Music' . . . it will be here a thousand years after we are all gone.

> IT'S GREAT! IT'S WONDERFUL! IT'S EXCITING! IT'S AMERICAN! And I am very proud to have helped expose the 'Big Beat' to music loving AMERICANS—instead of suppressing it. SO—LET'S ROCK 'N' ROLL!"
> —Alan Freed liner notes to *The Big Beat*,
> an MGM album by Sam "the Man"
> Taylor issued in 1955

By early 1955, a battle was waging among record manufacturers regarding the long-playing record. The 10" size was still standard, but the ground swell on enthusiasm for the 12" LP eventually would carry the day. Jazz labels were very much in the forefront on the move to the larger size. Original Broadway cast albums, classical projects, and Hollywood soundtracks were also important in the final decision making. There was very little LP production from either blues or R&B since single releases were the norm in those fields.

Norman Granz had been using 12" LP for his JATP concert discs, as well as his studio Jam Session series, since his move to independent distribution in 1953. Much of the Clef 10" series had been devoted to the reissue of sides originally on Mercury. The switch to 12" exclusivity came to the Granz labels before any other independent label. Of the majors, Columbia, which had a 12" line as well as ten-inch LPs, had great success with the larger format via jazz projects such as Duke Ellington's *Ellington Uptown* and Benny Goodman's *The Famous 1938 Carnegie Hall Jazz Concert*.

The death of Charlie Parker in March 1955 served to spur Savoy into launching a series of 12" albums. Three of the first nine releases in the Savoy 12000 series would be Charlie Parker reissues. Prestige quickly followed suit: its last session recorded for 10" LP was in June of 1955. All Atlantic LPs from 1955 forward would be 12." Other labels fell into place, and by mid-1956, the 10" LP was history.

The 78 rpm record was also on the way out. By early 1956, the 45 would overtake the 78 in popularity with the Southern market (especially blues and gospel) the only holdout. In the middle of the year, Columbia announced a gradual phaseout of the 78. There were 78 issues on many labels until the end of the decade always issued in conjunction with a 45 release and in ever-diminishing quantities. While there would be experiments with prerecorded reel-to-reel tape for albums, not every label pursued this, and nobody was successful with reel-to-reel sales.

Radio was becoming more and more important. While there were network stations still presenting their mix for their virtually all-white audience, black music formats were on the rise, and black disc jockeys were no longer the rarity of the previous decade. More importantly, black music was routinely being programmed as part of the music mix at pop stations. The disc jockey had become as important a part of a teenager's life as a math, English, or history teacher. If the disc jockey had become the messenger in terms of introducing new musical trends, performers, and songs, then Alan Freed had become the Pied Piper.

ALAN FREED

Freed's approval of a new record would often be the key to its success. Certain labels favored by Freed could count on his help on the air; others would need to have the right record. Payola was rampant throughout R&B radio, and everyone was paying Freed. Yet the myth persists than Alan Freed played only records he was being paid to play and that those labels who didn't pay him had no chance.

Actually, Freed stuck his neck out by playing the original version of a hit song. Cover records, usually white artists covering a hit R&B song for a major label, were often featured on pop stations and sold in white neighborhoods where an R&B record would not be stocked. At the same time, Freed could not afford to stick with a clearly inferior song since that would turn off the listening audience. He would get dozens of new records every week, and finding an unknown gem by a new artist was still part of what made his the most important radio show in the country. There would be the occasional exception such as Count Basie's "Every Day I Have the Blues," but for the most part, it had to have the big beat. It had to be rock 'n' roll.

At the start of 1955, Alan Freed was heard on WINS, New York, six nights a week; and his program was being syndicated to stations across the country. In January 1955, he presented his first stage show in New York, "The Rock-'n'-Roll Ball," at St. Nicholas Arena. The arena held six thousand, and it was sold out both nights with a reported gross of $27,500—most tickets selling for $2. In a postconcert trade paper ad, it was claimed that thousands were turned away. Another unusual aspect of the production was that all sales were in advance and that 70 percent of tickets were sold through sixteen designated record stores. The only advertising was done on Freed's radio show.

Performers included Big Joe Turner, Fats Domino, the Clovers, the Moonglows, Clyde McPhatter and the Drifters, the Harptones, Red Prysock's band, and the Buddy Johnson Orchestra featuring Ella Johnson and Nolan Lewis.

There was no question at all that R&B was the fastest-growing part of the popular music business. Activity in the field, including record sales and concert appearances, was estimated at a gross of $25,000,000 for 1954.

When Freed came east, his manager was Lew Platt, who had worked to build his name and image throughout Ohio. In New York, things were different, and Platt was soon found to be the odd man out as Morris Levy took over most aspects of Freed's career. By the summer of 1955, Platt was gone.

In that summer of 1955, Alan Freed and his various enterprises were expanding in a number of directions.

Freed continued to present stage shows in the New York area. His "Rock-'n'-Roll Easter Jubilee" appeared at the Brooklyn Paramount Theater and did $107,000 for a weekly gross, breaking the house record that had stood since 1932. Shortly thereafter, the show played a week's engagement in Boston followed by a three-day stand in Providence promoted by the Gale Agency.

The Freed stage shows continued to break records with the gross for his Labor Day stand at the Brooklyn Paramount estimated anywhere from $154,000 to $178,000 for a week's run. Before the end of the year, there were plans for a ten-day stand in Manhattan, and there was talk of Freed taking a big band into Birdland! Alan Freed who last played trombone in high school was the hottest thing in the music business.

There was a trade paper item about Freed signing a contract with Coral, but within a couple of weeks, the deal fell apart. Another trade paper story mentioned the fact that Freed had written or cowritten fifteen songs in the past year. It is unlikely that Freed ever composed any of the songs. He may well have suggested a title or a key line, but for the most part, this was simply another form of payola. Songwriting credits and publishing agreements were used as currency by labels to reward DJs who had helped break a record in the marketplace. Freed was the most obvious beneficiary, hardly the only one.

Alan Freed was spreading his wings in 1956, and Morris Levy was wheeling and dealing. Among the new deals was one for a CBS Radio Camel Rock-'n'-Roll Dance Party show.

The network was able to get a national sponsor in Camel cigarettes. In time, he would be appearing opposite his own WINS radio show on Saturday night! Also in the works were movies: the first of which would be **Rock Around the Clock**.

The Count Basie band, probably at Levy's suggestion, had been the house band for the CBS shows. The band had also played the last Freed stage show of 1955, a hugely successful stand at the Academy of Music in Manhattan. The radio programs were recorded in advance, and some emanated from Los Angeles while Freed was making the movie. In reality, the Camel Rock-'n'-Roll Dance Party broadcasts were as much about Count Basie as they were about Alan Freed. The band and Basie vocalist Joe Williams had almost half the selections on each show, and the two guest stars had two songs apiece. With guests such as the Chordettes, the Rover Boys, and Tony Bennett, the content of some shows was a long way from the music Freed had championed. It soon became clear to everyone that the Basie brand of swing was like a fish out of water at a rock-'n'-roll show. The teenagers were not interested in Basie's music.

But in the meantime, the stage shows were creating a sensation. The estimated net was $240,000 for the ten-day 1956 "Easter Jubilee of Stars" at the Brooklyn Paramount. The nature of the stage shows was very short sets with Freed functioning as an emcee to introduce the dozen or so acts who would rotate over a six- or seven-show day. The New York City police had to restrict traffic from the area surrounding the theater; the crowds were so thick. Inside the theater, there were police in the aisles to keep order. Despite the huge success of the show, the Basie band was not on hand. On stage was a big band fronted by Sam "the Man" Taylor and featuring Big Al Sears. The time for a change had arrived.

Bob Thiele of Coral Records had been trying to structure a deal with Freed for over a year. Freed was no stranger to conflict-of-interest situations, but to work for Coral in some sort of an A&R capacity was out of the question. But now came an opportunity: Freed wanted a big band on all his shows, but there didn't seem to be any one orchestra that could do everything he needed. Thiele said, "Why not form your own band?" Alan Freed would realize his dream and have his own band: the Rock-'n'-Roll Big Band.

THE ROCK-'N'-ROLL BIG BAND

In order to make this band work, the obvious choices were the arrangers and musicians who had been part of the bands that had played for Freed at his various shows. Enter Leroy Kirkland who along with Jesse Stone, Sammy Lowe, and Ernie Wilkins would provide the bulk of the original charts for the band. On the stage shows, the band would provide accompaniment for many of the singing groups; but in the studio, the band would have to have its own personality. Kirkland became Freed's music director and was in charge not only of hiring the musicians to play the record dates but the stage shows as well. And the musicians came: Taft Jordan from Duke Ellington via Chick Webb, Lloyd Trotman from the Atlantic Records house band, Panama Francis from Lucky Millinder and Cab Calloway, Jerry Potter from the Buddy Johnson band, and Heywood Henry from Erskine Hawkins, among many others.

Jack Hooke (1916–1999) was a partner, with Teddy Reig, in Royal Roost Records. He had known Alan Freed since 1952 and had provided advice to Freed for some of his earliest Ohio concerts. In addition to Royal Roost, Hooke had various other music industry interests, including publishing, artist management, and an association with Morris Levy. Because Freed and Levy trusted Hooke, he was given the title of Freed's manager. He was also involved in organizing Freed's stage shows.

It was Hooke who produced the Coral albums. But before the first album was assembled, there was a single: "Teener's Canteen"/"Right Now, Right Now." In hindsight, it seems likely that this two-tune session was put together very quickly. Both tunes were written by Big Al Sears (in fact, "Teener's Canteen"—as "Tina's Canteen"—had already been recorded, for Coral, by him). They were recorded in March 1956, and it would be another two months before additional recording was resumed in order to complete enough material for an LP. Both songs were performed live on the June 2 edition of the Camel Rock-'n'-Roll Dance Party. "Right Now, Right Now" became the Alan Freed band's theme song.

The first album was titled *Rock-'n'-Roll Dance Party*, meant to capitalize on the connection to the radio series; and it included four vocal covers that are so awful, it is surprising that Freed let them appear under his own name. But the eight instrumentals by the band are very much in the tradition of the great bands of Lucky Millinder, Erskine Hawkins, and Buddy Johnson and pointed a new potential direction for big bands. If the big band was to be a part of the Freed stage shows, it had a built-in audience; it had the most powerful persuader as an advocate and a musical product featuring originals by Sears, Stone, Kirkland, Budd Johnson, and Freddie Mitchell that rocked the house. The band that first recorded for Coral was eleven pieces, but in time, it would grow larger and would include two drummers to emphasize the big beat. In mid-1956, Alan Freed was at his peak. Ahead would be television, more movies, and more big band albums.

COUNT BASIE

If Count Basie and Alan Freed proved to be an incompatible pairing, the Basie band just shrugged its shoulders and continued to gain popularity. A new drummer, Sonny Payne, and a new vocalist, Joe Williams, each of whom joined the band in December 1954, had powered the Basie band back to the top.

Joe Williams (1918–1998) was from Chicago and had worked with the Lionel Hampton band during WWII. At that time, he sang mostly ballads sharing the vocal chores with Dinah Washington who was assigned the blues material.

His first musical meeting with Basie came during the summer of 1950 when the Basie combo was appearing in Chicago at the Brass Rail, without a singer. Williams, working locally with Red Saunders, would occasionally sit in with the group. Yet when Basie reformed his big band in 1952, he hired a woman named Bixie Crawford to be the vocalist. After having little impact on the band, she left in the summer of 1954, and Basie again had no singer.

He had done tours with Billy Eckstine and made records with Al Hibbler during the early years of the reformed band, so the sound of a male vocalist must have been on his mind after Joe Williams sat in with the band again, during the summer of 1954. On Christmas Day 1954, Joe Williams officially became a member of the Count Basie band.

"Every Day I Have the Blues" featuring an Ernie Wilkins arrangement and a Joe Williams vocal proved to be the biggest record of Count Basie's career. The song, written by bluesman Memphis Slim, had previous hit versions by Lowell Fulson in 1950 and B. B. King (which was on the charts when Basie recorded it). Williams had been singing the song around Chicago and had recorded it for Checker in 1952. The Wilkins arrangement made a big difference: the record had a twenty-week stay on the charts, peaking at #2.

Percival "Sonny "Payne (1926–1979) provided the flash and sizzle that had been lacking with the excellent Gus Johnson in the drum chair. Payne, the son of Louis Jordan drummer Chris Columbus, had come to Basie after several years with Erskine Hawkins. A natural showman, he would spark the band until his departure in 1964, and his feature "Old Man River" was one of the most popular items in the Basie book.

The Basie band was loaded with great veterans, and the younger members of the band such as Thad Jones and Frank Foster not only knew the Basie tradition but also added to it. The core of this group stayed together into the next decade and very quickly became a band with swagger and confidence. This was a band that could walk the walk *and* talk the talk. It was very different from the band that came out of Kansas City in 1936 and had existed in a similar fashion until its breakup in 1950.

Gone were the head arrangements and emphasis on great soloists. Instead there was an ensemble capable of playing all kinds of music. There were plenty of blues-based flag-wavers, but in addition, there were now more flutes and mutes. Basie biographer Albert Murray recognized this difference and assigned the phrase "New Testament Band" to the band that was reformed in 1952.

Norman Granz had recorded lots of Basie studio material in two mammoth sessions in January and July 1956. The more than thirty titles would be collated and issued over time, but Granz was in the process of folding all his labels into the new Verve imprint, and when this was finally accomplished, he would have dozens of Clef and Norgran titles to reissue. Verve was originally formed to feature the work of Ella Fitzgerald but would now feature all of Granz's artists, in separate numerical series for jazz, pop, and traditional jazz.

The last eighteen months of Count Basie's tenure with Clef/Verve would have two live albums recorded: *Basie in London* (actually recorded in Sweden in September 1956) and *Basie at Newport* (which would feature some of the JATP stars as guests) recorded at the 1957 Newport Jazz Festival. The period produced only one three-tune studio session for use in a movie. In retrospect, this seems like a missed opportunity. Williams had recorded an album of pop material with the band, and his blues material had been collected in a Clef album that became one of the label's best sellers.

At the same time, the band was clicking with exceptional arrangements: Wild Bill Davis's trio arrangement of "April in Paris" had been adapted for the big band, and another R&B chart success resulted; Frank Foster's "Shiny Stockings" was one of several exceptional originals by this writer, and veteran guitarist Freddie Green's "Corner Pocket" became known as "Until I Met You" when a lyric was added. There may have been reasons not immediately obvious for that period of neglect; but suffice it to say that by the fall of 1957, Count Basie had signed with the newly formed Roulette Records, owned by Morris Levy. Basie would be produced by Teddy Reig.

The first album of the new agreement was *e=mc2* (often known as *The Atomic Mr. Basie*) and consisted entirely of Neal Hefti arrangements. It would prove to be the most celebrated album of Basie's career and regain any momentum lost in the previous year. The band personnel was enhanced by the arrival of Al Grey on trombone and the return, for a brief period, of Eddie "Lockjaw" Davis. By early 1958, Davis was gone again, replaced by Billy Mitchell.

The major change in the way Count Basie was recorded was that, for the most part, each album would be a specific project involving the work of one arranger. Among the arrangers who would create albums for the Count Basie band over the next few years were Hefti, Quincy Jones, Billy Byers, Benny Carter, and Frank Foster. Thad Jones continued to write for the band, as did Ernie Wilkins and, occasionally, Freddie Green and Frank Wess. It was also during the Roulette period that the band began joint recording ventures with singers: albums with Sarah Vaughan, Billy Eckstine, Tony Bennett and the vocalese group, Lambert, Hendricks, and Ross were among the projects.

Lambert, Hendricks, and Ross was a vocal trio featuring lyricist Jon Hendricks, vocal arranger Dave Lambert, and singer Annie Ross. In 1957, they had created an album titled *Sing a Song of Basie* for ABC Records. Hendricks supplied lyrics to the songs and solos of Count Basie and his sidemen from earlier recordings. This was vocalese dressed up to succeed. The following year brought forth *Sing Along with Basie* for Roulette, a big hit, which launched L, H, and R as a touring group. In 1959, they gained a Columbia Records contract and, in addition, became a very popular attraction on the Jazz Festival circuit. The group continued at a high level of performance until 1962 when Ross left the group.

Joe Williams was recorded as an individual artist by Roulette in addition to making records with the Basie band. He left in early 1961, and while the band would have a number of fine singers among its members, none would reach the status of Williams who would reunite with Basie on special occasions. The Count Basie band had reached the apex of stardom during the Roulette years. This celebrity would be maintained for the rest of Basie's career.

DUKE ELLINGTON

Duke Ellington had suffered major defections from his band beginning with the departure of Cootie Williams in 1940, through the deaths of Jimmy Blanton in 1942 and Tricky Sam Nanton in 1946, and the loss of Ben Webster, for the first time, in 1943. Yet the departure of Johnny Hodges, Lawrence Brown, and Sonny Greer, at the same time, in 1951 had forced change upon Ellington. The rhythmic innovations introduced by Louie Bellson provided the band with fresh inspiration. Upon Bellson's departure, Ellington tried Butch Ballard and Dave Black; and each, while competent, could not provide the spark that Ellington was seeking.

Sam Woodyard, who followed Black, was the answer. Woodyard (1925–1988) worked with organist Milt Buckner before joining Ellington in July 1955. Woodyard used the two bass-drum setup, but his beat was what made the difference. He gave the Ellington band the strongest backbeat it had ever had. If the "big beat" was what Ellington wanted, Woodyard could deliver. For the most part, the critics didn't like Woodyard and yearned for the classic sound of the early 1940s. In many ways, the arrival of Woodyard heralded a New Testament Ellington band.

The resurgence of the Ellington band was also helped by the return of star soloists such as Hodges (who rejoined the same day Woodyard came aboard), Brown (1959), and Williams (1962). Ellington would be writing extended works and creating individual features for band members more frequently in the future. His days of writing pop songs, despite the fact that some good songs emerged from his various endeavors, were virtually over. The new band gave its first demonstration of greatness at the 1956 American Jazz Festival at Newport, Rhode Island.

July 7, 1956, likely began as many other days did for Duke Ellington. He was scheduled to play an outdoor concert in Newport, Rhode Island. He was working on a suite dedicated to the Newport event that needed some more work. He had also decided to adjust the set list to include a feature for Paul Gonsalves, his tenor player, and a Rhode Island native.

"Diminuendo and Crescendo in Blue" had been a two-part 78 first recorded for Brunswick in 1937. Another version was recorded for Musicraft in 1946. When Ellington retooled the piece in 1951, he devised it as a two-part performance separated by a tenor sax interval for Gonsalves, who had joined the band in November 1950. When Ben Webster departed the Ellington band for the final time in 1949, Ellington had tried several players, including Jimmy Forrest, Charlie Rouse and Bo McCain, as potential replacements; and Gonsalves proved to be the keeper. In time, Ellington would feature Gonsalves in a variety of roles and would write material specifically for him, but for the immediate future, Gonsalves would inherit the tenor solos that Webster had played, and there was a need to establish something that had his identity as part of it.

There are no commercial recordings of the new arrangement before July 1956 and only two known performances captured on tape: a broadcast from Birdland in 1951 and a concert performance in California in early 1953, and because of its length, it was not a regularly performed staple in the Ellington book.

George Wein (1925–) was the promoter of the festival. A jazz pianist and nightclub owner from Boston, Wein had the backing of a couple with Newport connections and a considerable amount of tobacco money. His 1956 event would be the third annual festival, and the evening of July 7 would put his event on the jazz map forever.

It started with the Ellington band on stage to perform a couple of tunes for the benefit of Voice of America, which would broadcast the evening. The band would return to close the show.

Upon its return, the band demonstrated from bar one that it was ready. Ray Nance had an inspired trumpet solo on the band's theme, "Take the A Train," which was immediately followed by the introduction of a three-part "Newport Jazz Festival Suite." After ballad features for baritone saxophonist Harry Carney and vocalist Jimmy Grissom, the audience was barely stirring prior to the announcement of "Diminuendo in Blue and Crescendo in Blue." Things would change very quickly.

"Diminuendo" is mostly ensemble with interjections from trumpet and baritone, but then the stage is set for Gonsalves and his lengthy, twenty-seven chorus ride. The tempo here is perfect, and the rhythm section is completely locked in with Ellington adding vocal encouragement from the piano bench. As Gonsalves built momentum, a blonde in the audience wearing a black dress began dancing, and the crowd erupted. At the conclusion of the tenor solo, Ellington brought the dynamic level down before bringing it back up again in his piano solo that set up "Crescendo." With the return of the ensemble, Woodyard booted the band to a furious climax featuring Cat Anderson blowing high-note trumpet out in front of the band. And the place went crazy.

The event was recorded by Columbia Records; and the resulting LP, *Ellington at Newport*, became the best-selling album of the bandleader's career. Subsequently, there were newspaper headlines, a cover story in *Time* magazine, and immense publicity of the festival and the album. Ellington was back, but he was not the only beneficiary of this remarkable turn of events: George Wein would soon supplant Norman Granz as the nation's foremost jazz promoter, and the festival would be known to all as the Newport Jazz Festival.

LIONEL HAMPTON

While many American musicians were dealing with the R&B to rock-'n'-roll transition in 1956, Lionel Hampton spent much of the year in Europe. He was still fronting an eighteen-piece orchestra and recorded with the big band in Paris in January and Madrid in August. He also recorded three small-group albums, in May in Paris, for three labels. While there were still quality players in the Hampton band, the unit suffered because of the leader's inability to come up with the material equal to that performed by his bands of the previous decade. So often a set list or recording session involved reworkings of "Hey-Ba-Ba-Rebop," "Hamp's Boogie Woogie," and "Flyin' Home." This coupled with the low pay for sidemen meant a long slow decline for Hampton. He would continue to seek out and find quality younger musicians, but he couldn't keep the best ones. At this stage of the game, a chair in the Hampton band would be considered an entry-level position for an aspiring musician.

If Hampton didn't exactly embrace rock 'n' roll, he did renew acquaintances with Alan Freed. Freed, by 1957, was making a movie each year; and the Hampton band was featured in **Mister Rock and Roll**. Little Richard, Chuck Berry, and the Moonglows were among several other groups in the film. In terms of recording, Hampton was recorded in Germany and Israel during 1958; but clearly, his approach to music was more visual than the average band of the time. Capturing the pandemonium that Hampton created in a stage show was nearly impossible on record. Increasingly, his recordings featured him in a small-group context where his talents were permitted to shine without the attendant hoopla that surrounded his big band performances.

There were two big band studio albums that demonstrated what the band was all about. The first, for Clef/Verve in 1955, featured the working band with Eddie Chamblee on tenor and special guest Buddy Rich on two tunes. The second, for Audio Fidelity in 1959, was a twenty-one-piece band including two drummers, with former Hampton sideman Cat Anderson added to the trumpet section. There were versions of "Flyin' Home" and "Air Mail Special" on each album.

In the early 1960s, Hampton would start his own record label, Glad-Hamp and by 1965 reduce the size of his band to nine pieces. He was still capable of reforming the big band for special occasions such as the 1967 appearance where the band rocked the Newport Jazz Festival. In the 1970s, Hampton would regularly take a big band to Europe for summer festivals. Whether those bands consisted of all-star sidemen, as they did in the 1970s, or fresh young talent, which was the rule during the 1980s, Hampton himself was always inspiring. This phenomenal musician continued to record into the 1990s, making great music and entertaining audiences around the world.

BUDDY JOHNSON

Buddy Johnson's band fought hard to maintain its position through the mid-1950s. The move to Mercury and the work with producer Bob Shad had provided minor hits for the band during 1955 and 1956 even though sales were not as strong in previous years. The core of the band had remained intact for some time, but Johnson's audience was overwhelmingly black, and the ability of the band to attract younger listeners or to find more of a white following was largely unsuccessful. The closing of the Savoy Ballroom would remove its home base from New York City, and when the Mercury deal finished at the end of 1957, the end was in sight. An album done for Roulette in 1958 was a solid musical effort and revealed more of the band personality than some of the late Mercury singles. When the band stopped traveling in 1959, it was the end of an era. Buddy Johnson had a publishing catalog that would sustain him, but his sister Ella never performed live after the band broke up.

Apart from Ellington and Basie, the black big bands were fading from the scene in the late 1950s. That did not mean that the sidemen had stopped contributing. Many of the star soloists had long since become leaders of small combos. The trend had started with the small clubs on New York's 52nd Street, Central Avenue in Los Angeles, or 47th Street in Chicago. The jazz stars of the big bands become better known as a result of what they did away from the big bands: jam sessions, engagements booked while the big band was on hiatus, guest spots on a club or concert stage, and the opportunity to appear on a JATP show were just some of the ways a great player could find a larger audience. But record dates were the most important way to advance in this highly competitive world.

NORMAN GRANZ

The mercurial Norman Granz was still a major force in the jazz business in the mid-1950s. JATP was feeling the heat from some of the R&B package shows but was still an overwhelming success as a touring attraction. Granz had been the personal manager of Ella Fitzgerald since the late 1940s, but her recordings were done for Decca. When Fitzgerald came to his new Verve label, Granz began to pay more attention to her than the established stars of JATP.

Verve was conceived a full-line label with different numerical series for different sorts of music. Buddy Bregman and Barney Kessel were hired to arrange (and produce) much of the pop material. Kessel, who recorded for Verve under the pseudonym Rock Murphy, managed to produce a hit single of "I'm Walkin,'" the first record by teen idol Ricky Nelson. While Ella Fitzgerald was the dominant Verve artist, there was room for the occasional special project (Oscar Peterson with strings, a vocal album by Buddy Rich, a couple of Bob Scobey albums) and a wide variety of mostly one-shot albums by pop singers. During 1956, Ella Fitzgerald was involved in an immense number of separate projects: Cole Porter and Duke Ellington multirecord

Songbooks, duets with Louis Armstrong, live concerts, and pop single sessions.

On the other hand, apart from his concert appearances, Flip Phillips hadn't recorded an album in three years. He would continue being a key member of JATP through 1957. Illinois Jacquet did an album for Clef and one for Verve between 1955 and his departure in 1958. Granz was touting a new pair of saxophone stars in Sonny Stitt and Stan Getz, and he added the Modern Jazz Quartet to JATP domestic tours in 1956 and 1957. The times were changing; and Granz had to find a way to keep up with the competition that now featured jazz festivals, competing jazz tours (such as the Birdland shows), and rock-'n'-roll caravans.

In the fall of 1957, Norman Granz had his JATP concerts in New York, Chicago, and Los Angeles recorded. It was standard procedure for Granz to do this since he would choose the best concert to release on record, and on rare occasions, he would mix and match performances from different concerts for release. The Chicago concert was recorded in stereo for the first time while the Los Angeles show was done in mono. Nothing from New York was used for release.

The records from the 1957 tour would be titled *Jazz at the Opera House*, honoring the location of the Chicago concert. Instead of a box set or a double album, as the last JATP issue from 1955 had been, the Opera House series would be individual albums. There would be volumes from Ella Fitzgerald, Coleman Hawkins–Roy Eldridge, and Stan Getz–J. J. Johnson and an album shared by the Oscar Peterson Trio and the Modern Jazz Quartet in addition to the customary LP by the JATP All-Stars. Between the time the concerts were recorded and the records arrived at retail, some very unusual things happened.

The mono albums were issued in the spring of 1958, but the performances were those from Los Angeles, not the Chicago Opera House. In his opening remarks on the All-Stars album, Granz announced that "it was Jazz at the Philharmonic night in Los Angeles." Critics pounced on this, and the All-Stars album was pounded in print. Even stranger is the fact that a drum feature for Jo Jones was initially part of the album, but it was very quickly replaced by a version of "Stuffy" that featured the combined Getz-Johnson and Hawkins-Eldridge groups.

If the All-Stars album (which featured Lester Young, Flip Phillips, Illinois Jacquet, Sonny Stitt, the Oscar Peterson Trio, and Jo Jones) took its lumps, there was nothing but unqualified praise for the rest of the albums. It wasn't until the stereo albums were issued over a year later that another unusual discovery was made. It was determined that the mono and stereo versions of the Hawkins-Eldridge set had different A sides! The Getz-Johnson and Ella Fitzgerald albums were completely different despite the fact that the cover art and liner notes were identical. Continuing the unusual, an album titled *The Oscar Peterson Trio at the Concertgebouw*, purporting to be concert recordings from Amsterdam, was actually the Chicago Opera House material! It wasn't until the CD era that all the details were sorted out.

How could something like this happen? Was Granz simply not paying attention? Had his interest in the flagship brand of his empire waned to the extent that he no longer cared about JATP?

In the spring of 1958, Granz presented a limited European tour of concerts featuring Ella Fitzgerald and Oscar Peterson to sold out houses. Perhaps it was here that he realized that JATP was becoming too much of a burden. Some of his original stars such as Young and Jacquet were becoming more difficult to deal with, and the next generation of stars such as Miles Davis and John Coltrane showed no interest in the competitive jam session concept at the heart of JATP. The last year was 1957. The days of Jazz at the Philharmonic as a touring organization in America were over. How quickly things changed!

Granz, who was now living in Switzerland, was more interested in reducing his operations. In 1960, he sold Verve to MGM; and apart from producing Ella Fitzgerald LPs, he was rarely involved in recording projects for the next decade. He would continue his managerial role with Ella and Oscar Peterson. His promotional efforts were increasingly based on the European continent. Soon he became known as the man who could arrange tours for Miles Davis, Ray Charles, and John Coltrane in addition to JATP. He also promoted nonjazz performers. He may have sold his record business, but he would be back.

ATLANTIC RECORDS

Nesuhi Ertegun (1917–1989) joined Atlantic Records on January 1, 1955. He joined his brother Ahmet and Jerry Wexler, and this triumvirate would run Atlantic Records for the next twenty years. Nesuhi's initial assignment was to develop a 12" LP line and to create a jazz roster. Ertegun came to Atlantic from Los Angeles where he had been active as a teacher of jazz history, an editor of small jazz magazines, and a label owner. He recorded the Kid Ory band in 1944 for his Crescent label, and those recordings were some of the most important documents of the New Orleans jazz revival. He married Merili Morden, owner of the Jazzman record store as well as the Jazzman record label, who was also deeply involved in promoting the revival. Crescent was folded into Jazzman, and the entire label was sold to Good Time Jazz in 1952. When the marriage broke up, Ertegun, who had been teaching at UCLA and doing publicity for Good Time Jazz, was ready for something new. Lew Chudd of Imperial records asked him to start a jazz line, and when Ahmet heard the news, he invited Nesuhi to come to New York and become a partner in Atlantic. Ahmet and Wexler were the hottest R&B-producing team in the country, and between recording and promoting their numerous hits, their plates were full. Original Atlantic partner Herb Abramson was away on military duty, and Nesuhi would have plenty to do.

While Nesuhi Ertegun would contribute much to the LP catalog over the years, his first and in some ways most important contribution to the label was the introduction of the songwriting team of Jerry Leiber and Mike Stoller to Atlantic. While in California recording some West Coast jazz artists, Nesuhi had been asked to produce a session on the Drifters, the very hot Atlantic R&B group, who were appearing locally. The label wanted to cover a hot song, "Adorable." Needing additional material, Ertegun sought out the pair, then operating Spark Records, to see whether they had something appropriate. The session produced a #1 R&B hit in "Adorable" but also, a second top 10 R&B hit, "Ruby Baby," written by Leiber and Stoller.

In his approach to jazz recording, Nesuhi had more in common with Norman Granz than his New York label neighbors such as Prestige or Blue Note. Through the years to come, Atlantic jazz would be most successful at taking artists who had achieved a breakthrough in the marketplace and help them get to stardom. Ertegun's first signings were artists such as Chris Connor, Shorty Rogers, and Milt Jackson. Within a year, the Modern Jazz Quartet and Charles Mingus had arrived, and the label was instantly a player in the jazz field.

Ray Charles (1930–2004) would be recorded in a jazz context as a trio pianist in 1956 while his band would be recorded as a unit on several occasions. Ray Charles had no hit albums on Atlantic, but his singles had found a huge audience among the black community. It started with a session cut in Atlanta in November 1954. After a few years of hanging out in New Orleans, recording with Guitar Slim and Tommy Ridgely, Ray Charles had come up with a band of his own.

The sound of four horns was something Ray had featured for some time, but it was often his piano trio fleshed out with studio players. For the first time, Charles had a working band that could be recorded. A key member of the unit was Texas tenor saxophonist Don Wilkerson (1932–1986) whose solos on "I Got a Woman," "This Little Girl of Mine," and "Hallelujah I Love Her So" would be repeated note for note by David Newman when Wilkerson left the band. Much of the material recorded by Charles in the mid-1950s was derived from gospel sources. This fusion of blues and gospel is where soul music begins.

And those songs were huge: "I Got a Woman," "A Fool for You," and "Drown in My Own Tears," #1 R&B hits. The Cookies, a female vocal group, made their first appearance on the latter. Within a year or so, they would become the Raeletts and become a permanent part of the Ray Charles band.

Ray Charles would often play alto sax with the band. When Hank Crawford in 1958 and Leroy Cooper, the following year, came aboard, that no longer became necessary. Ray Charles had his three-saxophone (and two-trumpet) sound: the sound of a modern blues band. The entire band hit its peak with the enormous hit "What'd I Say" in 1959.

The Atlantic Records executive staff was seasoned and expert in what they did, but there had been changes on the R&B side as the label adapted to changing trends. With the exception of Ray Charles, who always did *his* thing, *his* way, many Atlantic groups moved away from R&B with a conscious attempt at attaining a whiter sound. This began in 1956 and continued throughout the decade. There were white vocal groups, sometimes a chorus, added to the funky R&B underpinning. This was the influence of arranger Ray Ellis whose success on the label with Clyde McPhatter ("Treasure of Love"), Chris Connor ("I Miss You So"), and Ivory Joe Hunter ("Since I Met You, Baby") demonstrated to Atlantic that the right combination of ingredients could create a wider audience for the records. Soon there were white choirs behind Big Joe Turner, Chuck Willis, and even the Drifters.

This approach continued in the work of Reggie Obrecht and Stan Applebaum who followed Ellis. The result was a diminishing number of assignments for Jesse Stone and Howard Biggs, arrangers of Atlantic sessions for many years. In reality, the change had been coming for some time and was forced on Atlantic by a confluence of events that broke up the great Atlantic rhythm section.

Van Walls and Ahmet had a fight about something or other, probably money, in late 1955. As a result, Van Walls completely disappeared from the Atlantic scene and in fairly short order from the New York scene entirely. He was rediscovered working in Canada more than thirty years later. His place was taken by Ernie Hayes, Mike Stoller, and a variety of studio musicians.

The success of "Love Is Strange" put Mickey Baker on the road for more than two years. Immediately, Atlantic sessions moved to a two-guitar sound with the players almost always being white studio musicians. It would be the next decade before a single individual (Cornell Dupree) would again be entrusted with the guitar chair.

Connie Kay, so often the key drummer on Atlantic R&B dates since 1951, joined the Modern Jazz Quartet in the spring of 1955 and by the end of the year had given up doing R&B dates. The slack was taken up by Joe Marshall and, most importantly, Panama Francis. Only bassist Lloyd Trottman, of the original cast, was left.

Ahmet Ertegun and Jerry Wexler had been the great producing team in R&B, but as the decade grew to a close, it became apparent that they would not be able to continue working together. When they hired Leiber and Stoller to produce the Drifters in 1959, that was essentially the end.

They had reached the mountaintop, and in order to stay there, the producing tasks had to be divided. In time, Ahmet would be the point man on most of the California pop and English rock while Wexler stayed with his first love, R&B, which was rapidly becoming something different. Nesuhi Ertegun was hardly out of the mix and took on the task of international A&R. He would occasionally collaborate with Ahmet, Wexler, or both on album projects by artists such as Big Joe Turner, Ray Charles, or Bobby Darin. His jazz division was making major strides: in 1959, both John Coltrane and Ornette Coleman joined the label. Of all the independent labels that were formed during the race music era, Atlantic, in a bit more than a decade, had stepped out to the head of the pack.

INDEPENDENT JAZZ LABELS

If Atlantic Records was growing and becoming whiter, Savoy was headed in a different direction. Fred Mendelsohn had been a partner with Herman Lubinsky in Regent Records, a 1947 venture that lasted only one year. Mendelsohn had continued to make records for a variety of labels before returning to Savoy in late 1953. The R&B side of the label had slowed to a crawl despite a promising roster of artists headed by singers Billy Wright and Varetta Dillard. Jazz was represented by Cal Tjader, Don Elliot, and Marian McPartland. The biggest-selling artist of the label was the gospel music group the Famous Ward Singers.

Mendelsohn jump-started the R&B roster by bringing in Nappy Brown, Wilbert Harrison, Big Maybelle, and Little Jimmy Scott. New gospel signings included the Davis Sisters and the Drinkard Singers. Beginning in 1954, Ozzie Cadena began to produce jazz LPs.

Cadena assembled a number of Charlie Parker LPs that hit the market shortly after Parker's death. Indeed, there was considerable repackaging of jazz recorded during the Teddy Reig era as well as material from labels purchased by Lubinsky. For new sessions, Cadena got off to a good start with strong-selling albums by J. J. Johnson–Kai Winding, Cannonball Adderley, and Milt Jackson (*Opus De Jazz*). Cadena also recorded the first albums by Donald Byrd and Ernie Wilkins. Almost all the Savoy albums were one-shots, and exclusivity among jazz artists was very rare. Hank Jones and Kenny Clarke were regulars, and many albums recorded with Clarke as the leader appeared under the names of others.

Mendelsohn departed in late 1956 to head up a revived De Luxe label for the King organization. This left Cadena with the R&B to do as well as jazz. R&B recording went into steep decline, but Cadena was still making quality jazz LPs into 1960.

When Mendelsohn returned to Savoy in 1960, he concentrated almost exclusively on gospel. Within a short time, Savoy would become the largest and most successful black gospel label in the country.

Of the other independent jazz labels of the time, Prestige, Blue Note, and Riverside were making major strides. The 12" LP was their product and, with the exception of the occasional 45 rpm single, their only product. Unique cover designs and extensive liner notes were a part of each album.

Prestige was the most active and in 1959 had launched a major expansion: the revival of its original label, New Jazz, and the creation of Bluesville, Moodsville, Tru-Sound, and Swingville, as well as additional labels for folk, ethnic, and spoken-word recordings. Bob Weinstock stepped away from the recording studio and concentrated on the business side and from that point forward put Prestige in the hands of a succession of different recording directors.

The first and most productive of all was Esmond Edwards. Edwards was raised in Harlem and brought a black perspective to Prestige. He had begun with the label by driving musicians from New York to the suburban New Jersey studio of Rudy Van Gelder. Soon, he was shooting cover photos and designing album jackets. When he was appointed recording director in the summer of 1958, the direction of the label began to change. Before long, both Eddie "Lockjaw" Davis and Shirley Scott had been signed. Within a short time, the Prestige roster would turn over almost completely. A new approach was on the way.

The Blue Note label was started, immediately after the famous Spirituals to Swing concert, in January 1939, with the recording of Albert Ammons and Meade "Lux" Lewis. The first three years of the label were spent recording few artists on an occasional basis—it was really a part-time venture. As demand for records increased during WWII, Blue Note expanded. Blue Note was known from the beginning as a label that first and foremost recorded top-quality hot jazz. Alfred Lion of Blue Note often relied on the recommendations of certain musicians when it came to modern jazz.

Tenor saxophonist Ike Quebec (1918–1963), who had recorded a series of exceptional small band sides for Blue Note from 1944 to 1946, first brought Thelonious Monk to Lion's attention. Quebec was long associated with Cab Calloway but had been scuffling with a drug problem for much of the 1950s. In 1959, Lion thought that Quebec, with his big sound and affinity for ballads, might be able to cut singles for the jukebox market. Shortly thereafter, Quebec became an official member of the Blue Note family. He would not only record his own sessions but would also appear on albums with other Blue Note artists and recommend artists for the label to sign. Dexter Gordon, Don Wilkerson, Leo Parker, and Fred Jackson were Quebec suggestions.

Riverside Records was a New York label founded by Bill Grauer and Orrin Keepnews. The label began by reissuing traditional jazz and blues on 10" LPs but by 1954 had begun a series of new recordings in the modern jazz vein. The label had signed Thelonious Monk early on and was in the process of building a solid roster of modern jazz artists when in mid-1958, Keepnews (1923–2015) began recording Cannonball Adderley. This was the beginning of a highly successful relationship for both men.

Julian "Cannonball" Adderley (1928–1975) was then a member of the Miles Davis Sextet, one of the two or three most popular modern jazz groups. He had arrived in New York in July 1955 and been a Mercury recording artist for three years. He had led his own quintet during that period but had joined Davis when the group broke up. He would attain the sort of position within Riverside that Ike Quebec had at Blue Note. He would have his own record dates, appear with other leaders, and recommend (and even produce) other artists. When his reformed quintet began recording in 1959, it quickly became the best-selling act on the label and one of the most popular groups in the country. Riverside expansion included a second jazz label, Jazzland, and the Battle label, for blues and gospel issues.

Vee Jay records in Chicago was another relatively new entrant to the jazz business. Founded by Vivian Carter and Jimmy Bracken in 1953, the label had a very strong roster of blues (Jimmy Reed, John Lee Hooker), doo-wop (the Spaniels, the Dells), and gospel (the Staple Singers, the Swan Silvertones). They decided to launch a jazz line in 1958. Chosen to head up the division was Sid McCoy, a longtime associate of the owners and a popular Chicago DJ. Vee Jay quickly built an impressive jazz catalog led by hit-making saxophonist Eddie Harris.

Thus, as the 1950s turn into the 1960s, we have black men in charge of recording at two important jazz labels and key black musicians providing major input at two others. At no other time up to that point had black voices had as much to say about who got recorded and what kind of records they would make.

BILL DOGGETT-SIL AUSTIN

The musician who made the biggest impact during 1956 was organist Bill Doggett (1916-1996). He had been recording for King since 1952 in a variety of settings: trio, quartet—often with Percy France on tenor sax, and with a vocalist. He was making ballad albums and R&B singles, many of which he composed himself. His drummer, Shep Shepherd (1917–), had been with him almost from the beginning; and during 1955, Doggett added Billy Butler (1925–1991) on guitar. The final piece of the puzzle came aboard the following year with the arrival of Clifford Scott (1928–1993) on tenor sax.

On June 16, 1956, the band cut "Honky Tonk," an instrumental that the band had worked up at a dance in Gary, Indiana. From the first note of Billy Butler's truly inventive guitar solo, an irresistible groove was established, and the tenor sax solo that followed was on the same level. The performance was edited into a two-part single: part 1 guitar solo, part 2 tenor sax solo. The leader didn't solo at all!

But Bill Doggett laid the foundation with Shepherd and bassist Carl Pruitt (added for the recording session). And what a foundation it was! Part 2 of the single hit #1 on the R&B chart during a seven-month stay and rose to #2 on the pop chart. It was the biggest R&B instrumental of all time. The band had other top 10 R&B hits with "Slow Walk," "Ram-Bunk-Shush," and "Hold It."

Doggett did not stop making albums. An Ellington tribute found Scott playing as much alto sax as tenor. On other projects, he occasionally played flute. More horns were added to the group with Candy Johnson (on tenor and baritone sax) and trombonist Lawrence "Tricky" Lofton used most frequently. At one point, the band reached nine pieces.

When the King contract expired in 1960, Doggett signed with Warner Brothers for three albums and then went to Columbia for another three. Good as the resulting music was, the albums went nowhere in the marketplace. The big white labels could effectively sell a Miles Davis or Dave Brubeck, but organ combo music of the soul jazz idiom was outside their area of promotional expertise.

The core of the Doggett group split up after the King contract. Scott went to Los Angeles where he was on the scene, mostly as a sideman, for the next fifteen years. Sometime in the late 1970s, he returned to his hometown of San Antonio, Texas, and continued to play with reduced visibility. Scott was one of the finest blues players of the era, and one only wishes there had been more examples of his splendid work.

Originally a Philadelphian, Butler settled in New York where he became a prominent sideman in record studios and Broadway pit bands. He was often recalled by Doggett to play on record dates. Butler emerged as a jazz player where he was often employed from the 1960s onward. He made four LPs of his own for Prestige and was recorded in France notably for the Black & Blue label.

Shepherd settled in San Francisco working well into the twenty-first century. At one point, he switched to trombone and fronted an organ trio!

Doggett's follow-up to "Honky Tonk" was "Slow Walk," but that record was a cover of an even bigger organ-tenor sax single by its composer, Sil Austin.

Austin (1929–2001) had contributed key solos to R&B hits throughout the era. He came up with Cootie Williams and had recorded for Jubilee before signing with Mercury. After leaving Tiny Bradshaw in 1955, Austin hit with "Slow Walk," which made it to #3 on the R&B chart. This made him a touring attraction, and he broadened his sound to include sweet ballads ("Danny Boy" was another hit). Like his contemporary Sam Taylor, he recorded ballad albums for the Japanese audience. He also had a very large following among the Jamaican people.

Sil Austin left his New York base in the early 1980s and moved to Atlanta where he invested in a string of car wash locations. Rediscovered in the 1990s by the New Orleans–based Black Top label, he returned with all his abilities fully intact.

JONAH JONES

Another veteran musician who came to the fore during the mid-1950s was Jonah Jones. Jones (1909–2000) had worked with several bands during the 1930s, but his tenure with Cab Calloway was his longest and best-known association. It lasted, on and off, from 1941 to 1952. Yet before Calloway, Jones had made some remarkable records with Stuff Smith from 1936 to 1939, mostly for Vocalion. His playing on those sides is that of a hot, open-horn specialist in the Louis Armstrong tradition. In the early 1950s, he worked and recorded with an Earl Hines group that featured two vocalists, Etta Jones and Helen Merrill, as well as trombonist Bennie Green.

Jones had recorded sessions of his own for Keynote, Commodore, and Swing (France), often with players from the Calloway band, from 1944 to 1946; and the results were superb small-group swing. After leaving Calloway, Jones resumed recording while on a European tour and upon his return to the United States began appearing in small New York clubs, such as the Embers, with just a rhythm section. It had been suggested to Jones that by using a mute and serving up a less raucous brand of jazz, he might be able to find a niche for himself between the Dixielanders on one hand and beboppers on the other. It was the right decision.

He recorded first for Bethlehem and RCA, but in 1957, he began a seven-year stint with Capitol that yielded nineteen LPs! After that, there were deals with Decca and Motown that produced another eight albums. The Jones approach featured his muted trumpet in the context of a tight shuffle rhythm with the drummer using wire brushes. It proved to be instantly popular; and the first three albums, *Muted Jazz*, *Swingin' on Broadway*, and *Jumpin' with Jonah*, were Billboard pop chart items in 1958. At the time, the prevailing critical opinion suggested that the recordings were commercial sellouts, but closer listening reveals classic swing in three-minute miniatures where the soloist never overstays his welcome.

Jones's arrangement with the Embers ultimately culminated in a deal to play twenty weeks per year at the club. With this sort of security, Jones was able to maintain a solid following for many years, playing a largely white circuit. While one wouldn't think of Jonah Jones in the same breath as the Modern Jazz Quartet musically, each group was four black men, in tuxedos, performing for an increasingly white audience. Musically, the Jones group was closer in approach to his Capitol Records labelmate Louis Prima and his Las Vegas–based gang. In fact, it wouldn't be long before Jonah Jones was working frequently in those same Las Vegas hotels.

The success of Jonah Jones created a virtual cottage industry for trumpet players. Soon there were albums by Shorty Baker (King), Johnny Letman (Bethlehem), Joe Wilder (Savoy, Columbia), Harry "Sweets" Edison (Roulette), Henry "Red" Allen (Prestige, Columbia),

Taft Jordan (Mercury, Prestige), Roy Eldridge (Verve), Buck Clayton (Vogue), Joe Newman (Coral, Prestige), Rex Stewart (Design, Grand Award), Cootie Williams (Prestige), and no fewer than nine albums by Charlie Shavers (MGM, Everest) all featuring trumpet and rhythm section. More modern players joined the parade as Kenny Dorham (Prestige), Blue Mitchell (Riverside), and Lee Morgan (Blue Note) made their only quartet albums during this time. Even Dizzy Gillespie made two Verve albums during 1958 where Les Spann, on guitar and flute, was his only frontline partner. In most cases, these players would revert to a quintet or larger band, featuring other horns, for future recording.

COZY COLE

Beginning in 1968, the drummer with the Jonah Jones Quartet was Cozy Cole, an old associate from the Calloway days. Cole (1909–1981) was one of the first black musicians to work on a network radio staff orchestra when he left Calloway to join CBS in 1942. He led some exceptional small-group record dates for Keynote, Continental, Savoy, and Guild during the war years. From 1949 to 1953, he was a member of Louis Armstrong's All-Stars.

By the mid-1950s, he was a fixture on the New York scene and frequently on display at the Metropole Café, a Times Square club noted for booking the best black swing players.

Charlie Shavers, Henry "Red" Allen, and Coleman Hawkins were among the most frequently heard stars. Cole was a regular in the Allen group that also featured J. C. Higginbotham, Buster Bailey, and Claude Hopkins. His feature in the group was a lengthy solo on "Caravan."

Dick Hyman arranged a recording date for Cole on the Grand Award label in 1956. The date included Rex Stewart, Tyree Glenn, Hawkins, and Hopkins; but the recorded version of "Caravan" lacked a single release and was originally issued on a 10" LP at a time when that configuration had begun to fall out of favor with retailers. Another recording of "Caravan," for an English label two years later, suffered a similar fate: no single release and a 12" release that found Cole's music shared with music from another bandleader. The album was available in the United States only as an import.

Shortly after this, Cozy Cole made a recording with a group of New York studio pros that turned into a true phenomenon. According to Cole, a fan approached him at the Metropole one night and wanted to finance a new version of "Caravan." With a version on the market and a second version available in England, Cole was reluctant. When the fan proved to have the ability to bankroll such a project, Cole met with Hyman and suggested that "Topsy" might be worked into a two-part single as a drum feature. Hyman wrote the arrangement, and it was issued on the Love label.

Until that time, "Topsy," written by swing era veteran Edgar Battle, was best known in the 1937 Decca recording by Count Basie, which was in no way a drum feature. The Love single shot to the top of the charts, hitting #1 R&B and #3 pop! While Cole never had another record approaching the sales of "Topsy," he did manage to get out on the road with his own band in the wake of the record's success. He now became a recording leader in his own right, making albums for King, Charlie Parker, Coral, and Columbia during the 1960s. After joining forces with Jonah Jones, the group went to Europe for the 1974 Nice Festival, and Cole was recorded there. Cole's final record date was a 1977 tribute to Armstrong, under the aegis of one his great admirers, Lionel Hampton.

BENNIE GREEN

Another artist who made a breakthrough of sorts was trombonist Bennie Green (1923–1977). Originally from Chicago, Green had been a part of the Earl Hines band during the 1940s and would rejoin Hines for a while after his stay (1948–1949) with Charlie Ventura and his Bop for the People group. Beginning in 1949, Ventura recorded for RCA Victor and was the beneficiary of major promotion from the label.

Prior to that, during the 1948 recording ban, Ventura had recorded for Bob Shad's Sittin' in With label. Several of the group's best known tunes such as "Euphoria" and "I'm Forever Blowing Bubbles" came from that session. As the only black member of the band, Green's abilities were not on display to any great degree, but being an acknowledged member of a hit group surely didn't hurt.

He had made some small-group recordings for Jubilee and Prestige before Shad, at Decca for a brief stay between stints at Mercury, got him a session in July 1953. Among the items recorded that day was "Blow Your Horn," a solid jukebox item that became Green's signature tune.

Chronologically Green was from the bebop era but not really a part of it. His style featured his big sound in a sparsely noted attack that emphasized blues feeling. He had much in common with fellow Chicagoan Gene Ammons. Green worked a combo in the 1950s often featuring either Charlie Rouse or Billy Root on tenor sax. Frequently recorded from 1955 to 1961, his albums stand up very nicely many years later.

J. J. JOHNSON

Green was far from the only trombonist to make his mark at this time. J. J. Johnson (1924–2001) was the greatest of all bebop trombonists, yet he needed a day job in the early 1950s in order to keep his head above water. What changed things for him was a 1954 Savoy record date that paired him with fellow trombonist Kai Winding (1922–1983). This quickly became a working band, and the J&K group was quite popular during 1954–1956.

The group recorded for RCA's X label, Prestige, and Bethlehem (the most popular) and five LPs for Columbia. After breaking up, Johnson returned to leading his own groups, with time-out only to join Miles Davis for a brief spell. A talented writer/arranger, Johnson followed Quincy Jones to Hollywood in the late 1960s and was more active writing film scores than playing jazz. By 1977, he was back to playing on a more or less regular basis, and he made some marvelous recordings for the next twenty years.

ALAN FREED

Alan Freed had all his ducks in a row in 1958. There were movies, TV shows, local and national radio shows, local and touring stage shows, and big band recordings. There was now a considerable amount of competition in all these fields. The opposition in television came from Dick Clark and his Philadelphia-based television show, **American Bandstand**, on the ABC network. There were dozens of local television shows with similar formats by the end of the decade.

On the stage-show front, the major competition on the touring front had been the Biggest Show of Stars, operated by Washington, D.C., promoters Irvin and Israel Feld. The Feld tours had been a part of the scene before Freed's shows began traveling and were booked by GAC, a major booking agency. Other agencies assembled R&B tours; but the Feld series, which lasted well into the 1960s, was the best organized and would often string together three months of one-nighters. By comparison, Freed's tours, while competitive for talent, were not nearly as extensive. They were also expensive to mount since, unlike the other tours, Freed's big band was part of the show.

The sixth album by the Alan Freed band, *Alan Freed Presents the King's Henchmen*, had been completed in February 1958. The instrumentation was reduced to nine pieces, by eliminating the brass. The henchmen included Sam "the Man" Taylor, Count Hastings, and newcomer King Curtis. Yet the "king" in the album title was not a reference to Curtis but to Freed who had been billed as "the King of Rock 'n' Roll" for some time. The band for the stage shows continued to have seventeen or eighteen pieces. The road band was often led by former Count Basie saxophonist Earle Warren.

Despite the successes, all was not smooth sailing for Freed at this time. The major labels and ASCAP publishers were taking potshots at the music on a continual basis. As rock 'n' roll continued to build momentum across the country, Freed was the most obvious target for the wrath of white citizens' groups and politicians opposed to the music.

On March 20, Jack Hooke and Freed mounted his most ambitious tour yet, a six-week, sixty-eight shows in thirty-eight cities route covering the Northeast, Midwest, and Canada. This was a huge roll of the dice since previous Alan Freed tours had amounted to a few shows along the East Coast in a short period. Now he would be in direct competition with Irving Feld's Biggest Show of Stars, 1958, which had done an eighty-day tour the previous year and had been running shows of that magnitude for several years.

Despite the fact that the domestic economy was not good and that unemployment was high, **The Big Beat** show was a smash at the outset, grossing $150,000 in its first ten days. Then, on the evening of May 3, 1958, something happened.

The Freed tour was playing a one-nighter at the Boston Arena, in downtown Boston. Best known as a college hockey stadium, the arena seated about five thousand. This particular edition of the show featured Larry Williams, Jo Ann Campbell, Screamin' Jay Hawkins, as well as other acts and the Alan Freed band. They would perform in the first segment while Jerry Lee Lewis and headliner Chuck Berry would play after intermission.

Boston had been a problem for Freed during 1956. Unruly kids had charged the stage during a show, causing a confrontation with police. After the resulting melee, some seats were torn up, and there was considerable damage to the venue. At the conclusion of the evening, Freed, who had been questioned by the police and released, made some disparaging remarks about the cops to a group of reporters. There were more problems when Freed's show came to Boston the following year, resulting in a ban on rock-'n'-roll shows.

How much those remarks lingered in the minds of local officials is not known, but there had been a dramatic increase in the amount of vandalism and violence at rock-'n'-roll shows in much of the country. There had been a brawl at one of the Feld shows in New Haven, three weeks prior to the May 3 date. The Boston press, no fans of rock 'n' roll, trashed the music on a regular basis and warned the public in advance of what might happen when Boston's mayor, John Hynes, lifted the ban not long before Freed's scheduled arrival.

The full house at the show was racially mixed, and from the beginning, there were problems with roughhousing and evidence of drinking among the patrons. Police were in the crowd and backstage, but the performance continued without much trouble until Jerry Lee Lewis started a medley of his Sun hits and kids left their seats to start dancing. The police started to react when Hooke told them that such a response was not unusual and that Freed would handle it.

The kids calmed down until Chuck Berry came on to close the show, and the place exploded again. This time, there was more confrontation with the police, and Freed told the crowd that the cops, who had turned on the house lights, were opposed to them having fun.

Although Freed's remarks were not intended to incite the crowd, that is exactly what happened, and fights broke out. Chuck Berry ran for cover, and the show was over. Outside the arena, in the street, for a time, there was general mayhem; and someone was stabbed. In spite of this, the streets were cleared with no escalation of violence. Freed and Hooke were generally unaware of what had happened outside the building.

The aftermath found the press alleging girls raped, knife fights in the arena, and a huge riot in the street featuring teenage gangs. That coverage of the event forced cancellation of four of the five remaining Freed shows. On May 8, Freed found that a Massachusetts grand jury had indicted him on charges of inciting to riot, and he faced a substantial prison term if convicted. The fortunes of Alan Freed, the King of Rock and Roll, had begun to turn.

In short order, Freed resigned from his New York flagship WINS, when the station refused to back Freed in his battle to defend himself. He was indicted a second time in Boston on May 14. The following day, he pleaded not guilty to both charges and was released on $3,000 bail. On May 20, he was hired by WABC, a clear-channel station, at a substantial increase in salary. Freed's attorneys moved for dismissal of the Boston charges but were denied, and a trial date was set for January 1959.

The fifth motion picture to star Freed, **Go Johnny Go**, had been scheduled to start shooting in January 1959. It would be released in April. Chuck Berry had a featured role; and other musical performers included Jackie Wilson, the Cadillacs, and the Flamingos. There were several white acts as well. In terms of script and overall quality, this was the best of the Freed films. While still a good cut below the average Hollywood fare, **Go Johnny Go** was a huge improvement over the earlier films.

While Freed's New York shows over Labor Day and Christmas both exceeded $200,000 in gross revenues, all was not well in Freed's relationship with WABC, who had demanded a piece of the stage shows. There were restrictions on what Freed could play on air, and while his playlist was not nearly as restrictive as the newly arrived Top 40 format, Freed had to do certain things differently. In addition, his personal life involved a second divorce, a third wife, and lots of child support. Around this time, the investigation into television quiz shows with reportedly rigged results was under way. By year-end, the quiz show had virtually disappeared from the commercial television networks.

When Freed returned from shooting **Go Johnny Go**, WABC put on the pressure, demanding 75 percent of Freed's on-air salary in advertising to support his stage shows. On the other hand, his **Big Beat** television show, featured daily on WNEW-TV, from 5:00 PM to 6:00 PM, since June 1958, was given a Saturday slot as well in April 1959.

All this seemingly normal business-as-usual activity was soon to take a backseat to the mounting legal problems.

The Boston case was finally settled in November 1959. It resulted in a $300 fine for Freed but thousands in attorney fees to cover the eighteen months in time it took to conclude the matter. The congressional committees that had been investigating fixed TV shows now focused their attention on the record industry. The payola scandal was at hand.

There was no federal statute against payola in 1959. What Freed and other New York DJs were charged with was the violation of a New York state law against commercial bribery. There were different forms of payola: everything from the "$50 handshake" in the memorable phrase of Hy Weiss, owner of Old Town Records, to elaborate booze and hooker arrangements for visiting DJs set up by the record labels. The publicity generated by the infamous 1959 Disc Jockey Convention in Miami served to heighten the intensity of the scrutiny. In November 1959, the payola investigations shifted into high gear. By the end of November, Alan Freed was no longer on the air in New York.

Freed was indicted on charges of commercial bribery in February 1960. In a few short months, Alan Freed had gone from the King of Rock 'n' Roll to a pariah virtually unemployable in New York. The TV show was gone; the radio show was gone; the movies were gone; and after one final stage show at the Apollo Theater in Harlem, in February 1960, those would also be gone. By May of 1960, he was in Los Angeles doing an afternoon slot on KDAY. While showing some initial promise, Freed's stay at KDAY lasted only fifteen months. A final radio stop at WQAM in Miami in September 1962 lasted less than ninety days.

Alan Freed was being bled to death by his legal problems. As with his Boston indictment, he was ultimately fined $300 after pleading guilty in the payola indictment. When he paid it in March 1963, the payola scandals may have been over for him, but it took thousands of dollars in lawyer fees to settle the case. A year later, the IRS came calling. On January 22, 1965, Alan Freed died, stone broke.

The Alan Freed Rock-'n'-Roll Big Band had died long before that. While it may be fanciful to suggest that there might have been a way for a big band, in the black swing tradition, to function within rock 'n' roll, the fact is that the band is fondly remembered by people who attended the Freed shows. The records they made are variable in quality, yet when they are good, they are very much the equal of a Buddy Johnson or Erskine Hawkins record from the same period.

PAYOLA

As for the relationship between radio and jazz, that was changing as well. The AM band would, in its music formats, become increasingly compartmentalized. The days of block programming were receding in the rearview mirror while tightly selected playlists were now the province of a program director. Top 40 would become the dominant music format, and in time, the Top 40 might actually mean the top 15! Country, soul music, and other music specialist stations would become rigidly segregated in their musical approach. For jazz, the future would be on FM radio.

The payola relationship between record labels and radio would continue uninterrupted. In most cases, the program directors would be the beneficiaries of label largesse, but there were ways devised to make certain that anyone who had to be paid was paid. As the years passed, new and elaborate methods of record promotion were devised, many of them run through local distributors or independent promoters. This later group gained considerable power in the 1970s and 1980s as more scandals were brought to light. Record labels used independent promotion people as buffers between themselves and the radio people. In terms of payola to jazz DJs, there was always some of that; but after the 1970s, when jazz tended to be heard more on public radio stations, it virtually disappeared.

As the decade drew to a close, jazz record people had carved out their own turf. Managers and agents, in short supply in the early 1950s, grew in numbers and professional competence. They were able to move their groups through a circuit of clubs in the Northeast, Midwest, and West Coast that kept leaders working. The proliferation of jazz festivals created additional work and opportunities for exposure during the warmer months.

The passing of the Federal-Aid Highway Act of 1956 would, in time, permit musicians to move more freely via the Interstate Highway System. In time, coast-to-coast highways such as I-90, I-80, I-40, and I-10 would cut considerable time from city-to-city travel. Of course, there was a price to pay for this. Much of the land used for these highways came from black neighborhoods. Cities such as Detroit, Chicago, Cleveland, New Orleans, and Los Angeles would have the heart of traditional black neighborhoods completely destroyed.

Mobility became an engine for growth in jazz. Even air travel was relatively inexpensive. It was an era when great jazz groups were created and sustained. The jazz business had become more professional in every way. As 1960 came into view, things would only get better.

Hank Crawford 1985 by Joe Rosen

HANK CRAWFORD

"ESTABLISH YOUR OWN THING FIRST and then branch out. Get an identity. After you learn the basics, reading and technique, the rest has to come from you."

That advice by Hank Crawford was offered to aspiring young musicians constantly and consistently for many years. Crawford was a prominent combo leader for almost thirty years. He toured nationally and internationally and recorded more than thirty albums as a leader or co-leader during his distinguished career. Yet his five-year association as saxophonist and arranger with Ray Charles provided Crawford with much of his own identity.

Bennie Ross Crawford was born in Memphis, Tennessee, in 1934. He acquired the nickname 'Hank' during his years at Manassas High School because of a stylistic resemblance to well-known local alto saxophonist Hank O'Day. O'Day has been cited by other Memphians, notably Sonny Criss, as a player with a strong powerful tone.

His own highly personal tone was his calling card. Yet he was also fortunate to have been exposed to a wide variety of music during his formative years.

"In Memphis you heard the whole thing. You could wake up early in the morning and hear gospel music but before long you would hear Eddy Arnold or some other country music. The best jazz musicians had to play rhythm & blues because that was the only work that was available. People in Memphis really like the blues."

Crawford was a teenager when BB King was a disc jockey on WDIA. He was still in high school when the Beale Streeters (Johnny Ace, Bobby Bland, Earl Forrest, Rosco Gordon and Junior Parker) were scuffling in Memphis trying to get a break. He not only remembered the Midnight Rambles (amateur contests conducted by Rufus Thomas at local theaters), but was an occasional participant, winning on one occasion with a note-for-note reproduction of Illinois Jacquet's "Jet Propulsion" solo.

His own identity had begun with private piano lessons at age nine. Crawford kept up on keyboards, sometimes using an electric piano in his own groups and sometimes playing it himself either in live performance or on recordings. While in high school he was a member of the Manassas Rhythm Bombers, a sixteen-piece band that was playing advanced Woody Herman and Stan Kenton charts years before other schools would even acknowledge jazz. Manassas was the school where famed bandleader Jimmie Lunceford had introduced jazz as part of the music education curriculum in 1927. Lunceford's first band, The Chickasaw Syncopators, was recruited from Manassas students.

After attending Jackson State, Hank transferred to Tennessee State and was in the middle of his senior year when Ray Charles heard him. Despite the fact that he had completed his major and needed only eleven credits for graduation, in January, 1958, Hank went on the road with the Ray Charles band playing baritone sax. Crawford's family remained in the Memphis area and he returned to the Bluff City for extended stays on many occasions.

The Charles band was only seven pieces at the time. John Hunt and Ricky Harper were the twin trumpets, while doubling alto sax and tenor sax was David "Fathead" Newman. The Charles band really came together as a unit in 1958 and the Atlantic recordings from Newport and the Newman album *Ray Charles Presents Fathead*, which featured the Charles band, present strong evidence of this fact. Hank continued to play baritone sax until Leroy "Hog" Cooper joined in 1959 at which time he played alto and never looked back. Interestingly enough Newman had also played baritone when he first joined Charles in 1954. There are few if any Crawford solos with Ray Charles but his strong tonal presence as the lead saxophonist gave the Charles band a truly distinctive sound.

It was as an arranger that Hank made his greatest contribution to the Rat Charles sound. It was the *sound* of the seven-piece band as arranged by Hank Crawford that lingers in the memory of so many people. More than any other similar sized group this was the sound of a modern blues band. Over time Hank appeared with a number of vocalists, providing his distinctive horn charts in order to enhance the soulful mood of the singer.

Despite the fact that Ray Charles left Atlantic for ABC records in 1959, Atlantic executives, especially Nesuhi Ertegun, took an interest in Hank. Demand for Newman's performance of "Hard Times" from *Fathead* had spawned a 45 single, and the new Ray Charles lineup with Crawford, Newman and Cooper on saxes had an irresistible sound. By 1960, Hank was the music director for Ray Charles and had made his Atlantic debut album, *More Soul*. It is here that listeners first became aware of the soulful, singing sound of the Crawford alto saxophone.

The two trumpet, alto, tenor, baritone sound remained Hank's arranging trademark for his entire career. With Charles, Hank travelled everywhere. During the early years much of the work was in southern dance halls but, as Ray Charles became a full fledged star, more concert work and European tours became the norm. In all those years, before the appearance of the star, the band would play its own short set.

"Ray would remind us if we were playing a dance that he didn't want us to get too complex; but aside from that we could play what we wanted. I played piano on a lot of those sets. Sometimes when we'd come into Philadelphia at Pep's or The Showboat we would play some hipper things. We'd play a few numbers to establish a groove and then branch out. Ray always had good tunes in his book. I remember "Tin Tin Deo" and a lot of Horace Silver things."

The decision to leave the Charles organization came in 1963. Despite the joyful music, all was not calm in the Charles camp. Ray Charles' narcotics addiction would frequently make life difficult for those around him. Crawford had been recording for Atlantic through all these years and certain songs, such as "Misty", "The Peeper" and "Whispering Grass" were getting strong air play. Hank felt that the time had come to take advantage of the reputation he had built and to try things on his own. In June, 1963, after the Charles European tour, Hank formed his own seven-piece band. Ray had a big band now so those wonderful small band arrangements were stored away in Hank's trunk at the Crawford family home in Memphis. They were not played by anyone for many years. Despite the fact that he was a part of the Ray Charles organization for less than six years, the affiliation would be the first association most fans would make in thinking of Hank Crawford.

Mac Rebennack remembers the early Crawford band on a trip to New Orleans creating an absolute sensation. The five horn lineup left room for only bass and drums for rhythmic support.

"When Hank would solo, there was nothing behind him. Nothing! I had never heard anything like that before."

The Crawford band though it differed slightly in instrumentation, was the last in a long line of blues-based big/little bands that first appeared in the mid-40s. Illinois Jacquet was one of the first while Arnett Cobb, Earl Bostic and James Moody were other models. If the sound of the Ray Charles band had an influence on Hank it probably came from the fact that unless he played it himself, there was no piano in those warm-up sets for Ray Charles.

"I've always had a difficult time with piano players. Too many of them have a natural tendency to alter the chords. It always seems to clash with my thinking."

The Crawford band was based in Los Angeles and was extremely popular during the mid-60s. Many excellent musicians passed through the ranks. At one time, Jimmy Owens and Marcus Belgrave were the trumpeters while Wendell Harrison and Wilbur Brown were among the tenor players and Howard Johnson played baritone sax. Bassist Charles Green was a longtime member of the group and the drummers included Carl Lott and Milt Turner. The Crawford band played all the key black venues in Los Angeles.

Hank added a guitar in 1965 and at one point vocalist Austin Cromer was singing with the group. At its peak, the band had a book of more than 150 arrangements and featured work by Owens, Gerald Wilson, Phineas Newborn Jr. and Teddy Edwards as well as Hank himself.

By 1967, the payroll had risen to eleven pieces and it became too much of a load to carry. He disbanded and returned to Memphis where he stayed more than two years. During this time, he worked a smaller group that included guitarist Calvin Newborn and occasionally, Belgrave. The group did a lot of travelling to Chicago, New Orleans and Texas so Hank continued to make his presence felt on the national scene.

In 1970, he moved to New York. Shortly thereafter he left Atlantic. For his final album, he couldn't even get a big enough budget for a horn section, his signature sound. He had been an Atlantic artist since 1960 and the company had grown into a conglomerate deeply involved in current rock and pop music.

"I began to feel like a number rather than an artist toward the end. When I joined Atlantic they were a small company but when I left they had gotten very big. It seemed as though the vocalists were getting all the attention. Still, I have no bad feelings toward Atlantic."

Being a jazz artist in New York in 1970 with a track record but without a recording contract was actually something that proved to be beneficial; a case of being in the right place at the right time. Creed Taylor was about to start a second label and was looking for proven talent.

Taylor's CTI imprint had been established as a joint logo with A&M during a three-year period that Taylor had produced for A&M. Taylor struck out on his own with CTI in 1970 and had big selling albums almost immediately with Freddie Hubbard, Stanley Turrentine and George Benson. When Taylor added a second label, Kudu, Hank Crawford was the second artist he signed.

What is especially interesting about his stay at Kudu is that the treasured identity of Hank Crawford found a completely different direction. During the eight years that Crawford was involved with Creed Taylor he was not called upon as an arranger. At Kudu, Hank was a soloist.

In a 1974 interview, he remarked on the situation at Kudu. "They do everything first class here. The engineering is top quality-the arrangements, everything. I haven't had any problem in picking my material and I'm very happy with what Don Sebesky and Bob James have written."

The modus operandi for the Kudu sessions would find Hank playing with the rhythm section to establish the basic feeling. Arrangements for strings and/or horns would be added later. This is essentially the way one produces for a singer and indeed this is Creed Taylor's greatest contribution. He proved with CTI/Kudu as he had earlier with Verve and A&M, that jazz records could be sold in enormous quantities using that formula.

Unfortunately, Taylor was almost too successful. Problems with distribution hounded the labels, and major companies were not slow to raid the CTI artist roster. Large record labels are always convinced of the superiority of their distribution systems and, in the cases of a George

Benson or a Grover Washington, Jr., the artists proved themselves capable of sustaining a career level that justified a major label recording contract. Not all artists are so fortunate. Hank Crawford had his biggest hit with a 1976 Kudu album, *I Hear A Symphony* which was on the Billboard Soul LP charts for thirteen weeks.

By the end of the 70s, the CTI/Kudu situation had completely unraveled. After a couple of years of not recording, Hank signed with Milestone Records, a division of Fantasy. His Milestone releases returned him to his horn-rich blues sound and coupled him with stars of equal magnitude (organist Johnny Hammond, tenor men Houston Person and David "Fathead" Newman) while utilizing a crop of experienced session players (Dr. John, Wilbur Bascomb, Jr. Bernard Purdie and guitarists Jimmy Ponder, and Melvin Sparks). His 1991 album, *Portrait*, contains a first: a cover photo of a smiling Hank Crawford! Dental surgery repaired a gap in his front teeth which had forced him to be close lipped in all previous cover photos.

In 1986, he joined forces with organist Jimmy McGriff. They recorded together as co-leaders for Milestone in addition to their own separate projects. McGriff's manager, Maxine Harvard, took over booking and they became a top shelf touring attraction for the next fifteen years. A new generation of fans would think of Hank as the saxophonist in one of the last travelling soul jazz groups.

In person, the Crawford-McGriff band was only four pieces but neither leader had a particularly outgoing personality so the introductions and announcements were handled by Wayne Boyd, the guitarist! On record the albums were intended to focus on the sound of the group. George Benson, Billy Preston and Cornell Dupree were guests on early albums.

The material recorded by the band drew from the entire spectrum of black music. Jazz standards from the books of Ellington, Basie, Clifford Brown or Horace Silver would be paired with R&B standards, pop ballads and originals by each leader. The closing song for each performance would be "Lift Every Voice and Sing" by James Weldon Johnson, best known as the black National Anthem. Unlike many musicians, this band had a dress standard: tuxedos were the rule.

The group switched to Telarc for two albums in 1994-95 before returning to Milestone in 1996. The mix of jazz tunes, blue ballads and original material that had marked Hank's earlier Milestone albums was resumed while bassist Stanley Banks and pianist/organist Danny Mixon were now part of the proceedings. Two more albums co-led with Jimmy McGriff were also recorded.

In 1998, Barry Dolins of the Chicago Blues Festival called. They were presenting Ray Charles and wanted to reunite Ray with his original horn section. So Hank went into his trunk and dusted off those wonderful small band arrangements and they were played once again by Hank, David "Fathead" Newman, and Leroy Cooper along with Marcus Belgrave and Phillip Guilbeau for an enthusiastic audience of more than 50,000.

Belgrave (1936-2015) had settled in Detroit after leaving Ray Charles. He did a considerable amount of session work at Motown but always kept a jazz presence. Beginning in the late 1960s he was a mentor to many of Detroit's finest young musicians. His own work was often featured in edgy modern jazz settings yet as time passed he began playing jazz of all styles and assumed the role of elder statesman. He would play on Hank's final album in 2000. He recorded several CDs of his own in various settings in the last years of his career.

Guilbeau (1926-2005), who started with the Paul Williams band, was discovered by Ray working in Washington D.C. He probably had more solo space than any of the trumpet players who passed through the band. He had left the Ray Charles band in 1965 for a stay with the Count Basie orchestra and, later, was instrumental in promoting the funk group Black Heat before returning to Charles in the mid-1970s. His solo playing can be heard on the Williams hit, "The Hucklebuck" while Ray featured him prominently on his *Genius + Soul=Jazz* album for Impulse.

Newman (1933-2009) was a well known leader of his own groups and recordings. Always Hank's first call for a tenor player and often found as a co-leader of groups with Hank, the two worked together less frequently once the Crawford-McGriff combo was launched but were often teamed up on record. Newman who recorded solos with Ray Charles on alto, tenor, baritone and flute was a prolific recording artist with more than thirty albums under his leadership.

Leroy Cooper (1928-2009) had been working in Florida for many years. He got his start in the late 1940s with the Ernie Fields band and had returned to his native Dallas working and recording with Buster Smith (Atlantic). His lengthy tenure with the Ray Charles band would last until the mid-1970s. At one point, Cooper weighed well over three hundred pounds but his old band mates were delighted to find Cooper at least 100 pounds lighter when he arrived in Chicago. This reunion would be the first time the three reedmen had played together in many years.

It would also be the last time. Shortly after completing his Milestone album, *The World of Hank Crawford*, in 2000, Hank was felled by a stroke and was simultaneously diagnosed with prostate cancer. He returned to Memphis and rarely played again.

Hank Crawford's recording career has been well represented on CD. One of his Atlantic producers, Joel Dorn, managed to get almost all of Hank's Atlantic albums back on the market and the Milestone albums are not difficult to find. While some of the Kudu albums have not been made available on CD there is a chance that they will be in the future.

When he died on January 29, 2009, Hank Crawford was the third of that fabulous Ray Charles reed section to die in that same month. Cooper had passed on January 15 while David Newman had succumbed to pancreatic cancer on January 20. This spooked a lot of fans who felt that there must have been some serious voodoo reason for this to have happened. One veteran observer spoke for many people when he suggested that Ray was simply getting the band back together and that he called Hank last because he couldn't find the arrangements. He wanted to remind Hank to bring his trunk.

RECOMMENDED RECORDS:

Soul Of The Ballad, with Marty Paich Orchestra, 1963 (Atlantic LP); Help Me Make It Through The Night, 1972, (Columbia CD); Midnight Ramble, 1982, (Milestone CD); Soul Survivors, with Jimmy McGriff, 1986, (Milestone CD); The World Of Hank Crawford, 2000, Milestone CD).

SOUL JAZZ

"Now we are about to play a new composition by our pianist, Bobby Timmons. This one is a jazz waltz. However, it has all sorts of properties. It is simultaneously a shout and a chant. Depending upon whether you know anything about the roots of church music . . . meaning soul church music, not Bach chorales . . ."

—Julian "Cannonball"
Adderley introducing his group's performance of
"This Here" to a nightclub audience
in San Francisco, October 1959

THEY BEGAN AS TWO-PAGE ADVERTISEMENTS usually in the middle of *Down Beat* magazine. *Down Beat* was then a biweekly publication, and these ads did not run in every issue. When they did, the right-hand page would be devoted to Moodsville, New Jazz and Swingville, subsidiaries of the parent label, Prestige. The left-hand page was the one that attracted attention because it was there that the term *soul jazz* first appeared in print. Three columns of albums would be displayed featuring Gene Ammons, Shirley Scott, Brother Jack McDuff, Johnny "Hammond" Smith, Willis "Gator" Jackson, Bill Jennings, Jimmy Forrest, and others.

Soul jazz? What was this? You can search the history books and reference works, but you won't find any mention of it. Soul jazz parallels hard bop, avant-garde, and the earliest fusion (more often called jazz/rock). The era of its impact begins shortly after the arrival of the 12" LP, and it was well over before the arrival of the CD.

As rhythm and blues turned into rock 'n' roll in the '50s, so did bebop become hard bop. There was little difference in the approach of the jazz players except that they had a longer period with which to express themselves. In the '50s, soul jazz was, roughly, equal parts black swing and rhythm and blues, with a smattering of gospel and modern jazz influence. Its performers may not have utilized rhythm the way the modernists did, but the drummers would know the key licks of an Art Blakey or Philly Joe Jones. The adventuresome harmonies favored by modern composers would not necessarily be heard in an organ combo; but Miles Davis or Charlie Parker tunes, especially if those compositions were blues, would be in the repertoire of most groups, as would the popular R&B hits of the day. Danceable tempos were an important ingredient: expected and delivered in almost every song. If a soul jazz group played Charlie Parker's "Now's the Time," they might play Parker's melody with a feeling closer to that of "The Hucklebuck," the R&B hit based in part on Parker's tune. Soul jazz was entertainment first. Within a short period, it became the preferred social music of big city black adults. The initial impact of soul jazz was felt strongest in the northeast. Philadelphia, Newark, and New York were favorite stops of the organ combos. Yet by the mid-'50s, there were plenty of organ bars in Chicago, Cleveland, Detroit, and Los Angeles as well. In fact, by that time, it was a rare urban community that did not have one or two clubs featuring the Hammond organ.

WILD BILL DAVIS

At midcentury, the Hammond organ began to emerge as a popular instrument in the black community. Jazz writer Stanley Dance recalled hearing organ in the Cootie Williams band of 1949 at the Savoy Ballroom. But the man most responsible for the success of the new instrumental sound was William "Wild Bill" Davis. Davis left Louis Jordan in mid-1948 to experiment with the organ sound. A lot of people thought he was crazy.

The organ's function as a part of the black church services made it a sound most black people were well acquainted with. Popular entertainers such as Fats Waller and Count Basie had recorded on pipe organ. Yet

Wild Bill Davis conceived a new trio sound with organ, guitar, and drums. This was the beginning of soul jazz.

It took a while for Davis to develop his sound. In June 1951, he made his first recordings for Okeh featuring former Louis Jordan bandmates Bill Jennings on guitar and Chris Columbus on drums; and by that time, everything was in place. The musical rapport achieved by the group was imitated everywhere. While the records were not big hits, coming at a time of the 78 to 45 rpm changeover, they were especially popular on jukeboxes in black neighborhoods.

Davis kept the trio sound intact when Floyd Smith replaced Jennings; but when Calvin Newborn and, later, Dickie Thompson played guitar in the Davis group, they were frequently joined on record and, in time for live performances, by a variety of tenor saxophonists.

William Strethen Davis (1918–1995) was born in Missouri, raised in Kansas, and attended Wiley College in Texas. His first professional experience was with the Milton Larkin band in Houston. He played guitar and was an assistant to chief arranger Cedric Haywood from 1939 to 1942. He joined the Louis Jordan band in 1945 as pianist and arranger.

Davis's replacement in the Jordan group was Bill Doggett, and Doggett was also captivated by the sound. He had played organ behind Ella Fitzgerald on several of her scat-singing hits. On May 1, 1952, Doggett recorded as a sideman for Roost Records. The leader of the session was Eddie "Lockjaw" Davis, and the first organ-tenor sax album was made. The sound really gained popularity during 1952.

The competition among the New York–based black music labels of 1952 was fierce. Everyone was trying to get into the organ sound. Willis Jackson used organ in his Atlantic session of May 23 that resulted in "Gator's Groove" and "Rock, Rock, Rock." Hal Singer had organ on his Savoy session of August 21. Prestige was using organ in sessions with modern jazz performers such as Joe Holiday, Annie Ross, and Zoot Sims. Bill Doggett recorded with trombonist Vic Dickenson for Blue Note.

Pianists were doubling on organ to a much greater extent, and studio veterans such as Hank Jones and Dick Hyman were recording on organ on an almost daily basis. Nationally known pianists such as Sir Charles Thompson, Milt Buckner, Gerry Wiggins, and Marlowe Morris began experimenting with the instrument. Doggett and Buckner, as well as emerging talent such as Jackie Davis and Doc Bagby, had spent a lot of time in Philadelphia; and in time, the Quaker City would provide the new sound with its greatest performer.

If the activity and enthusiasm for organ groups was growing throughout the 1950s, it would take the 12" LP to move the music forward. There would always be 45 rpm singles issued for the jukebox trade, but in large measure, what sold to the soul jazz audience were albums.

EDDIE "LOCKJAW" DAVIS

In July 1952, Eddie "Lockjaw" Davis (1921–1986) was featured on "Paradise Squat" with the Count Basie band. Basie, who had learned the instrument from Fats Waller, played organ on the tune; and the performance resulted in a big record. At the end of July 1953, Davis left the Basie band to form his first trio. Organist Doc Bagby and drummer Charlie Rice completed the group. The group first recorded for Roost but switched to King in 1955. The group recorded five LPs over the next three years, and the last two featured Shirley Scott who replaced Bagby in 1956. After more recording done for Roulette and Roost (now associated with Roulette), the group that by then found Arthur Edgehill on drums was well established.

It was this group that Esmond Edwards heard one night at the Apollo Theater. He expressed great enthusiasm when mentioning this to his boss, Prestige owner Bob Weinstock.

Weinstock had a relationship with Davis that went back to the short-lived Birdland label in 1950. He had signed and recorded Shirley Scott a few weeks before agreeing to do a one-shot album with the Davis group. Bassist George Duvivier, who recorded with Scott, became a part of the Davis recording unit; and for the album *The Eddie "Lockjaw" Davis Cookbook Volume 1*, Jerome Richardson was added on flute and tenor. In the recordings done for King and Roulette, the Davis group stuck to short single-length performances. On his first Prestige album, Lockjaw stretched out. The highlight was a twelve-and-half-minute slow blues, "In the Kitchen." When the album was issued, that track got most of the airplay, and Lockjaw had a hit album.

Between the time that the album was recorded and the time it was released, Weinstock had decided to turn over the A&R direction of Prestige to Esmond Edwards. With Prestige set to undertake the expansion noted in the *Down Beat* advertisements, Weinstock needed to keep a closer watch on the business side of things. One of Edwards's first moves was to sign Eddie "Lockjaw" Davis to an exclusive contract. The tandem of Davis and Scott was recorded together, under Davis's name and in support of other artists, eleven times in less than two years! Shirley Scott was making her own albums, and their growing popularity suggested that sooner or later she would have to become the leader of her own group. But during the pivotal years of 1958, 1959, and 1960, Prestige was undergoing a transformation that would set it apart from its competitors. The success of the organ-tenor sound established by Lockjaw Davis had brought similar stylists to Prestige.

During the early 1950s, when Ira Gitler or Weinstock had been producing for Prestige, the musicians signed were modern jazz players who, when they worked in New York, would appear at clubs that specialized in modern jazz such as Birdland, Café Bohemia, or the Village Vanguard. During 1959, tenor saxophonists Arnett Cobb, Hal Singer, Willis Jackson, and Buddy Tate first recorded for Prestige. One significant fact about these signings is the connection to clubs in Harlem. Eddie "Lockjaw" Davis was a mainstay at Count Basie's Lounge while Buddy Tate had been resident at the Celebrity Club since 1951. Willis Jackson was one of a number of rotating groups who appeared several times a year at Small's Paradise, and Arnett Cobb had gotten his start as a bandleader at the Baby Grand.

ARNETT COBB

Arnett Cobb (1918–1989) was born in Houston, Texas. He worked with the Milton Larkin band in his hometown before joining Lionel Hampton to replace Illinois Jacquet in 1943. He set the Hampton band on fire and helped to spur the band to its greatest success. Upon leaving Hampton, he had formed a six-piece band and had taken on Ben Bart, at Universal Attractions, for management. Just as his bandleader career was getting started, he had serious back surgery that kept him out of action for over a year. When he resumed in 1950, he got a recording deal with Columbia. He first session produced "Smooth Sailin'," a solid seller though better known in the Ella Fitzgerald version.

If Cobb had no big hits, his band worked steadily being equally adept at playing clubs, doing studio work, or backing R&B groups on theater tours. His Columbia recordings were transferred to Okeh; and that relationship was followed by brief encounters with Mercury, Atlantic, and Vee Jay.

It was in 1956, driving in heavy rain, returning from a job in Connecticut, when he sneezed. He awoke in a hospital with his legs crushed. It was more than two years before he returned to active playing. From this point forward, he played on crutches. When he was booked to record with Lockjaw Davis in January 1959, nobody knew exactly what to expect.

The album recorded that day, *Blow, Arnett, Blow*, was an exceptional piece of work. Cobb was accompanied by Wild Bill Davis, his old friend from Texas, recording under a pseudonym. Seven more albums were taped over the next eighteen months, and they proved to be the best of Cobb's career.

In the mid-1960s, Cobb returned to his hometown and was based there for the rest of his career. His injuries restricted his ability to tour, but in time, he resumed. He became a major attraction in Europe during the 1970s.

BUDDY TATE

George Holmes "Buddy" Tate (1913–2001) was born in Sherman, Texas. His early professional career was spent with Midwestern territory bands such as T. Holder, Andy Kirk, Troy Floyd, and Nat Towles. He joined Count Basie in 1939 upon the death of Herschel Evans. His tenure with Basie lasted until 1948 after which he settled in New York, soon beginning a more than twenty-year stay at Harlem's Celebrity Club. Tate was a powerful blues player, and away from his own groups, he was most associated with other ex-Basieites such as Buck Clayton and Dickie Wells. He was also a regular attraction in Europe beginning in the mid-1960s. His soul jazz connection is based on sessions under the leadership of Wild Bill Davis and Milt Buckner for the French Black & Blue label. He was an active freelance player from the mid-1970s until the mid-1990s, often appearing in tandem with players such as Jay McShann, Al Grey, and Paul Quinichette.

In 1960, Big Al Sears, King Curtis, Jimmy Forrest, and Budd Johnson joined the Prestige family. They were recorded in twos, threes, and fours. Considering the fact that Davis and Coleman Hawkins were already Prestige regulars, this amounted to an overwhelming roster imbalance in favor of tenor saxophonists. The organists were coming as well. Brother Jack McDuff, Johnny "Hammond" Smith, and Larry Young became Prestige artists during this time.

If soul jazz seems to have arrived, it didn't last for Lockjaw Davis.

When Shirley Scott decided to form her own group, Davis was convinced that Johnny "Hammond" Smith would be her replacement. Smith, however, had other ideas; so Davis shifted gears and formed a two-tenor group with Johnny Griffin. The group recorded for both Prestige and Jazzland, and while the music was superb, it failed to find an audience. By the end of 1962, that group was history; and the following year, Davis announced his retirement to become a booking agent. He would return, but rarely would he return to the organ and tenor sound that he helped pioneer. He rejoined the Count Basie band in 1965, and he remained until 1974. From that point until his death, Davis worked in tandem with Harry "Sweets" Edison, with all-star groups assembled by Norman Granz and as a single picking up rhythm sections.

As a saxophone stylist, Davis was one of the unique figures of the postwar era. He was as big-toned as many of rhythm and blues stars, but his harmonic conception was truly his own, and his solo style of having rasps, growls, smears, or farts in almost every bar of his work tended to make it impossible to duplicate.

Shirley Scott (1934–2002) joined forces with Stanley Turrentine and formed one of the finest organ trios on the circuit. A Philadelphian, her style was vastly different from most organists of the time and reflected the influence of Milt Buckner rather than Jimmy Smith. After the group with Turrentine broke up, she continued to work trios, always with a saxophone included. As a recording artist, she was one of the most prolific of the era, recording thirty-seven LPs from 1958 to 1973. About half of those feature her with bass and drums, but the remainder find her leading units of varying size and instrumentation.

New Jazz was the first of Bob Weinstock's labels going back to 1949. Prestige was started so that the more experimental sounds would not be mixed up with the more accessible jazz of Prestige. The 1959 arrivals served to further compartmentalize the music. New Jazz was revived as an LP label while Swingville and Bluesville were formed to concentrate on specific styles. Moodsville was created to feature ballad programs by instrumentalists from all the labels. Several of the saxophonists were recorded in ballad programs for Moodsville while others were recorded for Swingville in contexts somewhat removed from the soul jazz sound of the parent label. All this amounted to lots of producing for Edwards. Yet the best of all the soul jazz saxophonists was still away. It would be June of 1960 before Gene Ammons was paroled.

The appointment of Esmond Edwards to his position and the work that he was doing did not go unnoticed. By 1959, Sid McCoy was well established in the jazz department at Vee Jay while the influence of Cannonball Adderley at Riverside and Ike Quebec at Blue Note was beginning to make itself felt. That these four men all were making key suggestions or decisions during the same period meant that black influence was being directly applied on the jazz record business to a greater extent than ever before. While each of these labels would be aware of soul jazz, not all of them did much about it. Prestige, as noted, was rolling straight ahead with its soul jazz roster; but Blue Note had been slow to react probably because they already had the greatest soul jazz artist under contract and was not about to let anyone else dim his luster.

JIMMY SMITH

James Oscar Smith (1925–2005) is largely responsible for the modern sound of the organ. A WWII veteran, Smith was raised in Philadelphia and had studied both piano and bass before beginning a professional career. It was during his stay with the Don Gardner band (which began in 1952) that he made the transition from piano to organ. He spent long hours working on the sound of the instrument, especially his bass lines. When he formed his own trio in September of 1955, the instrumentation may have been identical to Wild Bill Davis's group, but nothing else was.

Before Jimmy Smith, many of the records made that featured organ used a bass player. This is because the organ bass was played by foot pedals, which tended to sound muddy. Jimmy Smith invented a way to synchronize the foot pedals with the left hand, which resulted in a cleaner, more distinct bass line. His discovery by Blue Note Records in 1956 brought this sound to a national audience. Getting that sound on record was the achievement of a Hackensack, New Jersey, optometrist named Rudy Van Gelder.

Van Gelder (1924–2016) began recording for his own enjoyment and gradually made it his sole profession. He brought an approach to recording that was scientific rather than mechanical. His technique, which pioneered the multiple-microphone mix and featured a judicious use of reverb, had always appealed to musicians. When he recorded Lennie Tristano for Tristano's Jazz Records label, Van Gelder got billing on the 78 label! He had been introduced to Blue Note by saxophonist Gil Melle and by 1954 was doing all their recording.

Van Gelder was an independent contractor; and in addition to Blue Note, he was working for Prestige, Savoy, and, later, Impulse and Verve, among others. He would be the organists' favorite engineer of all time. Yet getting the Jimmy Smith sound required a lot of experimentation. By February 1957, the problem had been solved, and Jimmy Smith's organ sound had been captured completely.

If the sound of Jimmy Smith's bass conception took a while to master, his right-handed brilliance was there from the beginning. So much of what Wild Bill Davis, Bill Doggett, and Milt Buckner played focused on chords and a full orchestral sound. Each man was an accomplished arranger, so it was natural for them to think this way.

Jimmy Smith was a virtuoso soloist—a much different species! He was also one of the greatest blues players in the history of jazz.

While Van Gelder remained the one engineer of this period who could get the best organ sound on record, every new organist was working very hard to duplicate the sound that Jimmy Smith was putting forth. Jimmy Smith recorded for Blue Note until 1963, and his work for the label was very consistent. Indeed, Jimmy Smith's Blue Note output can be taken as a virtual primer for aspiring organists. His biggest albums for Blue Note were *Midnight Special* and *Back at the Chicken Shack*, both of which were recorded on April 25, 1960.

That morning, tenor saxophonist Stanley Turrentine opened his front door in the Germantown section of Philadelphia to be greeted by Jimmy Smith. Smith was on his way to Blue Note to record and asked Turrentine if he would like to come along? Turrentine did.

That spontaneous decision helped to produce, in one afternoon, the two single biggest albums in Blue Note history up to that time. Both records cracked the Billboard album charts, a rarity for jazz labels at the time.

But Smith's greatest popularity came when he left Blue Note. In 1962, Smith had been "loaned" to Verve, now owned by MGM, and had made an album, *Bashin'*, that featured, on some tracks, a big band arranged by Oliver Nelson. One of those tracks was "Walk on the Wild Side." The idea of wedding the organ to a big band was a fairly new sound. With *Bashin'*, the combination of Jimmy Smith, Oliver Nelson, and Rudy Van Gelder had achieved what would be, to that point, one of the two or three biggest albums ever by a black jazz artist.

The effect of this was not lost on Smith. He realized very quickly that the larger recording budgets, greater promotional effort, and superior distribution facilities could be a huge benefit to his career. He signed with Verve in 1963. The deal was negotiated by Smith's manager Clarence Avant, who had come up under Joe Glaser and who knew how to wield real clout.

Jimmy Smith became the most popular jazz musician of this era and one of the most popular of all time. He was often ignored by the white press, but his record sales were phenomenal. His albums routinely sold in the 100,000-and-up range, and their chart results were quite astonishing. Between 1962 and 1967, Jimmy Smith's Verve albums were in the top 20 of all pop albums five times with *Bashin'* reaching #10. His entries on the R&B LP charts (not in existence until 1965) were routinely near the top with *Respect, Organ Grinder's Swing*, and *Got My Mojo Workin'* (a #1 R&B album) the major achievers.

Jimmy Smith's working groups were trios prior to his early-'70s move to California. Guitarists such as Thornel Schwartz, Eddie McFadden, Quentin Warren, and Nathen Page were members of the trio for various lengths of time. Ray Crawford was Smith's guitarist for much of his time in California.

The drummer in the Jimmy Smith trio during its halcyon years was Donald Bailey (1933–2013). Like Smith, Bailey was from Philadelphia and proved to be the perfect drummer for the group. After his 1964 departure, the trio never sounded quite as good. Bailey settled in Los Angeles and was quickly absorbed into the scene, working with great musicians of all styles. He is especially remembered for the unique beat he supplied for *Back at the Chicken Shack*, one of Jimmy Smith's most enduring favorites.

The recordings Smith did for Verve were similar in some respects to those he did for Blue Note. Rudy Van Gelder's studio was the location, and his own trio was used on occasion, but much more often, a large orchestra was employed. Arrangers Claus Ogerman and Lalo Schifrin worked on individual albums, but Oliver Nelson wrote the bulk of the most successful albums.

OLIVER NELSON

Nelson (1932–1975) had been signed to New Jazz as a saxophonist by Esmond Edwards. Appreciating his multiple abilities, Edwards gradually worked him into the Prestige mix. He began making sideman appearances with Lem Winchester, Johnny "Hammond" Smith, and Eric Dolphy—fellow New Jazz artists. Next came a three-tenor date with Jimmy Forrest and King Curtis. It was September 1960 that he did his first major arranging job: a big band album for Eddie "Lockjaw" Davis, *Trane Whistle*.

The year 1961 was the time that Oliver Nelson started to make an impact. Early in the year, he had been loaned to producer Creed Taylor to create a celebrated Impulse album, *Blues and the Abstract Truth*. For Prestige, he co-led another album with Eric Dolphy, wrote a strings album for Etta Jones, and arranged an eleven-piece band session for Gene Ammons. For much of the year, he co-led a quintet with Joe Newman that recorded for Mercury under Newman's name. In August 1961, Nelson appeared in tandem with Newman on his own *Main Stem* album and with Shirley Scott on her date, *Blue Seven*. The fall of 1961 found Nelson completing his first major orchestral album, *Afro-American Sketches*.

During the first few months of 1962, he had arranging tasks for Etta Jones, Frank Wess, and Jimmy Forrest albums. His final appearances on Prestige were arranging for singers Faye Adams and Jimmy Grissom. By this time, he had finished work on his first collaboration with Jimmy Smith.

Upon leaving Prestige, Nelson recorded one-shots for United Artists, Verve, and Argo before signing with Impulse. He would record for Impulse and with former Impulse producer Bob Thiele on Thiele's Flying Dutchman label until his 1975 death. Almost all his post-Prestige work involved writing and large orchestras. If his work as a blowing soloist is heard mostly on Prestige, there are countless examples of Oliver Nelson's arranging artistry. His work, more than any other jazz writer, embodies the orchestral sound of the 1960s. The combination of Jimmy Smith's organ and the orchestra of Oliver Nelson sold more albums than any other similar combination in jazz history!

GENE AMMONS

Gene Ammons (1925–1974) had been a Prestige artist on and off for more than a decade when he returned, in 1960, from an almost two-year jail term from his first major narcotics conviction. His tenor sax battles with Sonny Stitt had been solid-selling singles, and a series of jam sessions produced intermittently popular albums in the late 1950s. Yet the period between 1960 and 1962 is when the Gene Ammons legend really took off.

Ammons's first recording upon his return resulted in the album *Boss Tenor*, an enormous hit. There was more to come, yet Ammons was still an out-of-control junkie at the same time his popularity was soaring. The label support and managerial guidance taken for granted for hit jazz artists today were generally nonexistent in the early 1960s. Yet when Ammons played an organ bar, people came from all over to hear him. While he was not the innovator Jimmy Smith was, Gene Ammons was the other giant of the soul jazz idiom.

The Ammons style was based on a commanding tonal presence and great interpretive ability. His method was to play fewer notes but to make each one count. An exceptional ballad player, Ammons was equally at home with a slow or medium-tempo blues; but his ability to put his personal stamp on pop songs such as "Canadian Sunset," "Angel Eyes," or "Exactly Like You" gave him a dimension rarely found in other saxophonists. Apart from *Boss Tenor*, the albums *Jug*, *Angel Eyes*, and, especially, *Bad Bossa Nova* were huge hits.

Despite the fact that Jimmy Smith had been recorded extensively since first joining Blue Note, the label had pursued no more organists. Apart from Smith sessions using some of the label's horn-playing artists in a jam session format, Blue Note hadn't even used organ in the rhythm section! It would be 1961 before another organist leader appeared on a Blue Note album. The decision to move more in a soul jazz direction likely came from discussions Alfred Lion and Frank Wolff had been having with Ike Quebec.

Quebec had been a Blue Note artist in the 1940s and remained close to the Blue Note partners. Quebec soon became part of the Blue Note inner circle. Among his tasks was to ensure the timely arrival of certain Blue Note artists to record dates. But Quebec was more than a babysitter; his recommendations were taken seriously. Originally from Newark, he knew about the hot young New Jersey–based organists: players such as Larry Young, Rhoda Scott, John Patton, and Freddie Roach.

If Blue Note was now emulating Prestige in the hunt for organists and the pursuit of soul jazz, it should also be mentioned that there had been some shakeup among the other labels. Savoy had stopped recording jazz almost completely by 1961 while Atlantic, apart from the work of Hank Crawford and David "Fathead" Newman (both veterans of Ray Charles's band), preferred to concentrate on more adventuresome performers such as John Coltrane, Ornette Coleman, and the Modern Jazz Quartet. Pacific Jazz, which had pioneered West Coast jazz in the early 1950s, was now a solid contender with the Curtis Amy–Paul Bryant combo, Richard "Groove" Holmes, pianist Les McCann, and the Jazz Crusaders carrying the soul jazz banner. As the jazz wing of Chess, Argo was deeply involved with artists such as Ramsey Lewis, Ahmad Jamal, and James Moody. Riverside was one label where the soul jazz potential was growing but not from the organ side of things. The key artist at Riverside was alto saxophonist Julian "Cannonball" Adderley.

CANNONBALL ADDERLEY

Adderley had left the Miles Davis Sextet in 1959 to form a new quintet with his brother Nat on cornet and pianist Bobby Timmons. These were key sidemen since each was a composer of considerable ability. Timmons had written "Moanin'" for Art Blakey and would contribute "This Here" to the Adderley group's first album for Riverside.

Each of these songs contained harmony with obvious links to gospel music. Timmons, Horace Silver, and, to a certain extent, Charles Mingus were developing a new kind of jazz repertoire. Nat Adderley fit right in; and his composition, "Work Song," was another outstanding example of the new genre.

The repertoire of jazz players has always been eclectic. The popular songs of the moment had provided source material since the beginning of the music. Yet the new soul jazz repertoire was being derived from blues, gospel, and folk roots—not Tin Pan Alley, and certainly not the Brill Building! The difference between what Lockjaw Davis was doing in his organ-tenor group and what Cannonball Adderley was doing was considerable. Davis's group used standard ballads or something with a Latin tinge for a change of pace from his hot, jivey, uptown jump. When Davis recorded "The Rev," the composition turned out to be a conventional slow blues.

The Riverside albums of Cannonball Adderley from 1959 to 1963 were best sellers; and among them were *In San Francisco, Them Dirty Blues, At the Lighthouse, African Waltz,* and *Jazz Workshop Revisited*. In addition, his group collaborated with vocalist Nancy Wilson; and a hit Capitol album, *Nancy Wilson/Cannonball Adderley*, was the result. The quintet format was expanded to sextet from 1961 to 1965 to include multi-instrumentalists Yusef Lateef or Charles Lloyd. In 1964, he signed with Capitol.

Cannonball Adderley was a knowledgeable, articulate spokesman for his music. Most of his best recordings were done before a live audience, and his announcements to that audience would often discuss the elements in his next selection. He began talking about music with roots in the church—and not "Bach chorales" as he was quick to point out. He began to talk about soul. The seeds of gospel that Ray Charles had planted in R&B had taken hold in jazz.

Adderley was permitted to produce LPs for the label by artists who were outside the mostly East Coast modern jazz coterie that made up the Riverside roster. Among Adderley's productions were albums by Dexter Gordon, Don Wilkerson (the Texas-based tenor saxophonist who had been a key member of the first Ray Charles band), and pianist Roosevelt Wardell as well as *The Sound of the Wide Open Spaces* album by two more Texas saxophonists, David "Fathead" Newman and James Clay. Adderley also produced sessions in Los Angeles and New Orleans, and not all his sessions were of the soul jazz variety.

WILLIS JACKSON

Willis Jackson (1928–1987) had come to Prestige not long after Eddie "Lockjaw" Davis. A Floridian who had attended Florida A&M with the Adderley Brothers, Jackson was an escapee from the frequently gymnastic demands of rock-'n'-roll tenor sax. He first gained notoriety in the small band led by Cootie Williams in 1948–1949 and was featured on the Williams recording of "Gator Tail," which provided Jackson with a nickname used for the rest of his professional life. He recorded for Apollo, Atlantic, and DeLuxe from 1951 to 1954, most of the sides utilizing his own seven- or eight-piece group that played clubs and R&B package shows. A highlight of his playing from his R&B years was a television appearance on Ed Sullivan's **Toast of the Town** in 1956 as a part of "Dr. Jive's Rhythm & Blues" segment. Jackson's feature was a less-than-two-minute instrumental that required him to kick off his shoes, sit down on the stage and bend over backward while squealing his brains out!

Jackson was a thoroughly professional bandleader whose quartets were always well rehearsed. He split much of his year between Small's Paradise in Harlem and the Club Harlem in Atlantic City where he worked the summer season. He brought with him a group that included future Prestige artists: Bill Jennings on guitar and Jack McDuff on organ. In Jennings (1919–1978), the slight left-handed guitarist, Jackson had found a player with an ability to provide ideal accompaniment as well as solo in a slinky, bluesy, highly distinctive style. McDuff, not yet Brother Jack, was capable of locking in with Jennings and drummer Al Johnson to create irresistible rhythmic grooves.

In a soul jazz context, Jackson, with his big tone and bluesy conception, found new life. Jackson's quartet included some tight arranging touches supplied by Jennings. The group's treatment of "The Man I Love" is an example of how an original arrangement could transform an old standard into something exciting and new. The albums recorded with this core unit and a variety of bassists and percussionists were exceptional. One, *Cookin' Sherry,* won the Grand Prix de Disc, a French award of the highest honor in 1962. Jackson also specialized in long, loose blues performances with a light yet insistent rhythmic pulse. His Prestige albums of the late '50s to early '60s have numerous examples of this special groove, and the one best remembered is "This'll

Get to Ya." What is more unusual is that the performance almost didn't get heard by anyone!

At more than ten minutes in length, "This'll Get to Ya" is long; but not overly so, for Jackson. It was left in the can after being recorded in February of 1960. When Jack McDuff left Jackson to form his own group in 1961, Jackson and Prestige were anxious to showcase the next Jackson band as soon as it came together. The Jackson group with McDuff had recorded plenty of material, and there would be time to deal with the excess sometime down the road. The year 1962 was an interesting time for Jackson in that the four albums he recorded that year used guest stars to good effect; but in 1963, he found a combination to his liking with a trumpet player, Frank Robinson; a new organist from Cleveland, Carl Wilson; and a hot young guitarist named Pat Martino.

Martino (1944–) was just eighteen when he joined Jackson, but he is *the* great guitarist of the era for pure playing ability. He made eight albums with Jackson and would later play on record dates with him in the 1970s. Martino's own career includes appearances in an organ group context among a variety of musical settings.

While Jackson made some splendid recordings over the next year, it seemed that some of audience was left behind. The consistent sales that had been achieved by the group featuring McDuff had fallen off. Still believing in the group, Prestige recorded Jackson live in the spring of 1964. What they didn't reckon with was Willis Jackson's knowledge of the American Federation of Musicians rules and regulations.

In any in-person recording during this time, a band would tape the three or four sets that they played during the evening and choose the best material for release. To Jackson, it appeared as though the label intended to record four LPs and only pay for one. He threatened to go to the AFM unless he was paid for all four. Bob Weinstock hit the roof. He paid Jackson but then released him from his contract! After assembly, the albums would be spaced out for release over the next eighteen months. Yet it would make no sense to issue four consecutive live albums by any band. Perhaps there was something left over from the earlier sessions Jackson had recorded. After all, McDuff had become a big star since leaving Jackson. He now had hit albums of his own and a quartet that was one of the most popular road bands of 1964.

The unreleased material was assembled into an album titled *Together Again* by Willis Jackson with Jack McDuff. The album title suggested a reunion, while in reality the two musicians had almost no contact over the past several years! Radio played a big part in breaking the album, and DJ personalities such as Joel Dorn on WHAT in Philadelphia and Ed Love on WCHD in Detroit got behind the album, specifically that more than ten-minute loose blues "This'll Get to Ya." The result was a smash of an album that built over more than a year and cracked the Billboard pop album charts. Prestige combed the vaults for still more and issued a second album titled, predictably, *Together Again, Again*. *Jackson*, who was now a free agent, cut one-shot albums for Cadet and Verve, before returning to Prestige in 1967.

JACK MCDUFF

While all this was going on, McDuff had made his mark. Jack McDuff (1926–2001) had learned much in his four-year stay with Jackson. He had also played on a lot of Prestige sessions, with Gene Ammons and Sonny Stitt—individually and collectively—and with artists as diverse as Betty Roche, King Curtis, Shakey Jake, and Roland Kirk. Originally a bassist, not only was McDuff a first rate soloist, he was an arranger with a highly personal touch. While his group was modeled on the Jackson quartet, it had its own unique sound. After some initial forays with units that included guitarist Grant Green and Jimmy Forrest or Harold Vick on tenor sax, he recorded a hit with a 1962 Prestige album, *Screamin'*. The session involved Leo Wright on alto and Kenny Burrell on guitar who were not McDuff sidemen, but much of the album's attention was focused on "Soulful Drums," a feature for his drummer, Joe Dukes. The success permitted McDuff to form his first national touring band.

That group included a veteran of the Chicago R&B wars, Red Holloway, on tenor sax; the soulful drummer from Memphis, Joe Dukes; and a nineteen-year-old guitarist from Pittsburgh, George Benson. There was strength in every chair of this band; and while each player, especially Benson, has achieved a great deal individually, what they accomplished as a group has rarely been attained by any jazz group regardless of personnel. The first album, *Brother Jack McDuff—Live*, while a solid hit, was not as live as one might think. The group had been recorded at the Front Room, a Newark nightclub, but the tapes had not been good. In exchange for scrapping the Front Room tapes, the band went into a recording studio, with an invited audience, kept the announcements from the Front Room session, and made an album that contained McDuff classics such as "Rock Candy" and "A Real Goodun." The follow-up album for Prestige, *Live at the Jazz Workshop*, was almost as popular. McDuff found most of his key players going their own way by 1966, and while his future groups never rose to the level of the 1963–1965 band, he always had well-disciplined, hard-swinging groups. It was not uncommon for Benson and/or Holloway to turn up on his record dates. But Joe Dukes was a big loss to the McDuff sound. Whenever Dukes was a part of the McDuff quartet, as he was on an intermittent basis, the group would find renewed vigor.

McDuff's recording after 1975 took an increasingly commercial approach, and it wasn't until the late 1980s when he began recording for Muse and Concord Jazz that he returned to what he did best.

The soul jazz explosion of the early 1960s had produced several other popular groups. The Shirley Scott–Stanley Turrentine group recorded for Prestige under Scott's name and Blue Note under Turrentine's. When Scott left Prestige, the group also recorded for Impulse and Atlantic before the group (and the marriage) broke up. The Scott-Turrentine road band was a trio while a bassist was usually added for recording dates. The recorded music was first rate.

LOU DONALDSON

Lou Donaldson, the versatile alto saxophonist, had been a part of the Blue Note roster since 1952. He recorded a solid seller in in the 1958 album, *Blues Walk*, which featured a jukebox favorite in the single version of the title track. A key component of the Donaldson sound was the use of conga drum in the rhythm section. The favored conguero was Ray Barretto (1929–2006). Barretto had made his recording debut on Atlantic with Arnett Cobb in 1955 and first recorded with Donaldson on the 1957 album, *Swing and Soul*. Donaldson felt that the conga drum would add a danceable element to the rhythm section.

Others agreed. Barretto was utilized on *Blue Gene*, a Gene Ammons album from April 1958; but on Prestige, he was most often found as an addition to the Red Garland Trio. The following year, he was on

Prestige dates by Cobb and Lockjaw Davis; and in 1960, Barretto and other conga players were regulars on Prestige dates.

Blue Note did not use Barretto or any conga player with great frequency. It would be 1963 before he contributed to a Blue Note hit, Kenny Burrell's *Midnight Blue*.

In 1962, Donaldson hooked up with organist Big John Patton and guitarist Grant Green for an album titled *The Natural Soul*, which would become Donaldson's biggest album to date. The key selection was Patton's tune, "Funky Mama." Donaldson began using organ in his working band and would continue to do so for the next fifteen years. His group became an incubator for soul jazz talent.

Big John Patton (1935–2002) was one of the first to emerge. Originally from Kansas City, he worked with Lloyd Price for four years in the late 1950s before switching to organ. The collaborations with Grant Green from 1962 to 1966 are his best remembered sessions. They recorded together under Patton's leadership, Green's leadership, or in support of others more than twenty times during that period. Of his Blue Note albums, *Along Came John* and *The Way I Feel* are outstanding. While Patton never had a bandleader career, his organ style had great blues feeling as a major component. He continued to record for Blue Note until 1970. His later years were interrupted by illness.

GROOVE HOLMES–LES MCCANN

The organists kept coming. Richard "Groove" Holmes (1931–1991), from Camden, New Jersey, had been discovered by pianist Les McCann working in Pittsburgh. McCann (1935–), a pianist of enormously contagious enthusiasm, had become a popular attraction around Los Angeles and had recorded albums with titles such as *The Truth* and *The Shout* for Pacific Jazz Records. The owner of Pacific Jazz, Richard Bock, had been one of those in the forefront of recording West Coast jazz, but times had changed, and Bock was at the center of soul jazz activity in Southern California. The success of McCann's gospel-ish trio and the well-remembered but short-lived organ-tenor sax combo fronted by Paul Bryant and Curtis Amy had given a soul jazz transfusion to the black music scene in Southern California.

Filling a role similar to those Ike Quebec and Cannonball Adderley had with their labels, McCann was a catalyst for more recording in the same genre by Pacific Jazz. Holmes, in his first three albums, had guest stars (including McCann, who supplied much of the original material). Ben Webster was a guest on his first album and Clifford Scott on the third, and these results proved to be musically solid yet failed to promote Holmes as a trio leader. On the other hand, *Groovin' with Jug*, a collaboration with Gene Ammons, was a solid sales item and helped to get the Holmes name out front. The organ-recorded sound on the Pacific Jazz albums was always less than the best, and that didn't help matters. While the early 1960s Pacific Jazz work is an adequate introduction to Groove Holmes, the best is yet to come.

Much the same could be said of Johnny "Hammond" Smith. Smith (1933–1997) was the best of all the organists on ballads. Born in Louisville, he came to prominence in Cleveland during the mid-1950s. Somewhat overlooked while on Prestige, where the bulk of his work was issued on the New Jazz label, he left for Riverside in 1962. His work for that label was curtailed by the label's bankruptcy in 1964. When he returned to Prestige the following year, tenor saxophonist Houston Person was part of his group. Smith would make some significant recordings for Prestige during the remainder of the 1960s. From 1971 onward, he was known as Johnny Hammond.

JIMMY MCGRIFF

Ralph Kaffel, the owner of California Record Distributors in Los Angeles, was sitting at his desk one day in October 1962. He got a call from Juggy Murray, the owner of Sue Records in New York. Murray had a new organ record, and he was requesting some quick promotional action.

The DJ copies had arrived, but both his promotion men were in the field, so Kaffel decided to drive the record out to KGFJ, an R&B station, himself. The station GM added the record immediately, and it was given to Larry McCormick who was on air at the time. On the way back, Kaffel heard the record on the radio. When he got to the office, there were dozens of calls from record stores asking about the record. It broke wide open in a matter of days. The record was "I Got a Woman" by Jimmy McGriff.

When the right elements (record, distributor, radio station, and retail outlets) were all in alignment, it was possible, at this time, for jazz records to break in the same way R&B records did. The right blues or jazz record fit easily within the KGFJ format.

While Los Angeles was a hot bed of soul jazz activity at that time, there were similar alignments in Detroit, Chicago, Philadelphia, and other cities with a large black population. Yet lose any one of the components and the whole thing could fall apart.

"I Got a Woman" also broke nationally. It became a top 20 pop single! Whether leading a trio or quartet, Jimmy McGriff (1936–2008) quickly proved to have a solid East Coast following; and while his label was not a jazz label, it knew the R&B promotion game well, and McGriff got much more black radio play than many of his counterparts. He followed up with two more successful singles, "All about My Girl" and "Kiko." McGriff sold singles better than most of his contemporaries.

McGriff left Sue for the United Artists–owned Solid State in 1966 and worked with producer Sonny Lester. This was a productive time for McGriff, and his energies were applied to several alternating projects. On the one hand would be McGriff's trio or quartet while the next album might be more orchestral, a live album, or have a special guest such as blues singer Junior Parker, with whom McGriff collaborated frequently. The best seller from this period was *The Worm*, which was a soul LP chart item for twenty-four weeks in 1969. When Solid State was folded into Blue Note, McGriff stayed with Sonny Lester. He was a key part of Lester's Groove Merchant label and, later, his LRC imprint.

McGriff's late 1970s material was heavily commercialized. His 1980s and 1990s work for JAM, Milestone, and Head First returned him to his straight-ahead ways. The albums sold steadily if not spectacularly, but the music was first rate. In 1986, McGriff teamed up with Hank Crawford, and those collaborations sold better than his own albums.

Jimmy Smith had taken everyone by surprise with *Midnight Special*.
In the early 1960s, sales of jazz albums would approach those of pop albums on rare occasions. However, they routinely outperformed

albums by R&B stars since that audience was oriented more toward single releases. But to be one of the top albums in the country was unheard of. In reality, it was just the beginning. The success of *Bashin'* created another milestone for Jimmy Smith. He was signed to Verve by the producer of *Bashin'*, Creed Taylor.

Taylor had started in the business with Bethlehem and moved to ABC-Paramount where he formed the jazz label Impulse. While at Impulse, Taylor produced *Genius + Soul = Jazz* by Ray Charles that combined the leader's organ with a big band. It was an album that was unique in Ray Charles's discography but in many respects would serve as a model for what Taylor would do with Jimmy Smith. Taylor came to Verve in 1961 after the sale to MGM by Verve founder Norman Granz.

While Verve was only one division of MGM, it was a huge operation in its own right, and Taylor was only one of several producers in its employ. He was easily the most successful. Whether it was working with artists held over from the Granz era such as Stan Getz and Johnny Hodges (whom Taylor paired with organist Wild Bill Davis) or his own signings such as Wes Montgomery, Cal Tjader, and Kai Winding, Creed Taylor knew how to make best-selling jazz albums. He would continue to do so for a long, long time.

By the mid-1960s, larger record labels, now aware of the soul jazz phenomenon, were taking a look at organ combo leaders. RCA signed Wild Bill Davis. Marlowe Morris, Bill Doggett, and Sir Charles Thompson would tape organ albums for Columbia. Jackie Davis had long been a Capitol artist. Groove Holmes had left Pacific Jazz by this time and had cut an unsuccessful album, with big band, for a Warner Brothers subsidiary. His next stop would not be a major label, but it would produce his most important record.

Holmes's first session for Prestige came in August 1965. It was a trio date with Gene Edwards on guitar and Jimmy Smith on drums. One of the tunes on the album, *The Soul Message,* was an Erroll Garner ballad, "Misty," given an up-tempo treatment with a rhythmic figure from the 1920s dance, the Charleston. The arrangement had been written by Slide Hampton and had been previously recorded by the Lloyd Price big band. Holmes's treatment of "Misty" became a hit single, reaching #44 on the Billboard pop chart. It ranked even higher on the Cash Box charts.

The album and single were pop chart items through most of 1966. In the same manner of the Willis Jackson–Jack McDuff material for

Prestige, Pacific Jazz retrieved some unreleased Holmes material from its archives and issued an album, *Tell It Like It Is*, that also made the charts. Holmes made a number of other solid-selling albums for Prestige, though none approached the level of *The Soul Message*. In 1968, he returned to Pacific Jazz where he had even less luck than in his first stint with the label.

While the big bands of Duke Ellington and Count Basie continued to thrive, they were virtually the last two black bands still with a nationwide itinerary. Yet the lure of big band leadership was something that would prove irresistible to popular entertainers such as Ray Charles and Lloyd Price. Charles would form a big band in 1963 and lead it for the remainder of his career. Along the way, he would record four albums devoted to the band itself. The 1960s band that Charles led was loaded with veteran players and was consistently interesting on its own. When he first got the band started, he was the recipient of arrangements written for the Billy Eckstine band in the 1940s. To hear Curtis Amy and Clifford Scott battling away on "Blowin' the Blues Away" may not have compared with Gene Ammons and Dexter Gordon, but it was great to hear anyway. In time, the band built up an impressive book from a variety of arrangers.

The Lloyd Price band was started a bit earlier and didn't last nearly as long. The band made but a single album of its own, yet that album featured the keyboard work and arrangements of James Booker, the New Orleans prodigy. Other prominent players who passed through the Price band included organist Big John Patton, saxophonists Red Holloway and Jimmy Heath, as well as trombonist-arranger Slide Hampton.

The future of the big band would move to the college campus where an increasingly large number of jazz programs began to emerge. In terms of performing bands, the models became those of Thad Jones–Mel Lewis in New York and Gerald Wilson in Los Angeles. These bands had recording contracts so that their work was available to the public, but neither traveled much beyond their home turf. The personnel of these groups tended to be increasingly random with musicians often choosing better-paying jobs instead of a Monday night jazz gig (in the case of the Jones-Lewis Orchestra). It should be noted that Dizzy Gillespie recorded several orchestral albums throughout the 1960s although he did not work regularly with a big band during the decade.

There were other big bands of the era that were fronted by arrangers for use on their recording studio projects. These bands never traveled and would appear infrequently, even locally, in person. Outstanding among them were those of Duke Pearson in New York and Onzy Matthews in Los Angeles. Each of these leaders made interesting records: Pearson for Blue Note, Matthews for Capitol. White bands such as those led by Louie Bellson, Maynard Ferguson, Terry Gibbs, Woody Herman, Harry James, Stan Kenton, and Buddy Rich (formed in 1966) had to compete with the "ghost" bands of Jimmy Dorsey, Tommy Dorsey, and Glenn Miller. Yet each was consistently coming up with quality jazz.

MODERN JAZZ COMBOS

Charlie Parker's only combos that were together for any length of time were his quintet from 1947 to 1948 with Miles Davis and Bird with Strings that first recorded in November 1949 and played regularly for the last time in 1952. While there would be occasional New York reunions for these groups, Parker's roadwork was usually played as a single.

Bud Powell led trios throughout the 1950s first with Curly Russell and Max Roach and later with George Duvivier and Art Taylor. In 1959, he began a five-and-a-half-year stay in France where his best trio included Pierre Michelot and Kenny Clarke. While all these trios were excellent, they tended to be supportive of the leader rather than fully interactive.

Dizzy Gillespie had devoted himself to his record label, Dee Gee, for much of 1951 and 1952. After the label folded, Gillespie signed with Norman Granz. He toured with JATP during 1954–1956 and made the best records of his career during this period. Big band sides; Afro-Cuban orchestral material; meetings with Stan Getz, Sonny Stitt, Sonny Rollins, or Roy Eldridge; albums with strings all contained the Gillespie magic. The sides recorded by the big band that toured for the State Department during 1956 and 1957 represent a high watermark for modern jazz big band recording. From 1958 to 1962, Gillespie had top-notch quintets first with Les Spann and Junior Mance, later with Leo

Wright and Lalo Schifrin. When he introduced a new quintet in 1963, it featured a budding star pianist in Kenny Barron and his old friend James Moody on alto, tenor, and flute. Moody and Gillespie were alike in that each had a joy of performing and entertaining. Many Gillespie fans claim this to be his finest small group.

The great modern jazz groups of the 1950s began with the Modern Jazz Quartet (1952) and the Clifford Brown–Max Roach unit (1954). The former with only one personnel change throughout its long history was very much an exception to the rule. The death of Clifford Brown in 1956 effectively brought an end to the latter; and while Max Roach led a series of interesting, unique groups over the next twenty years, he never led one that included someone with the singular talent possessed by Brown.

HORACE SILVER

The late 1950s to mid-1960s were the years of great groups coming together. So many of the prominent leaders who are household names today had their best groups and made their best records during this time. Art Blakey, Kenny Dorham, Hank Mobley, Horace Silver, and Doug Watkins had formed the Jazz Messengers in 1955 as a cooperative group. The history of cooperative groups is that when one person fails in his responsibilities, the entire group crumbles.

This one crumbled after an auspicious start. Recording as the Horace Silver Quintet for Blue Note in November 1954 and February 1955, the group came up with solid airplay items in tunes such as "Doodlin'," "The Preacher," and "Room 608" on two 10" LPs. Next up was a live session recorded at the Café Bohemia that produced two 12" LPs under the name the Jazz Messengers.

All this activity got them a Columbia Records deal. Alas, that contract was not as fruitful as it might have been. Kenny Dorham left and was replaced by Donald Byrd before the first album was recorded. By the time a second album was scheduled, the group had become Art Blakey and the Jazz Messengers with an entirely new band. Silver recorded an album for Columbia subsidiary Epic, including the remainder of the original group with Kenny Clarke or Art Taylor in the drum chair. While Blakey would spend the next two years doing one-shot albums with his Messengers for a variety of labels, Horace

Silver (1928–2014) went back to Blue Note, took the band (now with Louis Hayes on drums), and made the album *Six Pieces of Silver*, which contained another hit song, "Senor Blues."

Until this point, he had been doing Blue Note albums on a one-shot basis without exclusivity and without artist royalties. The contract he signed after *Six Pieces of Silver* was the first of many contracts that would keep Horace Silver a Blue Note artist for more than twenty years. He gave up the sideman work that had been so much a part of his career, not only for Blue Note but also for Prestige where he had recorded regularly with Miles Davis, Art Farmer, and Milt Jackson during 1954 and 1955. From 1957 onward, there would be one Horace Silver Blue Note album every year. Even after the sale of Blue Note to Liberty and, later, United Artists, the policy would continue. At a time when many artists were doing two or more LPs per year, Horace Silver had deliberately decided to limit his output. By doing so, he made each new album release an event, one that was eagerly anticipated by the jazz community.

While Horace Silver kept the same quintet with Blue Mitchell, Junior Cook, Gene Taylor, Louis Hayes, and later, Roy Brooks for more than six years, it wasn't until 1964 when he formed a new group that featured Carmell Jones and Joe Henderson that he recorded his most successful album, *Song for My Father*. That edition of his quintet did not last long; and from that point forward, during the rest of the 1960s, Horace Silver groups had more random personnel. Rarely was a combination of players employed for much more than a year.

This trend continued to the end of the decade; and then, for all intents and purposes, it stopped. Horace Silver albums throughout the 1970s were either devoted to various vocalists singing his lyrics or to concept albums that found his music with layers of brass, strings, woodwinds, or percussion. On record, the great Horace Silver Quintet sound had disappeared, and that was a major loss for jazz.

ART BLAKEY

Art Blakey (1919–1991) was a fiery, powerhouse drummer with an instantly recognizable beat. He was also an astute, intelligent combo leader whose Jazz Messengers were a basic training program for aspiring hard bop musicians. Once you had graduated from Art Blakey University, you could play with anyone.

After the Columbia period, Blakey freelanced the Messengers with albums for Pacific Jazz, Bethlehem (two LPs), Elektra, Vik (two LPs), Atlantic, and Jubilee. For most of this period, the band had a front line of Bill Hardman on trumpet, Jackie McLean or Johnny Griffin on saxophone, and Sam Dockery on piano. By the fall of 1958, the personnel had changed with young trumpet player Lee Morgan joining Benny Golson's tenor sax with another youngster, Bobby Timmons, on piano. This was an unbeatable combination.

Blakey had a long history with Blue Note. He was Thelonious Monk's drummer on the first Blue Note sides from 1947 and made an octet recording under the name Art Blakey's Jazz Messengers the same year. He had done session work for the label throughout the 1950s, as one of a group of drummers that included Kenny Clarke, Philly Joe Jones, Max Roach, and Art Taylor. But his signing an exclusive contract with Blue Note probably had more to do with his playing on two Blue Note dates in early 1958: the first with Jimmy Smith and the second with Cannonball Adderley.

On February 25, Jimmy Smith recorded four lengthy selections with Lee Morgan, Lou Donaldson, Tina Brooks, Kenny Burrell, and Blakey. One tune, "The Sermon," at twenty minutes in length, was not only one of the longest tracks in Blue Note history but also one of the great sustained grooves in the history of jazz. Without Art Blakey's beat, "The Sermon" simply would not have been as powerful.

Two weeks later, Blakey was present for *Somethin' Else* by Cannonball Adderley. Working in a rhythm section with Hank Jones and Sam Jones, Blakey supplied exactly the kind of beat needed to support Adderley and his frontline partner, Miles Davis.

Blue Note signed Blakey to an exclusive contract and had an instant hit with *Art Blakey and the Jazz Messengers* (later titled *Moanin'*, after the key track). Before Blue Note could get the band in the studio for a follow-up, Benny Golson departed. He was replaced by Hank Mobley, but by the summer of 1959, Wayne Shorter had taken over the tenor chair.

The next Blakey album, *The Big Beat,* featured what many people think is the best Blakey quintet. There was a certain amount of grumbling about Shorter. When he first arrived, he was not in the league of a soulful sophisticate such as Hank Mobley, but his talent developed. While sales of this album were not in the class of their last Blue Note release, they were better than most. For an eighteen-month period, this edition of Art Blakey and the Jazz Messengers made world-class hard bop, but by the end of 1961, the band had broken up, and a new entity formed, this time a sextet.

Bassist Jymie Merritt and Shorter were the only holdovers; but new members, Freddie Hubbard, Curtis Fuller, and Cedar Walton, would soon become stars in the jazz community. Not only were they exceptional players, each was a gifted composer.

The first Messengers album featuring the sextet was actually done while Morgan and Timmons were still in the band. It was done for Impulse on a loan basis. This arrangement, which included no payment to Blue Note, was helpful to Blakey in the sense that he was able to experience the superior promotion and distribution operations of a major label. Jimmy Smith, Stanley Turrentine, Donald Byrd, and Oliver Nelson were other artists who were loaned to larger labels during this period.

By 1962, Blakey's Blue Note deal had expired, and he returned to freelancing the band. He accepted a deal with Riverside shortly before the label went into bankruptcy. By the end of 1964, the band had broken up, and the Jazz Messengers would never again achieve the quality and consistency they had maintained during this period.

The problem was twofold. Blakey was not a horn soloist, so he was to an extent dependent on the quality of the frontline players. Nor was he a composer so that the original material had to come from a series of band members who would be appointed music director. At some point, the sidemen realized that they could be writing for their own groups. But make no mistake about it; Art Blakey did more for his musicians than any combo leader: he turned sidemen into leaders.

LEE MORGAN

Lee Morgan (1938–1972) was born in Philadelphia and after joining the Dizzy Gillespie band at eighteen began to serve notice that a major trumpet player had arrived. He joined Blakey in 1958, although he had been recording for Blue Note since late 1956. Apart from some albums done for Vee Jay and Jazzland between 1960 and 1962, Morgan remained a Blue Note artist for his entire career. His work with Art Blakey found him in the frontline company of Benny Golson, Hank Mobley, and Wayne Shorter from 1958 to 1961; and Morgan functioned ideally with each partner. He rejoined Blakey during 1964 but departed in less than a year to resume leading his own quintet. What propelled him back to leader status was *The Sidewinder*.

The album was recorded at the end of 1963 and hit the Billboard charts the following year. The title track was covered by a variety of performers and quickly became a jazz standard. Morgan continued to write funky originals for his Blue Note Records without changing his methodology. While he never had another hit the size of *The Sidewinder*, he never made a bad album. Still in his prime, he was murdered in a New York nightclub in 1972.

It is clear that the success of *The Sidewinder* coupled with that of Kenny Burrell's *Midnight Blue*, Donald Byrd's *A New Perspective*, Horace Silver's *Song for My Father*, and the Jimmy Smith catalog, made Blue Note a prime candidate for acquisition. In 1965, Blue Note was sold to Liberty Records. For a while, things were the same; but when Alfred Lion retired in the summer of 1967, things gradually began to reflect a more corporate point of view.

BENNY GOLSON–ART FARMER

Benny Golson (1929–) was a natural to take on a leadership role. In his case, it was a co-leader role: the Jazztet, in partnership with Art Farmer (1928–1999). The group had a recording deal with Argo, a Chess subsidiary; and the initial release, in 1960, *Meet the Jazztet*, was top shelf in every way. It featured Curtis Fuller, an outstanding trombonist and the hot new pianist of the moment, McCoy Tyner. It also had a key track, "Killer Joe," that got a tremendous reception at radio. Yet by the time of the second album by the group, some seven months later, the whole band except for the co-leaders was new.

The Jazztet made a total of six albums in a little more than two years. The last two were cut for Mercury, a larger and more powerful label. Nothing seemed to work for this star-crossed band. By the end of 1962, it was over. Farmer formed a quartet with Jim Hall on guitar and later a quintet with Jimmy Heath on saxophone. By the end of the decade, he had settled in Europe.

Golson headed in the other direction, eventually moving to California where he concentrated on writing for film and television. His elegant tenor saxophone playing did not appear on record for the rest of the decade. Although he returned to the instrument in the mid-1970s, times had changed.

DEXTER GORDON

Among the tenor saxophonists of the era, Dexter Gordon, Sonny Rollins, and John Coltrane stood out. Gordon (1923–1990) was originally from Los Angeles and got his start playing in the big bands of Lionel Hampton, Louis Armstrong, and Billy Eckstine during WWII. While he maintained a strong presence in his hometown, he cut an equally stylish figure in New York. His recordings for Savoy and Dial cemented his reputation as the first pure bebopper on his instrument. Much of the 1950s were missing for Gordon since he spent the time in Los Angeles at a time when the mostly white West Coast jazz movement was in vogue. He also spent some time in prison for narcotics violations. Gordon reemerged in the 1960s recording first for Jazzland and then Blue Note (1961–1965) and Prestige (1969–1973).

A move to Europe, first to Paris, then for a longer time, Copenhagen, kept Gordon under the radar in the United States from the period 1963–1975.

SONNY ROLLINS

Sonny Rollins (1930–) was born in New York and worked around the city with various leaders beginning in 1948. Rollins had signed with Prestige early on and was recorded with most of the Prestige leaders at one time or another, notably Miles Davis. He replaced Harold Land in the Clifford Brown–Max Roach group in 1955 and remained there even after Brown's June 1956 death. His Prestige albums of that period are nothing short of spectacular. There were six of them, each with a different pianist in either a quartet or a quintet setting. The music was rolled out slowly with the final album appearing in 1961.

At the conclusion of his Prestige contract, Rollins freelanced for a while, finding opportunities to record for Blue Note, Contemporary, and Riverside, among others. He was the leader of his own combos by this time, but by the end of 1959, he had gone into a self-imposed retirement. He emerged in 1962 and immediately got back into the fray signing with RCA Victor for a large sum of money. In 1965–1966, he recorded four albums for Impulse, including his compositions used in the hit movie **Alfie**; but by 1968, he was gone again. There would be no Sonny Rollins records between 1966 and 1972. When he began again with former Riverside owner Orrin Keepnews for Milestone Records in 1972, he quickly gained a level of celebrity and recognition that has continued unabated until today.

JOHN COLTRANE

John Coltrane (1926–1967) had been a part of Miles Davis's first working quintet beginning in 1955. Until that time, his career had been that of a journeyman, working without distinction with Dizzy Gillespie, Eddie "Cleanhead" Vinson, and Johnny Hodges. With Davis, he blossomed. Davis had broken up the group in late 1956 and had left for Paris where he worked on a film score. This move opened up new opportunities for John Coltrane.

Coltrane was a prominent sideman on many Prestige sessions during 1956 and 1957. He was available because he was working with Thelonious Monk on a steady, long-term job in New York. When he rejoined Miles Davis in 1958, he was traveling and not as available for sideman gigs. He had agreed to do one album for Blue Note prior to the time he signed with Prestige. The album was *Blue Train*, in time, the biggest seller among all his albums. There were three albums for Prestige done in 1957 under his leadership and nine more recorded during 1958. They were parceled out over time, the last one being issued in 1965.

After a two-and-a-half-year period with Atlantic (which included his first real hit, *My Favorite Things*, and his masterpiece, *Giant Steps*),

Coltrane was signed to the new Impulse label by Creed Taylor. By 1961, his classic quartet with McCoy Tyner, Jimmy Garrison, and Elvin Jones had been established.

The Impulse period produced a number of major accomplishments. Coltrane, throughout his career, was a great ballad player; and two of his most popular Impulse albums (*Ballads* and *John Coltrane–Johnny Hartman*) reflected this. Extended compositions such as *A Love Supreme*, another hit album, demonstrated another facet of his persona. Throughout the 1960s, Coltrane's music became increasingly radicalized.

By 1962, he had a unique arrangement with his record label. He would book time with Rudy Van Gelder, usually at night, record until he was finished, and leave. He would usually record three or four selections. Bob Thiele, his producer, was often not in attendance.

John Coltrane is an example of a musician whose stature, and record sales, grew after his death. While he was alive, he developed a strong following in the jazz community based on his work with Miles Davis and his own recordings. The early Impulse recordings were well received, but by 1965, he was developing a new audience of younger fans of all races while alienating some of the fans who had been in his corner for years. His music was moving further and further away from his 1950s style.

Since his death, every known scrap of music that survived him has been issued one way or another. It seems likely that if he had lived and continued to explore, much of this material would have been viewed as rehearsals or tests of a particular project and not brought to public attention.

After Yusef Lateef and Barry Harris moved from Detroit to New York in 1960, the great migration of Motor City musicians began to slow down. There would be others in years to come but nothing to approach the astonishing influx of talent that began in the mid-1950s.

MILT JACKSON

Milt Jackson (1923–1999) was one of the first, arriving in New York in 1945. He quickly came into Dizzy Gillespie's orbit and was a part of the Dizzy Gillespie Rebop Six that brought bebop to Los Angeles. The vibraharp, and its forerunner the vibraphone, was essentially a novelty instrument until Red Norvo, and especially, Lionel Hampton, brought it to prominence in the mid-1930s.

Jackson had a very different yet equally compelling approach to the instrument, one that was a major beneficiary of high-fidelity recording techniques of the 1950s. If Lionel Hampton was fast and hot, Milt Jackson was relaxed and soulful. He was a master blues player. In 1951, he recorded a quartet date with fellow Gillespie associates John Lewis, Ray Brown, and Kenny Clarke. With Percy Heath replacing Brown, these four men became the Modern Jazz Quartet. This group quickly became one of the most popular groups of the day. Connie Kay replaced Clarke in 1955, and the group maintained its popularity until it broke up in 1974.

Jackson was a recording artist before the creation of the MJQ and continued to be once the group took center stage. Early examples of outstanding work are his collaborations with Lucky Thompson for Savoy and Atlantic (1955–1957). He also pioneered the vibes-flute combination with Frank Wess on the hit Savoy album *Opus De Funk*. Jackson's frequent recording collaborators included Jimmy Heath, Ray Brown, and James Moody.

The MJQ was contracted to Atlantic beginning in 1956, and both Jackson and Lewis made their own albums for the label. Among the Atlantic albums was Jackson's *Plenty, Plenty Soul*, a meeting with likeminded artists Horace Silver and Cannonball Adderley. Quincy Jones arranged two Atlantic albums, and the two men became a mutual admiration society. Upon leaving Atlantic, Jackson spent the next several years recording for Impulse, Riverside, Limelight, and Verve and two highly celebrated albums for CTI. When the MJQ disbanded, Jackson began recording for Norman Granz and had an eleven-year run on Pablo. His final recordings were created for Quest/Warner Brothers in a deal arranged by Quincy Jones. With Jackson's death in 1999, something left jazz that has never been replaced. It was not merely the passing of a legendary and prolific contributor but the instantly recognizable, shimmering *sound* of what he did.

KENNY BURRELL

The road to stardom for Kenny Burrell (1931–) was a bit different from other Motor City jazzmen. He had the experience of working with Dizzy Gillespie and Oscar Peterson before moving to New York. Trim and handsome, Burrell fronted trios and quartets but was quite active in the recording studios where he was in demand for commercial music as well as jazz dates.

He quickly became the favorite guitarist of organists such as Jimmy Smith and Brother Jack McDuff. His tune "All Day Long" was recorded for Prestige by an all-star combo and, in its definitive treatment, by Jimmy Smith on Blue Note. *Blue Bash,* a Verve album he co-led with Jimmy Smith, was a big hit in 1963; and he appeared on McDuff's breakthrough album, *Screamin',* the same year. Away from organ groups, Burrell had strong-selling albums with *Midnight Blue* for Blue Note, also from 1963, and *The Tender Gender* for Cadet in 1966.

Unlike most artists, Burrell recorded for Blue Note and Prestige during the same period. A bit later, he was doing the same thing with Cadet and Verve. For the latter in 1964, he began a series of orchestral albums that further enhanced his star. It really didn't matter whether it was a trio or a quartet, a jam session, a solo guitar, or a large orchestra; Kenny Burrell dispensed consistent quality. And unlike Grant Green and Wes Montgomery who died young and George Benson who has concentrated on his pop side, Kenny Burrell has been prolific as a pure jazz artist. There are more than seventy-five Kenny Burrell albums.

THELONIOUS MONK

Thelonious Monk (1917–1982) while born in North Carolina was raised in New York from an early age. A professional pianist since his teens, he became known to musicians during the early 1940s while serving as the house piano player at Minton's, the fabled jazz club in Harlem. He worked with Coleman Hawkins during 1944 and 1945, making his recording debut with him and joining him for an ill-fated JATP tour on the West Coast. A close associate of Dizzy Gillespie, Monk was involved in the vanguard of harmonic change that was so much a part of bebop. He worked and recorded with Gillespie but in large measure went his own way once he began making his own records for Blue Note in 1947.

The sales of his singles on Blue Note were impossibly small but Alfred Lion stuck with him until 1952. A period with Prestige was followed by a six-year stay with Riverside. It is during this period when he was leading his own quartet in New York that his popularity began to grow. By the time of his last Riverside studio session for Riverside in 1960, Monk had become a regular attraction on the circuit. He appeared at festivals and toured extensively in the United States and internationally as well. The success came as his quartet developed a permanent sound aided by the presence of tenor saxophonist, Charlie Rouse. Over the length of their professional association, Monk and Rouse would develop a kinship similar to what Dave Brubeck and Paul Desmond achieved in the Dave Brubeck quartet.

When Monk signed with Columbia in 1962, he became a star. There are those who thought that he had been one for some time, but there is no question that the publicity and marketing departments at Columbia were helpful in building his career. Monk's credo was to be true to his own music and to let the public catch up to him. In that, he clearly succeeded. In 1964, he was on the cover of *Time* magazine.

CHARLES MINGUS

Like Monk, Charles Mingus (1922–1979) was a composer of immense talent. But like Art Blakey, he was at the mercy of his musicians to create the solo playing needed to make his music come alive. His own bass playing was unique and especially valuable in his own groups. It is hard to imagine that Mingus compositions would function nearly as well with someone else in the bass chair. The major influences on Mingus were Duke Ellington, Charlie Parker, and the black church. The first two revealed themselves almost immediately; the gospel influence emerged during his greatest period.

Mingus began as a professional musician in Los Angeles. By 1945, he began making his own records for a number of tiny independent labels. His experience was enhanced by important associations with the big band of Lionel Hampton and the trio of Red Norvo. After settling in New York in 1951, Mingus freelanced, working with a variety of leaders. In early 1952, he formed Debut Records that produced records by his partner Max Roach, Thad Jones, Lee Konitz, and others. The most noteworthy Debut album was *Jazz at Massey Hall*, the recording of a Canadian concert featuring a reunion of Charlie Parker, Dizzy Gillespie, and Bud Powell with Mingus and Roach.

Mingus took the name Jazz Workshop to describe his groups. His recordings could feature a piano trio or a large ensemble in an attempt at a classical-jazz fusion. He also did some accompaniment for a poetry and jazz session. Dannie Richmond joined Mingus in 1957 and was involved in almost all Mingus projects from this point forward. Trombonist Jimmy Knepper also became part of the cast that year and lent his presence to three albums (*The Clown*, *Tijuana Moods*, and *East Coasting*) that show the Mingus sound evolving.

In 1959, Mingus added the last major piece to his puzzle. Tenor saxophonist Booker Ervin became the major voice of many Mingus compositions over the next several years. Saxophonists John Handy, Roland Kirk, and Eric Dolphy were also key contributors to Mingus projects. The albums that Charles Mingus recorded from 1959 to 1963 form the basis for his greatness. Mingus was friendly with Teo Macero, Nat Hentoff, Bob Thiele, and, especially, Nesuhi Ertegun. These producers provided the setting for Mingus's finest work. But by 1964, Mingus had formed another label, Jazz Workshop, and for the next year recorded various concerts for album release. In 1965, he gave it all up and retired.

Mingus returned to action in 1970, and while he led several solid groups until his death, things were not the same, and the momentum that Mingus had achieved during his greatest period had disappeared. The return resulted in two Columbia LPs, but sales of both albums were disappointing.

QUINCY JONES

Quincy Jones (1933–) had come to New York as a trumpet player and arranger with Lionel Hampton. After settling in the city, he freelanced as an arranger and producer working on blues and R&B projects as well as jazz dates. Quincy Jones quickly became known as the most versatile young man about jazz in the city. He was writing arrangements for James Moody, Dinah Washington, Big Maybelle, and Count Basie while still in his early twenties.

He was the music director for the great Dizzy Gillespie Big Band of 1956 and 1957 that toured the world under the auspices of the US State Department. After studying in Paris with Nadia Boulanger, he organized a big band to appear in a new Harold Arlen/Johnny Mercer musical, **Free and Easy**. The band Jones assembled was an outstanding one. Among the featured players were such major talents as Clark Terry, Benny Bailey, Jimmy Cleveland, Jerome Richardson, Phil Woods, and Budd Johnson.

The idea was to open the show in Paris and move it to London where Sammy Davis Jr. would join the cast and finally to Broadway. Alas, the Paris engagement found the French and Algerians in the midst of a bitter political brouhaha, and that limited the potential audience. This caused the show to close two weeks before the London opening. When it was determined that the show would close and the band would be out of work, the members voted unanimously to stay together and pick up what jobs they could in Europe. After sticking it out for several months, the band gave up the ghost and headed back to America.

The Quincy Jones Orchestra returned in the fall of 1960 and worked sporadically for most of 1961 before disbanding for good. Jones would make splendid big band recordings throughout the 1960s, but he gave up touring. He took an executive position with Mercury Records and produced pop records as well as jazz artists. Along the way, in attempting to keep the band together, Jones had accumulated a considerable amount of debt. He took out a loan with his publishing company as collateral in order to settle that debt. It took him seven years to get his publishing back. Although Jones has never stated as much, it was quite possible that Morris Levy put up the money.

MORRIS LEVY

Levy had long been the "bank" for many jazz musicians. He had known organized crime connections; but Levy had also given Dizzy

Gillespie the money to buy a house, had bailed out Count Basie from some potentially embarrassing gambling problems, and had supported Bud Powell during some of his darkest hours. He was known as a man of his word.

With the closing of Birdland in 1965, Levy paid less attention to jazz. He turned his attention more toward the pop music business. By this time, he had become the bank for independent record men; and along the way, Roulette would acquire Rama, End, Gee, Gone, Roost, Jubilee, and Colpix, among many other labels. He was also a major player in the cutout business: the buying and selling of manufacturers' overstock and deleted titles. In addition, he built a chain of retail record stores, Strawberries.

Moving to California, Quincy Jones concentrated on composing and arranging but not jazz. He soon became the hottest black music man in Hollywood, scoring movies and television shows. If Benny Carter and Henry Mancini, among others, opened the door for Jones, he continued that tradition and helped Benny Golson, J. J. Johnson, and Oliver Nelson break into the field. When he returned to the recording studio in 1969 for A&M, he had a totally different approach to jazz.

MILES DAVIS

The protean figure of Miles Davis stood astride all this activity. At the turn of the 1960s, he was one of the few jazz artists with a major label contract. He had first recorded for Columbia in 1955. As a combo leader, Davis had an unerring ear for hiring the right sidemen. His first quintet, formed in 1955, featured John Coltrane, Red Garland, Paul Chambers, and Philly Joe Jones. Each of these players found immense popularity in the jazz community.

His change to a sextet in 1958 had brought Bill Evans (later Wynton Kelly) in to replace Garland and Jimmy Cobb to replace Jones, and Cannonball Adderley was added to the cast. This was the group that recorded *Kind of Blue*, an exceptional LP and the best-selling jazz album of all time. The rhythm team of Kelly, Chambers, and Cobb stayed with Davis until 1963 and over that time proved to be one of the finest sections in the history of the music. Coltrane introduced his own group in the spring of 1960, and Davis replaced him with Sonny Stitt and then

Hank Mobley. For a brief period, J. J. Johnson was added to the group with Mobley, but this sextet never recorded.

Kelly, Chambers, and Cobb left as a unit in 1963. It was their plan to work as a trio and to join forces with Wes Montgomery for certain engagements. The new Davis rhythm section of Herbie Hancock, Ron Carter, and Tony Williams was in place in the spring of 1963. George Coleman was used on tenor for about eighteen months. He was replaced by Wayne Shorter. This particular edition of the Davis quintet was the darling of white critics; but sales of the group's recordings, beginning with *ESP* from 1965, were disappointing. The last Davis combo recording with significant sales was *Seven Steps to Heaven* from 1963.

Davis meant much more to the black community than just a bandleader or trumpet player. With his matinee idol good looks and an individual and innovative fashion sense, Davis was a hero. When he appeared in a pinstripe suit at a 1961 Los Angeles concert, there was a gasp of astonishment from the audience. Within a week, anything with pinstripes was gone from hip Los Angeles clothing stores.

The company of beautiful women, an Italian sports car, and an attitude that kept much of the white media consistently off guard all contributed to the Davis mystique. Musically, he had managed to stay ahead of the pack. Whether it be the orchestral albums with Gil Evans, the modal innovations introduced on *Kind of Blue,* the ability to find and definitively interpret unlikely melodies ("Bye Bye Blackbird," "On Green Dolphin Street," "Someday My Prince Will Come"), or the ability to keep in touch with the tradition via his use of the blues, Miles Davis was numero uno. To stay on top, if his current quintet wasn't the answer, he would have to find something else.

The advent of the 12" LP at an affordable (less than $5) price had produced a vehicle for change in the musical choices of the black community. As the late '50s–early '60s generation of college students became attracted to jazz, it was not an unusual occurrence for young fans to debate the relative merits of Red Garland or Horace Silver in the same way they might compare James Baldwin and Ralph Ellison. The intellectual interest in the music was almost always focused on what was current and what was coming rather than what had been.

While there would be technical innovations that appeared during the 1960s, notably multitrack recording, the commercial market for products such as eight-track tape or cassette was limited. The former was used almost exclusively in vehicles while the latter had not yet resolved its audio quality issues. With the passing of time, eight-track would disappear while cassette would gain in popularity. The greater appeal of stereo rather than monaural recordings would show a continuing advance across the decade.

When President John F. Kennedy was assassinated in November 1963, Al Grey and Ahmad Jamal were recording for Chess; Grant Green, Freddie Roach, and Andrew Hill were completing albums for Blue Note while Paul Bley had recorded for Savoy, a rarity for 1963. Jimmy Witherspoon and Booker Ervin were in the studio for Prestige; and Cal Tjader, Wynton Kelly, and Oscar Peterson were cutting sessions for Verve. Little Johnny Taylor and the Impressions had hot R&B singles while Ray Charles, Count Basie, and Jimmy Smith were competing with Nancy Wilson and Bobby Bland on the pop charts because there was not a soul LP chart yet.

The sociopolitical scene in America began to reflect radical changes. The administration of Lyndon Johnson knew exactly how to wield power, and its ability to pass landmark legislation meant that many things that had stayed the same for a lengthy period were about to change. New laws affecting education, the environment, health care, and housing came into being very quickly.

The Voting Rights Act of 1964 was followed by the Civil Rights Act of 1965; and there was substantial resistance among whites notably, but not exclusively, in the South. Add to this, an escalating war that was not only being questioned but was also straining the nation's resources, both human and financial. There were full-fledged riots in communities such as Los Angeles, Detroit, and Newark. To some, the United States appeared to be unraveling. The Vietnam War had become increasingly unpopular. Troop strength that had been 23,300 after 1964 had mushroomed to more than 485,000 by the end of 1967. Press reports of atrocities and mismanagement of the war were becoming more frequent. There was widespread resistance to the draft.

There was talk of revolution among college students. Black activists such as Stokely Carmichael, Angela Davis, and H. Rap Brown were calling for Black Power. Pressure groups such as SNCC, CORE, and the Black Panther Party were making the slow but steady approach of the venerable NAACP seem outdated.

Yet the black community produced two outstanding personalities whose activities seemed to dominate the decade. One was a pugilist, the other a pacifist.

MUHAMMAD ALI

Cassius Marcellus Clay Jr. (1942–2016) was born and raised in Louisville, Kentucky. He began to train as a boxer at the age of twelve and by the age of eighteen had won championships in local and national Golden Gloves events as well as a pair of titles from the Amateur Athletic Union. The culmination of his amateur boxing career came at the 1960 Summer Olympic Games in Rome where he won the gold medal in the light-heavyweight division.

After turning professional, Clay began an uninterrupted march toward a heavyweight title fight with the champion Sonny Liston. Despite a 19–0 record, he was a heavy underdog when they met in 1964. Leading up to the fight, Clay began a campaign of publicity that involved mugging for the cameras, directing insults at the champion, and reciting poetry that predicted not only his own victory but also the round his opponent would fall. This sort of thing was expected in the professional wrestling world where exaggeration and burlesque were an accepted part of the game. Some boxing purists were offended. In truth, this behavior had been going on for some time, and Clay had been dubbed "the Louisville Lip." He was also right in his predictions about twice as often as not. Boxing had never seen anyone quite like Cassius Clay.

These and other antics made him hot copy for sportswriters, who expected him to get bloodied by the heavily favored Liston. When a thoroughly trounced Liston failed to answer the bell for the seventh round, Clay was the Heavyweight Champion of the World.

After the fight, Clay proclaimed that he had become a member of the Nation of Islam. He would announce shortly thereafter that he had taken the name Muhammad Ali. This announcement produced a firestorm of reaction.

Whites viewed the Nation as a threat while many blacks, especially devout Christians, condemned the move as well. Ali became a lightning rod of controversy, although it didn't affect his ability in the ring. He defended his championship on nine occasions and was successful each time.

In 1967, Ali was drafted and refused induction into the army. His request for conscientious objector status had been denied. He was soon stripped of his championship and denied a license to fight. In June, a court found him guilty of draft evasion. He remained free on bond as appeals were initiated. If his case was yet to be finalized, his status in the black community had not changed. Muhammad Ali was not only a champion but also a hero, who stood up to the white man.

MARTIN LUTHER KING

Martin Luther King Jr. (1929–1968) achieved his celebrity using methods that were virtually opposite those of Muhammad Ali. Born in Atlanta, he was educated at Morehouse University and Boston University where he received a doctor of philosophy degree in 1955. He had been an ordained minister since 1948.

King began his public advocacy of civil rights with his involvement in the Montgomery, Alabama, bus boycott of 1955. In 1957, he formed the Southern Christian Leadership Conference (SCLC) dedicated to the exposure of racial injustice. King was an advocate of the principle of nonviolence espoused by Mahatma Gandhi. The SCLC organized nonviolent marches and protests in conjunction with black churches throughout the South all in the service of civil rights reform.

In August of 1963, King was one of many speakers at the March on Washington for Jobs and Freedom. The event drew over 200,000 people, and while there were lots of folk music and several other speakers, it is King's "I Had a Dream" speech that is remembered. The event attracted significant television coverage. For the first time, most Americans were able to experience the power of King's eloquent oratory.

There is no question that Martin Luther King Jr.'s speech led directly to the passage of the Civil Rights Act. Not all of these marches and protests resulted in such success. The March 1965 marches on Selma, Alabama, were considered by young black militants to be a failure when King did not confront a mass of troops.

The first one on March 7, widely known as "Bloody Sunday," attempted to dramatize the need for a federal voter registration law. It had resulted in 770 arrests after bitter confrontations. Two days later, King led a second march, one that was not sanctioned because a judge had requested time to deal with a legal challenge to the march. He led his 2,500 marchers up to the troops, said a prayer, and turned back. Both of these events were shown on television and to see what actually was happening affected people in different ways. King may have avoided confrontation with white authority, but he found plenty of it within his own ranks. Soon Stokely Carmichael and his followers were using Black Power in antiwhite rhetoric. Young firebrands found the King methodology lacking.

King's advocacy and these marches can quite properly be linked to passage of the Voting Rights Act of 1965. By 1967, Martin Luther King Jr., perhaps feeling marginalized by the louder, more militant elements of the civil rights movement, sensed the need for a larger stage. He expressed his public opposition to the Vietnam War and began focusing his attention on poverty issues.

Despite the political frenzy of revolution, assassination, and general upheaval, the jazz business was doing quite well. One lurking problem was the mass migration of jazz players to Europe. In the 1960s, players such as Sonny Criss, Kenny Drew, Art Farmer, Dexter Gordon, Johnny Griffin, Carmell Jones, Duke Jordan, Horace Parlan, Rhoda Scott, Sahib Shihab, Hal Singer, Idrees Sulieman, Art Taylor, Mal Waldron, and Ben Webster all immigrated to European countries. If one factored in the premature death of outstanding players such as Clifford Brown, Sonny Clark, John Coltrane, Wardell Gray, Booker Little, Charlie Parker, Leo Parker, Oscar Pettiford, Ike Quebec, and Lester Young and the inactivity of major players such as Gene Ammons, Charles Mingus, and Sonny Rollins, the future could not look very rosy. The soul jazz groups were doing fine, and the modern jazz players were looking at the opening of international markets as opportunities. But what of all those open slots in American nightclubs or record labels? Who was going to fill them, and what kind of music would they be playing?

Grant Green 1961 by Frank Wolff

GRANT GREEN

THE SPOTLITE WAS A BAR and restaurant on Broadway, near Fifty-second Street, across the street from the original Birdland. It is long gone now; but in the late '60s, it was one of a number of midtown Manhattan locations where one could have a meeting with a musician, without being disturbed, in the middle of the day.

It was a sunny January day in 1969, and my reason for being at the Spotlite was to meet Grant Green for lunch. In my last meeting with Bob Weinstock, we had discussed the need for a guitarist who could provide a certain type of rhythmic comp in an organ combo setting and was capable of strong solo playing as well. I had convinced Weinstock to sign Billy Butler for Prestige. Butler was a thoroughly professional veteran of the New York studio scene as well as a former member of Bill Doggett's band. But he was not what we were looking for in this particular situation. Neither was Pat Martino nor Joe Jones, two other guitarists who were Prestige artists at this time. What we needed was a versatile player, capable of blending with other musicians who might not ordinarily play together.

Grant Green had been the answer for Blue Note Records in the early 1960s. From 1961 to 1965, Grant Green appeared on more Blue Note LPs than any other artist. He was used with leaders as diverse as Herbie Hancock and Ike Quebec; but he thrived with the organists Jimmy Smith, Baby Face Willette, Larry Young, and Big John Patton.

He was born in St. Louis on June 6, 1935. He came to prominence in his hometown working with local hero Jimmy Forrest, whose recording of "Night Train" had been such a huge record in the early 1950s. This apprenticeship was about three years old when Forrest recorded, in Chicago, for Delmark and featured Green on guitar. Two albums resulted from that 1959 session, but they were issued sometime after Green's initial splash had been made. The first album to appear on the market featuring his work was *Space Flight* by St. Louis organist Sam Lazar on Argo. He was brought to the attention of Blue Note by Lou Donaldson who recalled,

"I first heard him in East St. Louis at a club where he was working with just bass and drums. The club was run by a guy named Leo Gooden. I persuaded Leo to bring Grant to New York, and we got him together with Alfred Lion."

Donaldson was most important in getting Green established in the Big Apple, serving as coach and financial consultant during his first few months in New York. He was still a sideman and one without any leader credentials away from St. Louis. Their first recorded meeting, *Here 'Tis*, was a solid musical effort. However, Donaldson's next album from 1962 was a big hit, *The Natural Soul*. The album yielded a two-part single in "Funky Mama," and it was the side with Green's guitar solo that got all the airplay. By the end of 1961, it was clear that Green was a major new guitar voice. In addition to *Here 'Tis*, Green had appeared on fifteen Blue Note sessions during 1961!

The following year, he was voted the *Down Beat* magazine New Star award. He spent a year working with Brother Jack McDuff and was still remarkably active in terms of recorded appearances. He formed a trio with Big John Patton—later Larry Young—on organ. But instead of a steady rise to the top, his career seemed to be stuck in neutral. Along the way, he had acquired a heroin habit and began to gain a reputation for unreliability.

Blue Note, like most New York–area jazz labels, had to deal with a number of narcotics addicts during this time. There is no question that many of the best modern jazz players in metropolitan New York had drug problems at one time or another. Blue Note's solution was to have someone sleep at the residence of the key performer, hoping that this would enable the artist to get to the recording studio on time and in condition to perform.

When questioned about Green's habit, both Donaldson and McDuff indicated that it was the single reason they decided not to work with him any longer. Record dates were one thing, but being on the road with a junkie was no fun for a bandleader. And the record dates continued, especially for Blue Note, another eighteen sessions in 1962. Stanley Turrentine, Hank Mobley, Baby Face Willette, Ike Quebec, Dodo Greene, and Horace Parlan were just some of the players who wanted Grant Green on their record dates. And there were lots of his sessions as leader as well. Eighteen more sessions for Blue Note were taped in 1963. He, Patton, and drummer Ben Dixon had become a veritable house rhythm section at the label. Clearly, Alfred Lion was taken with Grant Green.

Things continued at a similar pace into March 1965 when he recorded his last Blue Note album as a leader, *I Want to Hold Your Hand*. There were a few more sidemen dates in 1966, but Johnny Hodges had brought him into the Verve Records orbit, and he cut three albums—the last two unreleased, the tapes apparently lost—under his own name in 1965. By mid-1966, things had ground to a halt. Grant Green the Musician had gone about as far as Grant Green the Junkie would let him go.

Green's condition was reasonably common knowledge among the jazz record cognoscenti at the time. There were rumors that he had done some time and had cleaned up. He had been inactive through most of 1967 and 1968, so perhaps this was just the right moment. I knew only that he seemed to be the one guitarist who could give my organ combo records the proper soul jazz pocket. I had to go through some handlers in order to reach him and was told that he could not be permitted anything with caffeine in it on record dates.

I had never met him nor even seen him perform prior to meeting him at the Spotlite. He was big, probably six foot two, well over two hundred pounds, easygoing, and relaxed. His hands were enormous. Over a sandwich and a couple of beers (Green drank hot tea), we became friends. In the forefront of Green's thinking was a plan to take his basic sound forward through the use of organ and vibes but with an underpinning of funk rhythms a la James Brown. He wanted to use Leo Morris (not yet Idris Muhammad) on drums. Funk was still a new concept in 1969. James Brown was clearly the most important, as well as the most popular, black music artist of the time; and Sly Stone was the hottest new artist on the scene. Funk was at the heart of what each group was about. Funk also had New Orleans roots traceable at least back to Huey Smith and the Clowns' late 1950s work. The New Orleans sound was returning to the popularity charts anew via the Josie label act, the Meters. Another New Orleanian, Mac "Dr. John" Rebennack, would describe funk as music that "leaves a lot of open space."

Green was willing to become a house guitarist on the Prestige organ dates, and we could agree on the number of albums per year and a publishing arrangement for his own albums, but the per-album advance was a major problem. Heavy on Green's mind was the large contract that George Benson had recently signed with A&M. Green wanted $1,500 per LP as an advance, and Bob Weinstock would only go $1,000. The insurmountable problem had arrived.

Looking at this situation with more than forty years' hindsight, it seems such a petty amount of money; but in Weinstock's defense, most new recording projects were losing money for Prestige in 1969. This despite the fact that albums were routinely completed for less than $3,000! What had happened was that all albums were being released only in stereo and that the monaural format that had coexisted with stereo had been eliminated in 1967. The black audience didn't buy many stereo albums. They thought in terms of monaural because 45 rpm singles were still monaural. The English rock groups and the rock critics of the day had convinced a good part of the fringe audience for jazz that jazz was no longer "what was happening." English rock fans bought a lot of stereo albums. There were a number of very good Prestige albums made at this time that didn't sell a thousand copies.

While we couldn't agree on an artist contract for Green at that time, perhaps it could be done in the near future. With no other contract at this time, he was more than happy to play the two sideman sessions that were offered to him. The first of these was with Ohio saxophonist Rusty Bryant.

The album, *Rusty Bryant Returns*, was only a moderate sales success; but significantly, most of that success came from the Detroit area. Radio station WCHD-FM was largely responsible as the key DJs, Martin Douglas and, especially, Ed Love, really got behind the album. Love was a big Grant Green fan, and much of the attention was focused on the guitarist.

(It should be noted that famous instrumentalists frequently will lend their presence to recording projects of acquaintances and friends alike. When this happens, it is understood that the record label will not attempt to exploit the artist contributing to the project any more than any other sideman. It therefore shouldn't come as any great surprise to find the guest stars playing beneath their accustomed level. This never happened with Grant Green. He always gave 100 percent of himself to any session we were both involved in.)

The news that Green was back quickly found its way to Blue Note where the guitarist renewed his relationship with original Blue Note partner, Frank Wolff. His appearance on Reuben Wilson's *Love Bug* album helped generate heavy sales, with Detroit once again leading the way. It wasn't long before Green returned to the Blue Note fold.

His first new album for Blue Note was *Carryin' On*, and it displayed exactly the qualities he outlined for me in our meeting. The contents included a James Brown hit and a Meters composition among the five-tune program. The most popular item on the album proved to be "Cease the Bombing," an original by pianist Neal Creque. Grant Green was back! And this time he wasn't playing what Alfred Lion wanted; he was playing what *he* wanted.

His next two albums, both from 1970, continued the formula. *Green Is Beautiful* was notable for another Creque composition, "The Windjammer," as well as selections by Brown and the Beatles. *Grant Green Alive!* was recorded in a Newark nightclub. It featured drummer Idris Muhammad, saxophonist Claude Bartee, and vibraharpist Willie Bivens, holdovers from earlier albums, and introduced young Ronnie Foster on organ. Both sold well, and by the end of the year, Green had decided to move to Detroit where he continued to surge in popularity.

Blue Note's Frank Wolff died in 1971, and the direction of the label shifted to the parent company (United Artists) staff located in Los Angeles. The chemistry between label employees and recording artists is something seldom discussed. Yet the situation of Grant Green in 1971, while not unique to him, was destined to have some ugly repercussions. Because Green had proved to be one of Blue Note's top-selling artists, his recording budgets were increased, and more care went into the cover art of his albums. The first album issued under the new Blue Note team was *Visions*, and it was a smash hit. The big song was a version of "Does Anybody Really Know What Time It Is." It proved to be the biggest album of Green's career.

Much of what he recorded for the label after this originated in Los Angeles. The sound of Grant Green that had been so carefully captured by Rudy Van Gelder was beginning to disappear in the Los Angeles smog. His last recording for Blue Note—*Live at the Lighthouse*—was done in April 1972. Despite the best-selling stature he had achieved, he was at odds with Blue Note. It was clear that he felt he didn't get all the money that was due him. He waited out his contract and went four years without making a new album.

Despite the fact that I had no direct business relationship with Green, I'd frequently get phone calls from the road—some gig in Cleveland or upstate New York. He would always have suggestions for upcoming recording dates—usually his own inclusion—but Green's price as a sideman had gone up, and it wasn't always possible to afford him.

We did get together for a live recording in Detroit in 1973 under Houston Person's leadership, where he was featured in an all-star quartet with Person, McDuff, and Muhammad. In characteristic fashion, he insisted on playing on some of the Person band tracks as well.

(During this particular engagement, there was much good-natured joking about attire. Person and his band had always worn suit and tie for their performances. Green, on the other hand, in keeping with the very casual bandstand dress codes of the time, might show up in a dashiki one day and a turtleneck the next time. When it came time for the press party prior to the actual recording session, Person appeared in a jacket and turtleneck while Green arrived in a very hip pinstripe suit that looked right out of the pages of *GQ*! Martha Jean Steinberg, the legendary "queen" of WJLB radio, was present that evening. Upon meeting the two men, who were standing together at the time, she praised Green for dressing so well.)

The last time I saw him was in 1976 at a club in Newark. He was playing mostly funk, but at one point in the evening, he stretched out to great effect on John Coltrane's "Impressions." It was shortly before his first album in four years was issued. He had waited out his Blue Note contract and then signed with Creed Taylor's Kudu label. It was Taylor's habit at this time to lay rhythm tracks first and bring in the soloist to overdub his performance. When I asked Green if his album was finished, he howled with laughter and suggested that I would know more about that than he would!

The album that was issued, *The Main Attraction*, was a decided disappointment. Much of Green's playing in the mid-'70s had been long soloing over seemingly endless vamps. In today's market where lengthy performances by "Jam Bands" are routine, this would not be a big deal. Here it seemed taken to an extreme, since the album contained only three tracks, and one was nineteen minutes long! *The Main Attraction* proved to be his only Kudu album. He toured as a part of a CTI all-star unit (working in tandem with Hank Crawford), but it seems unlikely that those concerts were actually recorded.

His final album was issued on the Versatile label in 1978. *Easy* found Green playing melodies once again. The album was well titled since the essence of Grant Green's style was that he made everything sound easy and relaxed even though the inner fire was always there. He never used tricks such as fuzz tone or wah-wah, always preferring his own crystal clear tone. The album showed up on some popularity charts but undoubtedly would have been more successful had Green been able to tour in support of it.

Green had been admitted to Harlem Hospital in New York in the summer of 1978 with a variety of ailments. At first there seemed to be little to worry about, but then as he was about to be released, he was held over for more tests. When he was finally released in December, he was given strict doctor's orders to fully recuperate before attempting to tour. Yet his mortgage was behind, and he had a slew of medical bills to pay, so he returned to the road almost immediately. Two weeks in Ohio were followed by a gig at the Lighthouse in California, and that was followed by a stint in Rochester. In the early morning of January 31, 1979, after returning from the Rochester gig, he suffered a heart attack and died.

His old friend Lou Donaldson had visited Green regularly while he was hospitalized. He spoke to doctors about the diagnosis but could never learn the extent of the problems. There were rumors about a slight stroke and blood clots. At the time of his death, I wrote the obituary for *JazzTimes* and let Lou Donaldson have the final word:

"He was a single-note exponent. His sound was such that you could identify it right away. All the top guitarists who came later—like George Benson and Pat Martino—have some of Grant's stuff."

And the obscurity that frequently follows death in jazz musicians seemed to be the likely fate of Grant Green. Yet in the years since his death, something truly extraordinary has happened.

His old label, Blue Note, underwent a remarkable metamorphosis. Dating from about 1985, the label, which had undergone periodic revivals since its halcyon days in the '50s and '60s, once again become a full-fledged recording entity. The executives led by Bruce Lundvall and Michael Cuscuna knew the Blue Note history and were determined to recapture its place at the top. New stars such as guitarist Stanley Jordan, pianist Michel Petrucciani, and vocalists Cassandra Wilson and Norah Jones were developed while Blue Note veterans such as Stanley Turrentine, Jimmy Smith, and Kenny Burrell returned to produce some of their best work. Yet nothing about the label and what it achieved in its phoenixlike rise to prominence can equal what has happened to the reputation of Grant Green. It started in Japan.

In 1977, King Records became the Japanese licensee for Blue Note. Michael Cuscuna was working for Blue Note assembling albums from unissued sessions—some going back to the 1950s—so that there would be an orderly tape vault at the United Artists headquarters in Los Angeles. He met with Yoiichi Nakao, from King, who had learned of the unreleased Blue Note albums. United Artists had no plan to issue these albums at the time but were not opposed to have them released in Japan. Nakao suggested that Cuscuna recommend candidates for Japanese release and to assign liner notes. Beginning in 1979, shortly after his death, Grant Green albums began to appear in Japan.

The Japanese people have long had a continuing interest in classic Blue Note albums of the past. In 1979, there were four Grant Green albums issued in Japan, two of them (*Gooden's Corner* and *Matador*) for the first time anywhere. King Records was able to create interest in the newly released albums by reminding fans that they were not available anywhere else. The following year, four more, including *Oleo* and *Remembering*, appeared. It continued.

No fewer than nine Grant Green albums from his first period with Blue Note (1961–1965) have been issued since his death. Most of these came to the US market via a domestic Blue Note reissue program while others were available as imports. These have been greeted with worldwide critical acclaim. In addition, his sideman appearances on other Blue Note albums, similarly discovered, have helped to raise his standing in the eyes of younger players everywhere.

At the time of his death, few would have suggested that Grant Green would be anything more than a misty memory for the few who still remembered his talents. Yet Grant Green has become a genuine legend: having fully attained his place alongside George Benson, Kenny Burrell, and Wes Montgomery as one of the great guitarists of the era.

RECOMMENDED RECORDS:

Sunday Morning, 1961 (Blue Note CD); *Grantstand*, with Jack McDuff and Yusef Lateef, 1961 (Blue Note CD); *Am I Blue*, with Joe Henderson and John Patton, 1963 (Blue Note CD); *Visions*, 1971 (Blue Note ICD-J); *Shades of Green*, 1971 (Blue Note LP)

FUNK AND FUSION

"You have reached Sweet Lou, straight-ahead alto saxophonist from the Bronx. No fusion, no confusion."
—Answering machine message on the phone of Lou Donaldson

WITH THE ASSASSINATION OF DR. Martin Luther King Jr., black America exploded. Whole areas of Washington, D.C., Detroit, Newark, and other cities erupted in full-scale riots. Boston, the scene of acrimonious race relations because of the busing of school children, was spared because of the combination of good luck, good politics, and James Brown.

The good luck was the scheduled concert of Brown at Boston Garden on April 5, 1968. The politics involved Mayor Kevin White and black city councilman Thomas Atkins agreeing that rather than cancel the concert, they would convince WGBH, the local public television outlet, to televise the show.

Brown was at a peak of popularity during 1968. His horn section with Waymon Reed, Fred Wesley, Pee Wee Ellis, St. Clair Pinckney and, especially, Maceo Parker was the finest of any soul band in the land. After leaving Brown, Wesley, Ellis, and Parker would contribute some very fine soul jazz of their own to the mix. The opportunity to see the James Brown show on television was a rare occurrence. It kept people off the streets and in their homes to witness a spectacular performance.

During the month that Martin Luther King Jr. was murdered, Kenny Burrell was recording his *Night Song* album for Verve, Stanley Turrentine was cutting *The Look of Love* for Blue Note, while Herbie

Mann, King Curtis, and Yusef Lateef were working on various projects for Atlantic. Otis Redding's "Dock of the Bay," Aretha Franklin's "(Sweet Sweet Baby) Since You've Been Gone," and James Brown's recording of "I Got the Feelin'" were top-selling singles while albums by Aretha Franklin and the posthumously released *Dock of the Bay* album by Redding were at the top of the R&B LP charts.

By the late '60s, more shakeout had occurred among the record labels. Both Blue Note and Pacific Jazz had been sold to Liberty Records of Los Angeles. Before the end of the decade, Liberty would be absorbed by United Artists. Atlantic was sold to Warner Brothers/7 Arts in 1968, while Chess and its jazz label (now called Cadet) would also be sold just prior to the 1969 death of Leonard Chess. Clearly, Prestige, still owned by Bob Weinstock, was becoming more isolated.

A major change in the record business occurred during 1967 when Columbia Records decided that it would no longer manufacture monaural albums. Not only was Columbia the number one label in the country, but its plants, through their Custom Pressing Division, were responsible for manufacturing the albums of many other labels. This decision changed the entire industry, and within a few months, all labels had fallen in line. From 1968 forward, monaural was used only for 45 rpm singles. The rest of the industry was soon entirely stereo, and for jazz, sales fell considerably. Hit albums would sell in hit quantities, but the average jazz album saw sales fall way off. Stereo albums were more expensive, and much of the market didn't yet own stereo equipment. Retailers demanded that the word *stereo* appear on the jacket of every item in their inventory. This led to the appearance on covers of the deadly phrase "electronically rechanneled for stereo," an admission of decidedly inferior audio.

THE CLUB CIRCUIT

The club circuit had been in place for some time. The specific nightclub might change from time to time, but if one went down, there was usually another to pick up the slack. Soul jazz groups who carried their own organ would often travel in a hearse that permitted the organ to be transported in the most convenient fashion. Others might use a panel truck or van to get around. Most of the work was above the

Mason-Dixon Line. Washington, D.C., was considered a "Southern" town with Jim Crow accommodation policies still in force at least until the mid-'60s. It was rare for a group to head into the Deep South with the exception of New Orleans or Atlanta. On the other hand, most of the smaller industrial cities of the Midwest had clubs along the soul jazz highway.

West of St. Louis, there was Kansas City or Omaha on an occasional basis with a better chance at finding a regular stop in Denver. There were clubs in Texas and Oklahoma, but they weren't really jazz clubs. Indeed, the wrong "style" of jazz could be a disaster in some of the nonspecialist locations. Patrons in such clubs expected to be entertained, and the performers had to keep that in mind at all times.

The West Coast offered Seattle and lots of different places in San Francisco, San Diego, and, especially, Los Angeles. An artist such as Richard "Groove" Holmes would work his way across country to Los Angeles arriving in January and return to the East Coast when the weather got warm. The demand for organ combos continued to be strong. When the scene first exploded in the late 1950s, it was possible for a good organ combo to connect with a major booking agency even if it had no record deal! While that was no longer possible, there was still a chance for a good organ combo to build a strong local, even regional, reputation without a record contract.

The singers who worked the circuit were usually accompanied by organ trios but not always. Men such as Jimmy Scott and Arthur Prysock were not very similar in stature or vocal quality, but they had one thing in common: they could deliver a sophisticated love song as well as anyone on the planet. A touch of the blues was always welcome, but in general, blues singers were not. To be too "down home" was to be "country," not a good thing. The female singers such as Etta Jones, Gloria Lynne, Della Reese, Irene Reid, and Dakota Staton were stylists with their own identity and repertoire. Dinah Washington and Nancy Wilson were models for up-and-coming women rather than Sarah Vaughan or Ella Fitzgerald.

If Vaughan and Fitzgerald had attained a larger share of the audience, much the same could be said of Joe Williams or Billy Eckstine. These artists were now simply too big for the small clubs that made up a majority of stops on the road. At one time, they may have worked those spots; but now they had moved up, crossed over, and developed a white following. Their tours would play larger, more expensive clubs and theaters/concert halls rather than smaller clubs in black neighborhoods.

Another artist who had found a way to appeal to a broader audience was pianist Erroll Garner (1921–1977). Garner, originally from Pittsburgh, had come up via the 52nd Street scene in New York before establishing his own trio. Shrewd management gained television exposure for him at a time when it did the most good. Garner made lots of records through the 1950s; but it was his Columbia albums, especially *Concert by the Sea*, that made him a household name. Garner had a huge white following.

Louis Armstrong (1901–1971) is the only other jazz musician to have accomplished this, and he had the benefit of starting a career in the 1920s and becoming a hero to his people in short order. Once again management played a major role in moving him up the ladder. His participation in Hollywood films and his appearances on radio with white stars (notably Bing Crosby) went a long way into moving him into the entertainment mainstream.

Unlike Louis Jordan who had that status but lost it, Armstrong was able to reinvent himself via hit records at different stages of his career. "Mack the Knife," a 1956 pop hit, was followed by a #1 pop single, "Hello, Dolly" (and a #1 pop album of the same name) in 1964. Many years after his death, in 1988, one of his recordings, "What a Wonderful World," became a hit single. There is no precedent artistically or commercially for Louis Armstrong.

BLACK RADIO

Radio was all about change. By the late 1960s, there were established formats across the AM band. The news/talk sound so prevalent today was first coming into existence. Top 40, the most successful music format, while still dominant, was beginning to show signs of age. There were still AM stations that had their own black music mix, and a jazz single could be aired if it had the right groove.

When promoting black music, label people in charge of working records would start things at the R&B station before moving their attention to the Top 40 stations. A black record had to achieve hit status on the black station before it had a chance to get played since white groups dominated Top 40 radio. Yet some black stations were so powerful in their own markets that certain artists and the right song could sell in enormous quantities with virtually no white radio exposure. "Precious, Precious" by Jackie Moore on Atlantic sold over one million copies in 1971 without ever cracking the top 10 on the R&B charts and getting only to #30 on the pop side!

Payola had never really gone away. It had become more sophisticated. While there were still cash payments to individual DJs, more often there were in-kind payments, often with drugs. Payola was endemic in black radio, but in many respects, it was even more blatant at white stations. Program directors or music directors were more often the beneficiaries.

This practice carried over to the FM band. Here you found stations that could accommodate vastly different approaches: there were now progressive rock outlets, free-form stations that could include all manner of musical styles, all-jazz and all-classical formats. The band that was barely in existence in the 1950s had mushroomed in the 1960s and by the end of the 1970s would become dominant in all music formats. FM was where albums were sold.

FRANKIE CROCKER

In 1971, Inner City Broadcasting, a consortium headed by New York politician Percy Sutton bought WLIB AM and FM. These stations were based in Harlem, and each had a black music format: the AM side was a dawn-to-dusk operation with an eclectic mix of gospel and R&B while the FM band was jazz. In 1971, Frankie Crocker was hired as program director, and WLIB-FM became WBLS. Crocker (1937–2000) was a flamboyant personality who had previously worked in the New York market at WWRL, the AM R&B leader, and WMCA, where the other DJs were white. Crocker introduced a new station slogan: the Black Experience in Sound.

The mix meant that prominent jazz artists such as Gene Ammons, the Crusaders, Cannonball Adderley, and Les McCann would be played alongside Stevie Wonder, Isaac Hayes, Aretha Franklin, and Earth, Wind, and Fire. If a jazz artist had the right feel or a soulful groove, he could fit right in. This idea spread like wildfire through the nation's urban radio markets.

Crocker himself set the standard for all the announcers, and in his afternoon drive-time shift, he used Jimmy Smith's "Flamingo" for a between-tunes music bed while his closing theme was King Pleasure's "Moody's Mood for Love." Not all stations used jazz to the extent that Crocker did, but the emergence of jazz-oriented soul groups such as Ohio Players or Kool and the Gang meant that jazz would be heard everywhere to some extent.

Jazz formats such as KBCA in Los Angeles, KJAZ in San Francisco, and similar outlets in Detroit, Philadelphia, Pittsburgh, and Seattle were the engines for increased record sales. And there were late-night jazz shows sprinkled throughout the nation. These could be very powerful stations. One such was clear-channel WHAM in Rochester, New York, which could be heard perfectly in the Chicago loop.

Although the term *soul* had succeeded *rhythm and blues* as the primary descriptive term for popular black music somewhere in the mid-'60s, it wasn't until 1969 that Billboard adopted soul LPs for its album chart designation.

In musical terms, the reference to soul meant the combination of Southern blues and music from the black church to form a new hybrid. The gospel training of popular black singers such as Sam Cooke, Aretha Franklin, and Johnnie Taylor would be successfully used in secular music. Yet "soul" was applied indiscriminately by the music media, often being used to describe anything that wasn't white.

"Rock 'n' roll" had faded as well. The roll went out with the British Invasion of groups such as the Beatles and Rolling Stones. "Rock" was now the popular derivative. In time, the term *fusion* would be associated with the jazz of the mid-'70s onward. Yet the fusing with jazz could come from a number of directions: Latin rhythms, popular dance grooves, the use of electronic instruments, vocalists, strings, whether employed in a conventional fashion or simulated electronically.

Jazz continued in a positive direction with the most exciting new breakthroughs coming from Lou Donaldson, Eddie Harris, and a veteran guitar player from Indianapolis, Wes Montgomery.

LOU DONALDSON

Lou Donaldson (1926–) had spent three years with Argo/Cadet, joining the label when Esmond Edwards moved there after departing Prestige in the fall of 1962. While Donaldson's seven albums for that label continued the direction of his last albums on Blue Note, the chemistry just wasn't there. Even though he was recording with many of the same players, the magic of the *Natural Soul* didn't happen. He returned to Blue Note in 1967 keeping one key sideman from his time with Argo/Cadet, drummer Idris Muhammad.

Muhammad (1939–2014), then Leo Morris, was a product of the New Orleans R&B scene. The emerging funk sound of R&B was a natural groove for Muhammad, and it fit perfectly with Donaldson on *Alligator Bogaloo*, his first new album released by Blue Note and an instant hit. It was followed by five more consecutive hits, a considerable achievement.

Muhammad would play drums on all the hit Donaldson's albums. Yet it took Blue Note almost two years before they began to utilize Muhammad on a regular basis with other artists. For Muhammad's part, it was a confusing situation. He had come to New York determined to play jazz, but what the jazz players wanted was his New Orleans street beat!

As soul jazz added funk rhythms to its bag of tricks, Muhammad and drummer Bernard "Pretty" Purdie (1941–), a pivotal member of the Atlantic Records house rhythm section, became the key timekeepers on the East Coast. Purdie succeeded King Curtis as the leader of the Kingpins, Aretha Franklin's touring band, upon Curtis's 1971 death. He and Muhammad became the house drummers at Prestige from 1969 to 1971. Muhammad and Purdie each recorded two LPs as a leader for the label.

Alligator Bogaloo also featured organist Lonnie Smith and guitarist George Benson. Smith would soon record for Blue Note and demonstrate his considerable ability for years to come. Benson had formed a quartet featuring Smith and baritone saxophonist Ronnie Cuber, after leaving Jack McDuff in 1965. Soon thereafter, the group had recorded for Columbia under the supervision of John Hammond.

Hammond heard great potential in Benson (1943–), not only as a fleet, Charlie Christian–influenced guitarist but also as a vocalist. The music he recorded for Columbia produced two LPs; however, they did not sell enough. Major label sales standards were considerably higher than those of independent labels. Benson sang a few songs on the Columbia albums, but the focus was on his guitar. The focus on singing would come later.

Lonnie Smith (1942–) had made three hit albums with Lou Donaldson before getting his own contract with Blue Note. His albums sold well, especially *Move Your Hand*, which spent sixteen weeks on the soul LP chart. He continued to work and record with Donaldson and has continued to be a top performer on his instrument with numerous recordings for a dozen or more different labels. Today, he wears a turban and is known professionally as Dr. Lonnie Smith.

RAY BRYANT

To demonstrate that one size did not fit all, consider the success of Ray Bryant. Bryant (1931–2011) was a pianist in an organist's town, Philadelphia. After a professional debut with Tiny Grimes and some early trio records made for Epic, he had apprenticed as the house pianist at the Blue Note in Philadelphia. In that capacity, he accompanied, and recorded with, artists as diverse as Miles Davis and Carmen McRae. When he made the move to New York, he worked with drummer Jo Jones in a trio context.

His initial impact came from the tune "Little Susie" in 1960. This brought him to the attention of John Hammond who produced him at Columbia. Right out of the box he delivered "The Madison Time," another Bryant composition, which contained overdubbed dance calls! The single hit #5 on the R&B charts and made it to #30 on the pop chart. The backing here featured Buddy Tate on tenor sax and a beat that had more to do with "The Hucklebuck" than "The Twist." Bryant continued to make jazz trio albums but did not have any other major hits until Esmond Edwards hooked up with him at Cadet.

Cadet was home to Ahmad Jamal and Ramsey Lewis. The label, a Chess subsidiary formerly named Argo, had considerable experience promoting piano trio records. Edwards had produced a solo album for Bryant on Prestige/New Jazz, but what he had in mind in 1966 was something completely different. He used a front line of two trumpets, for ensemble purposes only, in a soulful update on the Tijuana Brass sound! Of the three albums recorded with this sound during 1966, both *Gotta Travel On* and *Slow Freight* were hits. The former hit #5 on the R&B chart while the latter, not quite as popular, demonstrated Bryant's exceptional blues playing.

Another Cadet success story was that of Odell Brown (1938–2011). Brown led a Chicago-based organ group, the Organ-izers, that featured two saxophones. The band struck pay dirt with their second album, *Mellow Yellow*. The album had a ten-week stay on the R&B charts and even cracked the Top 200 pop LPs. A second album, *Odell Brown Plays Otis Redding*, from 1969, was also an R&B chart item. But by this time, Esmond Edwards was gone.

Edwards left Cadet to take Creed Taylor's place at Verve when the latter moved to A&M. Among his first signings was George Benson who had been dropped by Columbia. After two albums, an administrative error occurred: Benson's Verve option was not exercised in time. He became a free agent, and he signed with A&M. At A&M he would work with Taylor. Would Benson be the next Wes Montgomery?

WES MONTGOMERY

Montgomery (1925–1968) was raised in Indianapolis. After a period playing with Lionel Hampton, he had established a huge local following as the leader of an organ trio. In 1959, he was brought to Riverside by Cannonball Adderley. His brothers, electric bassist Monk and pianist/vibraharpist Buddy, were members of the Mastersounds, a Pacific Jazz group.

Montgomery recorded with his organ group about half the time. The remainder of his Riverside dates were cut with top-notch pianists such as Tommy Flanagan, Hank Jones, and Wynton Kelly. He also recorded with Cannonball Adderley, Milt Jackson, and others in straight-ahead jazz albums for that label. When he came to Verve and Creed Taylor in late 1964, he was treated to the same formula that had worked for Jimmy Smith: large orchestral settings enhanced by the richness of Rudy Van Gelder's audio.

Montgomery had a unique sound that utilized octaves, played without a pick. This sound was copied, at one time, by every young jazz guitarist. His Verve association is best recalled by his five smash albums of 1966 and 1967: *Bumpin'*, *Goin' Out of My Head*, *Tequila*, *California Dreaming*, and *The Dynamic Duo* (with Jimmy Smith). More than any other musician of his generation, Wes Montgomery had a sense of melody that could make current pop songs work in a jazz context.

The ability to create a pop singer's environment for a jazz soloist was the genius of Creed Taylor. Arrangers such as Bob James, Oliver Nelson, Claus Ogerman, Lalo Schifrin, and Don Sebesky did some of their finest work on Taylor sessions. Jimmy Smith and Montgomery were Taylor's two biggest stars at Verve, and when he decided to leave Verve in 1967, Montgomery went with him. The three A&M albums recorded during Wes Montgomery's last year were even more celebrated. *A Day in the Life* was a gold album and was on the soul LP charts for an astonishing sixty-three weeks. The following album, *Down Here on the Ground*, reached number 4 on the charts during a thirty-week stay. The posthumously issued *Road Song* was another hit album. The death of Wes Montgomery in June 1968 was a terrible blow to jazz.

Jimmy Smith stayed with Verve and saw his label begin to crumble. By the end of the decade, he and Stan Getz were the only two jazz artists signed to the once-mighty Verve label. Smith's last big hit, *Respect*, hit the charts near the end of 1967. Three Esmond Edwards's productions in 1968 found only modest success. Trying to recapture his mid-1960s magic, he attempted all manner of commercial recording with almost no luck.

RAMSEY LEWIS

For funky pianists, things had been looking up. Ramsey Lewis (1935–) had been recording for Argo/Cadet since 1956. His trio, with bassist Eldee Young and drummer Red Holt, was known initially as the Gentlemen of Swing. It was a polished group: bluesier than Ahmad Jamal yet as melodic as Red Garland. Thematic albums were successful for Lewis with albums such as *The Sound of Spring*, *The Sound of Christmas*, and *Bach to the Blues* among his many releases. In 1965, the group now known as the Ramsey Lewis Trio hit the jackpot with *The In Crowd*, a live recording at the Bohemian Caverns in Washington, D.C. This LP hit not only #1 on the R&B charts but also #2 on the pop charts, a stunning achievement. After one more live album, the trio broke up.

Lewis reformed with new bass and drums in 1966. Young and Holt, with a new pianist, formed Young-Holt Unlimited and had huge hit albums with *Wack Wack* (1967) and *Soulful Strut* (1969). The novelty of Young-Holt Unlimited wore off after a time, but Ramsey Lewis was here to stay. When Lewis moved to Columbia in 1972, he left behind a solid record of consistent sales from 1965 to 1971. A dozen of his Cadet albums were chart items, and several registered strongly on the pop charts. His persona changed at Columbia from that of a funky pianist with a wide repertoire to a fully electrified fusion artist who specialized in hit pop albums. The piano was often relegated to the background. The key album was *Sun Goddess,* a 1975 album that sold over a million copies. Lewis was a Columbia artist into the late 1980s and continued to have strong sales if not the spectacular results of *Sun Goddess*.

While Ramsey Lewis had a lengthy and important stay on Argo/Cadet, his label partner Ahmad Jamal (1930–) had achieved great success even earlier. Like Lewis, Jamal had hits with live performances. Not only was his 1958 Argo LP *But Not for Me/Ahmad Jamal at the Pershing* a huge album, at the time, it was the biggest selling of all Argo LPs. Jamal also had a pair of veteran sidemen in bassist Israel Crosby and drummer Vernell Fournier who contributed greatly to his sound. Later trios were not quite as successful, but Jamal was still making hit records in the mid-1970s.

Jamal was an enormous influence on Miles Davis who in a 1955 interview was quoted to the effect that "all my inspiration comes from Ahmad Jamal." What Davis especially appreciated was the use of "space," the relaxed, uncluttered rhythm section flow on Jamal's recordings. As an idea, it can be traced back to Buddy Johnson who would proclaim his band sound as "walk a little bit and let the rhythm flow through."

Ramsey Lewis wasn't the only artist who made the switch to electronics during this era.

Joe Zawinul (1932–2007) was the pianist in the Cannonball Adderley group and utilized electric piano on his composition "Mercy, Mercy, Mercy," which produced a #2 R&B single and a #1 R&B album hit with the album of the same name. This opened new vistas for the Adderley group and other hit albums such as *Why Am I Treated So Bad*, *Country Preacher*, and *Soul Zodiac* followed during the period 1967–1972. Zawinul went on to form Weather Report with saxophonist Wayne Shorter, and that group became one of the most popular fusion groups of the 1970s.

Gene Harris (1933–2000), leader of the piano trio the Three Sounds, had been on Blue Note from 1958 to 1962. He departed the label in 1962 and, after a three-year stay with Mercury, returned in 1966. After the retirement of Alfred Lion, the production of his albums began to get more elaborate, and he fell in with the current trend toward a more pop-oriented direction. Harris stayed with Blue Note through 1977 and had some strong-selling albums, though, much like Ramsey Lewis, his original trio sound had disappeared. Harris began a more than fifteen-year relationship with Concord Records in the mid-1980s where he made some exceptional albums as leader of an all-star big band, his own quartets or joint appearances with other Concord artists. None of these projects involved electric piano.

All the organists tried to incorporate the electric piano into their sound, but none was successful. The problem was one of identity. Those organists who had established a sound unique unto themselves were lost in the world of electric keyboards where an identity by touch was almost impossible. On electric keyboards, personal anonymity was the desired result. While electric piano became an automatic double for jazz pianists, not all of them dealt with electronics in the same way. Some didn't deal with electric keyboards at all.

Oscar Peterson (1925–2007) had been the pianist who, more than any other player, was acknowledged for his instrumental brilliance as well as his popularity. But at the end of 1965, something happened. His longtime bassist Ray Brown decided to come off the road and settle in the Los Angeles area. This partnership had been in existence for more than fifteen years.

The early years of the Oscar Peterson Trio had included either Barney Kessel or Herb Ellis on guitar, but when Ellis departed in 1958, Peterson switched to drums for his trio sound. The drummer of choice was Ed Thigpen who lasted until 1965, departing a few months prior to Brown. The Oscar Peterson Trios to come would feature fine players such as bassists Sam Jones and Niels-Henning Orsted Pederson and drummers Louis Hayes and Bobby Durham, but the rapport achieved in either of the earlier Peterson trios would be difficult to recapture.

Horace Parlan (1931–) had come to New York from his native Pittsburgh and found instant acceptance with Charles Mingus. His contributions to *Blues & Roots* and *Mingus Ah Um* are considerable. He was able to provide a blues and gospel influence that opened up Mingus to things that had been hinted at if not actually delivered.

Parlan also came into the Blue Note orbit. He had been working at Minton's in Harlem and was signed to Blue Note in 1960 and recorded seven albums in the next three years. He was often heard in the company of Booker Ervin, another Mingus sideman, as a part of the Playhouse Four, the Minton's house band. When things slowed down for Parlan, he settled in Europe. Still active, he has not returned.

Julian "Junior" Mance (1928–), a Chicagoan, had major associations with Gene Ammons, Lester Young, Cannonball Adderley, and Dizzy Gillespie before starting his own trio. While breaking in the group, he worked with Joe Williams and the Lockjaw Davis–Johnny Griffin combo. He has been one of the perennial favorites of New York fans for many years working duos and trios while maintaining a busy teaching schedule. A master blues player, Mance has appeared on countless record dates and and continued to work until his mid-80s.

The compositions of Bobby Timmons (1935–1974) that were hits for Art Blakey ("Moanin") and Cannonball Adderley ("This Here," "Dat Dere") would seem to have been enough to keep him in front of an audience, yet such was not the case. Despite an impressive number of trio recordings for Riverside, Prestige, and Milestone throughout the 1960s, he was unable to sustain a career as a trio leader. Illness hampered him continually in the later stages of his life.

Wynton Kelly (1931–1971) was another great pianist who died too young. He made his first trio records for Blue Note at age nineteen while working as Dinah Washington's accompanist. His reputation as an exceptional rhythm section player grew throughout the 1950s.

During his time with Miles Davis, from 1959 to 1963, he worked with bassist Paul Chambers and drummer Jimmy Cobb in what is generally considered the finest rhythm section of its time. That trio later worked with Wes Montgomery, but Kelly was unable to forge a career as a trio leader. His recordings for Riverside, Vee Jay, Verve, and Milestone are first rate; but they failed to find an audience.

His death at the age of thirty-nine was a tragedy for jazz.

HERBIE HANCOCK

Another pianist who followed Ramsey Lewis to Columbia Records was even more successful with the electronic sound: Herbie Hancock. Hancock (1940–) grew up in Chicago and was a member of Donald Byrd's quintet for three Blue Note albums recorded during 1961. Hancock's own Blue Note debut came in May 1962 with *Takin' Off*, a quintet date that featured Freddie Hubbard and Dexter Gordon. The key track was "Watermelon Man," which became a top 10 R&B hit in the version by Mongo Santamaria. In short order, he became the house pianist at Blue Note, appearing as a sideman on more than thirty-five Blue Note projects in the next five years. His own Blue Note albums followed the Horace Silver pattern: one release per year. These albums produced a number of jazz standards such as "Maiden Voyage," "Dolphin Dance," and "Cantaloupe Island," cementing Hancock's position as one of the finest composers of the era.

Hancock had joined Miles Davis in the spring of 1963 and stayed until he formed his own sextet in 1969 and signed with Warner Brothers Records. While a part of the Davis group, he began to see the potential for the use of electronic keyboards in his own music. After three uneventful years with Warner Brothers, Hancock signed with Columbia. His 1974 album, *Head Hunters*, was on the soul LP charts for forty-six weeks and sold over one million units. His next three albums were also hits and, significantly, crossed over to the pop charts. The hit-making potential that Herbie Hancock had flirted with since his debut had arrived.

He had a number of enormous hit albums, including a 1983 million seller, *Future Shock*, and was a Columbia artist until the late 1980s. He has been involved in film work in addition to his own pop and rock projects, but Herbie Hancock never misses an opportunity to play jazz piano with old friends. His popularity has continued over a long period, and his position as one of the most versatile music makers to emerge from the 1960s is secure.

DONALD BYRD

Hancock's first boss, Donald Byrd, also found a way to stardom above and beyond what he had achieved in the jazz world. Originally from Detroit, Byrd (1932–2013) came to New York in 1955 and quickly established himself as a major trumpet stylist. He freelanced with a number of different leaders and formed a working group, the Jazz Lab Quintet, with saxophonist Gigi Gryce, in 1957. This was followed by another co-led group with baritone saxophonist Pepper Adams that lasted into the 1960s. He began recording on Blue Note sessions in 1956 and recorded with most of the key Blue Note artists before his own first album in December 1958.

For the next five years, Byrd recorded quality hard bop quintet and sextet albums in the Blue Note tradition. In January 1963, he developed a new idea for the use of jazz with his aptly titled album *A New Perspective*, which blended jazz with choral music on original compositions with religious overtones. The album was on the Billboard Top 200 in 1964.

Byrd continued to make radio-friendly jazz albums into 1967. These sold well, especially *Slow Drag*, which appeared on the soul LP charts in 1969. His next album, *Fancy Free*, used flute, electric piano, guitar, and Idris Muhammad on drums. This album also performed well, but more importantly, it suggested a direction to Byrd. *Electric Byrd* continued the approach. In 1972, Byrd came into contact with Larry and Fonce Mizell, each of whom had an extensive background in pop music. Together they began work on an album that would take several months to complete. It would be titled *Black Byrd*. This was unlike anything Byrd had been involved with in the past.

The album was an example of pop-jazz fusion that was widely accepted at radio and panned by the critics. It involved a completely electric rhythm section, including synthesizer, with percussion and vocals and a relatively small amount of jazz. It was also a huge hit, gaining the #2 spot on the soul LP chart in a thirty-six-week stay. The same team was involved in four more LPs in the same vein, all of which were top 10 entries on the charts.

Byrd was an early advocate of jazz education, having earned several advanced degrees, including an LLD. He taught at several universities during the 1970s. In 1973, Byrd took a group of his Howard University students and formed the Blackbyrds. He produced this group on Fantasy Records, and the results were a series of hit albums that spanned the rest of the decade. Donald Byrd found extraordinary success as a pop artist and producer well into the 1980s. He continued to teach and lecture and even returned to straight-ahead jazz in the mid-1980s, when he made some conventional small-group albums for Milestone Records.

LES MCCANN–EDDIE HARRIS

Les McCann left Pacific Jazz for the Mercury-owned Limelight label in late 1964. His pop-gospel piano trio sound was beginning to wear thin. Different approaches were attempted on his Limelight sessions, but nothing seemed to click. In 1968, he was signed to Atlantic where he would work with producer Joel Dorn. Nesuhi Ertegun had brought Dorn, a Philadelphia disc jockey, to the label to help with jazz production.

The Dorn-McCann team connected immediately with a hit album titled *Much Les*. The key track was a ballad "With These Hands," sung by McCann. McCann had sung before with little impact, but now vocals became a more prominent part of his show. A 1969 live recording would dramatically demonstrate how important they had become.

The Montreux Jazz Festival in Switzerland was in its fourth year in 1969. Claude Nobs, the festival director, had become friendly with Nesuhi Ertegun and suggested he bring some Atlantic recording artists to the festival. The festival was equipped with a first-rate recording studio, so the label would have access to the recorded performance. Joel Dorn was brought along to help with the proceedings.

McCann and Eddie Harris were among the artists to appear. At the last minute on June 21, the decision was made for Eddie Harris to join the McCann trio. Trumpet player Benny Bailey was another last-minute addition. The results of that evening produced a landmark LP for the festival and a smash hit for McCann and Harris, *Swiss Movement*. The album powered by McCann's vocal feature, "Compared to What," reached #2 on the soul LP charts and stayed on that chart for more than eight months. A follow-up, *Second Movement*, was a 1971 hit. While McCann never again approached such rarefied standing in the record business, he continued to be a solid seller and is still active today.

Eddie Harris (1934–1996) arrived as a jazz artist about the same time as McCann, but his background was quite different. Raised in Chicago, he learned to play jazz during military service in the late 1950s. He burst on the scene with his first record date and a hit single, "Theme from Exodus," in 1961. Harris continued to record for Vee Jay into 1964, specializing in movie themes. Stylistically he was a bit unusual: his sparsely noted attack was not accompanied by a big tone such as that of fellow Chicagoan Gene Ammons. His was a light, airy sound more akin to that of Stan Getz. Harris signed with Columbia in 1964, but his stay produced three albums that achieved little impact. By 1965, he had arrived at Atlantic.

His first Atlantic album not only continued the theme trend with "Love Theme from the Sandpiper" but also featured an original composition, "Freedom Jazz Dance," that was recorded by Miles Davis and quickly became a jazz standard. His next venture brought forth something new.

The year 1966 was the time the Varitone or electric saxophone was introduced by the Selmer Company. Equipped with its own amplifier, the Varitone permitted all kinds of effects never heard before, notably the ability to play octaves. The process tended to dull the tone of the player, but this was less a problem for Harris than it was for other players. Harris introduced his use sparingly over his next two albums, but by 1967, he had it all together. *The Electrifying Eddie Harris*, propelled by the hit single "Listen Here" was one of the biggest jazz records in Atlantic history. The album was on the soul LP charts for forty-five weeks, peaking at #2. Electric guitars, electric keyboards, and now electric saxophones!

Other prominent artists picked up on the Varitone sound. Lou Donaldson used it because it allowed him to cut through a loud band without straining his embouchure. Sonny Stitt, on the other hand, used it because he had an endorsement deal.

Sonny Stitt (1924–1982) was ubiquitous during the entire era covered by this book. He had come to stardom during the bebop era and was equally proficient on alto or tenor sax (for a brief period in the 1950s, he also featured baritone sax). Stitt was the ultimate freelancer; he worked with all the booking agents and virtually all the record labels on a nonexclusive basis. Beginning in 1961, Stitt began working with organist Don Patterson and drummer Billy James. It was the only organized group that Stitt had been involved with in many years. The relationship lasted, on and off, into the 1970s, producing records on Jazzland, Atlantic, and Delmark but with greater frequency on Prestige where Patterson was also signed. Stitt recorded for other labels in an organ group context, but the working trio produced some of his finest work. If one was interested in hearing bebop played in an organ group context, this was the band that could do it. Stitt's endorsement of Selmer saxophones led to his association with Selmer's Varitone unit. The Roulette album *Stardust* that introduced the Varitone was Stitt's best-selling album of the period.

Eddie Harris continued to experiment with electronics and utilized a number of different units over time. He remained with Atlantic into the late 1970s when he began recording for smaller, mainly European labels and returned to the unamplified saxophone. Sonny Stitt followed a similar path, and his electric saxophone work was a thing of the past by the mid-'70s.

With the arrival of a new decade, the '70s, soul jazz could look back at a roughly twenty-year run. The music had changed considerably in that time. The black swing tradition was less prominent in the mix because little that was new had occurred in that music. Only Basie and Ellington remained of the big jazz bands, so relatively few soloists in the swing style were being developed.

Modern jazz had suffered a few bumps and bruises over the past twenty years as well. Modal playing, which was so much a part of the jazz scene in the '60s, can be found in the work of Larry Young but almost nowhere else among organists. And the avant-garde jazz of Ornette Coleman and Cecil Taylor had virtually no influence on soul jazz. The little clubs in black neighborhoods that had nurtured bebop and embraced the organ groups wanted nothing to do with the music dubbed "the New Thing."

The 1967 death of John Coltrane had created an opportunity for a tenor saxophonist with similar credentials to at least partially fill his shoes. Pharoah Sanders (1940–), who had been a part of Coltrane's last group, was the logical candidate. His 1969–1970 Impulse albums that featured vocalist Leon Thomas were staples of jazz radio and sold well. Stylistically, Sanders was very much like Coltrane, and his saxophone tone showed a spooky similarity to that of the master.

Chico Hamilton (1921–2013) was one bandleader who could claim some connection to the avant-garde in a very positive way. In his first group, the Chico Hamilton Quintet, he introduced guitarist Jim Hall and featured cello and flute along with bass and drums. Later groups featured early work from reedmen Paul Horn, Eric Dolphy, and Charles Lloyd, each of whom went on to contribute as bandleaders in the future. Hamilton kept this instrumentation through 1960 and on his Pacific Jazz and Warner Brothers LPs from this era.

He replaced the cello with trombone in the early 1960s but continued to attract strong young players. Guitarist Gabor Szabo, bassist Albert Stinson, and trombonist George Bohanon joined Lloyd and Hamilton for a group that had popular Impulse LPs with *Passin' Through* and *Man from Two Worlds* in 1963 and 1964, respectively. The key track from the latter was Lloyd's composition "Forest Flower: Sunrise, Sunset." Before Charles Lloyd left Hamilton in 1965, he had recorded two albums of his own for Columbia. Lloyd then signed with Atlantic where he assembled a new quartet featuring pianist Keith Jarrett.

Lloyd's 1966 albums *Dream Weaver*, with its key track "Sombrero Sam," and *Forest Flower*, which contained a live version of the title track, were enormous hits. The song "Forest Flower" became his signature tune. The new group stayed together through the rest of the decade and quickly gained a large white following. During much of the 1970s, Lloyd was involved with pop music and did not return to jazz until the mid-1980s. Jarrett, on his own, became a stalwart of the newly formed ECM label in the '80s, recording several enormously popular solo concerts.

Multitalented artists such as Yusef Lateef (1920–2013) and Rahsaan Roland Kirk (1935–1977) were often confused with the avant-garde because of the variety of the unusual instruments they employed. In fact, each was a deep-rooted swinger with abilities that spanned the entire spectrum of jazz.

Lateef was born William Huddleston and was raised in Detroit where he led one of the best modern jazz groups for several years until he moved to the New York area in 1960. An exceptional blues player on any instrument, Yusef Lateef is that rare jazzman: one who had a genuine personality on oboe. His tenor saxophone work is best heard on his earliest recorded work for Savoy, Prestige, Riverside, and Verve. A two-year stay with Cannonball Adderley brought him to wider attention. His soul jazz ability is on display on Grant Green's *Grantstand* album where he fits quite comfortably into the organ-tenor-guitar-drums combo. More involved in academia over the last twenty years of his career, Lateef's approach changed considerably, and his later playing bore little resemblance to his earlier work.

Kirk, from Columbus, Ohio, was blind from the age of two and attracted attention for the strange instruments (manzello, stritch) that he carried on stage so that he could play three horns at once! Like Lateef, he was a fine blues player who recorded in a variety of contexts. His soul jazz album *Kirk's Works* (Prestige) finds him in the company of Jack McDuff to good effect. Much of his 1960s work for Mercury/Limelight is of major league quality, and like Lateef, he came into his own when signed to Atlantic by Joel Dorn.

Herbie Mann (1930–2003) was another Atlantic jazz artist who had great success. He was brought to the label by Nesuhi Ertegun in 1960. Known as a jazz flute player throughout most of the 1950s, he switched over to a sound that worked for him: a rhythm section including vibes and one or more Latin percussionists. His treatment of "Comin' Home, Baby" led to a huge hit album, *Herbie Mann at the Village Gate*, in 1961. Because of the danceable element in his music, Mann had a wide following with many fans in the black and Latino communities.

He had another smash album in 1968 with *Memphis Underground* and became known as the ultimate synthesist in jazz. He would place himself in the middle of whatever musical genre he chose and find a way to make it work and still retain his own identity. This approach led to the most diverse catalog of any jazz artist of the period. He also managed to keep himself relevant: he was still recording for Atlantic in 1985!

If much of the print media attention devoted to jazz was focused on the bizarre and unusual, what had been happening in R&B was exciting and easily adaptable. Whether it was the increased use of gospel harmony in soul music or the innovative rhythms of funk, the creative torch had been passed from modern jazz to R&B. Soul jazz had always utilized dance rhythms of the moment whether it was the twist or the samba (so popular in bossa nova), but funk was a different game altogether.

The new dances such as the Latin bugaloo, the jerk, the shing-a-ling, and, later, the bump were all coming out of funk. Funk was making anything else seem old hat. Those soul jazz groups who could adapt easily to funk would prosper, while those who could not would begin to fall back.

THE CRUSADERS

One group that burst through during this time was the Crusaders. Originally from Houston, Texas, the group consisted of trombonist Wayne Henderson (1939–2014), tenor saxophonist Wilton Felder (1940–2015), pianist Joe Sample (1939–2014), and drummer Nesbert "Stix" Hooper (1938–). Sample played organ for a brief spell but soon switched to piano when the group made their first Pacific Jazz album, in 1961, as the Jazz Crusaders.

The band developed a large local following in Los Angeles, but sales of their albums were strong across the country. The group would add a number of different bassists to the core unit and for recording purposes began to use guitar when they changed labels first to Chisa and then Blue Thumb. It was here that they dropped jazz from their group name and where they found their biggest success.

The Crusaders proved to be one of the best-selling groups of the 1970s, making the soul jazz to fusion transition without missing a beat. Throughout the decade, they had fourteen hit albums, six of which hit the soul LPs top 10 and three of which (*Southern Comfort*, *Images*, and *Street Life*) sold in excess of 500,000 copies. Each of the members recorded their own projects during their great popularity, and each had hits! This was a rare and most remarkable accomplishment.

New arrivals were mingling with returning veterans. Gene Ammons returned from a seven-year prison sentence in late 1969. Ammons resumed recording for Prestige, and his popularity rebounded to equal, perhaps even surpass, his early 1960s peak. His first four LPs issued in 1970 and 1971 were all best sellers. Ammons maintained an extensive touring schedule, and his presence on the scene seemed to energize everyone. His quartet became one of the hottest groups on the circuit.

After an almost two-year hiatus, Grant Green had rehabilitated himself from a destructive heroin habit. He put together a group that utilized vibes and saxophone with organ and drums. Green resumed recording for Blue Note and started to have hit records. He also became a major attraction on the road.

Rusty Bryant (1929–1991) who was rarely heard outside Ohio began to record in a soul jazz context with considerable success. Bryant had some minor hits on the Dot label in the 1950s, when he fronted a small band featuring pianist Hank Marr. Singer Nancy Wilson got her start with this group.

When Marr (1927–2004) switched to organ in 1960 and got a Federal Records deal, Bryant became part of the Marr group. Guitarists Cal Collins, Wilbert Longmire, and James "Blood" Ulmer worked and recorded with Marr at one time or another. Yet Hank Marr stayed in Columbus and rarely traveled. For many years, he taught in the music department of Ohio State University.

Bryant was working as a single picking up rhythm players when he was signed to Prestige in 1968. He was originally recorded playing electric saxophone—both alto and tenor—in an attempt to ride the coattails of what Eddie Harris and Lou Donaldson had been doing. The electronics were soon put aside, and Bryant created a smash with *Soul Liberation*, a 1971 release that hit the Soul LP chart in Billboard. Without competent representation, Bryant was unable to cash in on this success but continued to play well in the style right up to his death.

Ivan Joseph Jones (1940–), a New Jersey guitarist, had impressed Bryant and Marr when they encountered him in Atlantic City in the mid-1960s. First heard on Prestige with Groove Holmes, he found fame as Boogaloo Joe Jones with a hit album (*Right On, Brother*). Despite the fact that he had no touring group of his own, Joe Jones was on Prestige from 1967 to 1973 and recorded eight LPs. He worked and recorded with the Willis Jackson band throughout the 1970s, but by the end of the decade, he had left the music business.

Tenor saxophonist Houston Person (1934–), who first recorded with Johnny "Hammond" Smith, became a prominent bandleader with a hit Prestige album, *Goodness*, to his credit. Person was hardly an overnight success. It took three years, three producers, and six albums before he had a hit. Bob Weinstock showed great faith in his ability.

He joined forces with singer Etta Jones in 1971, and the duo became a leading attraction on the circuit for more than thirty years. Person who had no manager and did all his own booking was, by the late 1970s, his own record producer as well. Truly the vertically integrated jazz musician! In the late 1970s, Person began a relationship with Joe Fields of Muse (later High Note) that continues to this day. In addition to producing his own albums, Person has produced dozens of artists for Muse/High Note.

Smith, now known professionally as Johnny Hammond, saw his own career take off upon joining Creed Taylor on Kudu Records. His first album, *Breakout*, had a twenty-four-week run on the soul LP chart in 1971; and in the same pattern as other successful artists, his last Prestige album, *What's Goin' On*, issued slightly later, also sold well enough to chart.

Lou Donaldson was riding a peak of popularity, and his band yielded another star discovery with organist Charles Earland. Earland (1941–1999), from Philadelphia, struck gold with his first Prestige album, *Black Talk*. The key track was an eleven-minute version of the pop tune "More Today Than Yesterday" with solos only by Earland and guitarist Melvin Sparks. The album was a soul LP chart item for forty-three weeks. A second album, *Black Drops*, contained Earland's version of "Raindrops Keep Falling on My Head" and was a solid hit as well. A live album, *Living Black*, was a third consecutive smash, and the Mighty Burner (Earland's nickname) had begun a career that would have many ups and downs but continued to his death with quality soul jazz. He had other chart albums for Mercury and Columbia, but much of his best work was done for the Muse label. His powerhouse performances made him continually popular on the nightclub circuit. On a concert program, *nobody* wanted to follow Charles Earland.

Earland was also the last major star of Prestige Records and the last hit-making organist to arrive on the soul jazz scene. With the hits of Gene Ammons, Charles Earland, and others, Prestige became a prime takeover target. Bob Weinstock had seen his distributors shrink from more than twenty to less than half of that. Despite the hits the label was producing, getting paid by those distributors was becoming increasingly difficult. The era of great independent distributers was almost over. There was massive consolidation under way; and the compressing of territories made regional, rather than local, distribution more the norm.

Weinstock negotiated a deal with Fantasy Records of Berkeley California and made arrangements to sell the label for a reported 3.2 million dollars. All of a sudden, the AFM threatened to kill the deal until an audit was done regarding back pension and welfare payments. Rather than call a lawyer to handle the dispute, Weinstock called his old friend and former partner Morris Levy. The problem promptly disappeared, and the sale was completed in May 1971.

More and more players were utilizing electronic keyboards. The electric piano which Ray Charles introduced on "What'd I Say" had gained great popularity in the Cannonball Adderley group of the mid-1960s. "Mercy, Mercy, Mercy" was a hit single in 1967 and launched a new wave of popularity for the Adderley quintet. Miles Davis, always an influence on modern jazz, began using electronic keyboards in his group and was experimenting with rock rhythms. *Bitches Brew*, his double Columbia album from 1970, was a big hit. It put him in touch with a whole new audience, and he never returned to his acoustic jazz roots. Electronic keyboards would play a major role in new groups such as Weather Report co-led by Joe Zawinul, a veteran of both the Adderley and Davis groups, and Wayne Shorter who had also been a member of the Miles Davis group.

CTI RECORDS

CTI left A&M distribution in 1970. Creed Taylor would now have his own label, and it would be independently distributed. He added a second label, Kudu, in 1971; and almost immediately they made a formidable tandem. He had contracted veteran jazz stars such as Stanley Turrentine, Hank Crawford, and Freddie Hubbard, among many others, and continued his vision begun at Verve and fine-tuned at A&M. These players who had been known and admired in the jazz community now became stars throughout the black community. Their album sales on CTI routinely doubled or tripled what they had sold for other labels.

Examples of how the public reacted to new CTI product are exemplified by the early releases of Freddie Hubbard and Stanley Turrentine. Hubbard (1938–2008) was from Indianapolis and had been a graduate of Art Blakey's Jazz Messengers. He was generally acknowledged as one of the finest trumpet players of the 1960s and had recorded seventeen albums for Blue Note, Impulse, and Atlantic with only one minor hit. The band for *Red Clay*, his first CTI album, featured Joe Henderson and Herbie Hancock in a quintet that produced more of a blowing session than anything else. Yet the album had a seven-week run on the Billboard soul LP chart, the first of his five consecutive hits on CTI.

Turrentine (1934–2000), from Pittsburgh, had played with a variety of groups (Lowell Fulson, Earl Bostic, and Max Roach) before launching his own career as a leader. Like Hubbard, he had been making albums since 1960, although his were mostly for Blue Note. On that label, he had made splendid music and his notable work as a sideman with Jimmy Smith or Kenny Burrell that contributed to hit albums. His own efforts tended to be well known among the hard-core fans, but apart from some modest success with two albums, he was unable to gain acceptance outside the jazz community. His first CTI album, *Sugar*, changed everything. It was a soul LP chart item for seventeen weeks and because of a provocative cover photo (by Pete Turner) was one of the most-talked-about albums of the year regardless of genre.

For Turrentine, the long career of first-class music was now paying off. For the rest of the decade, he would be one of the two or three most popular saxophonists. Lasting success was right around the corner.

Taylor was also developing new stars such as Grover Washington Jr., Bob James, and Deodato. Taylor had his finger on the pulse of the jazz audience in the early '70s. But beyond that, CTI and Kudu generated an enormous following in the black community. When CTI advertised, it tended not to be in jazz magazines. They chose *Essence,* a magazine with a large readership among upscale black women.

The record business does not operate in a vacuum, and the entire industry watched with wide-eyed disbelief as hit after hit poured out of the CTI/Kudu organization. When Esmond Edwards, back at Cadet again, used Bob James to arrange a Jimmy Ponder album and Fantasy used a photo by Pete Turner (who had been doing CTI/Kudu cover photography) for a Bola Sete album, the CTI people became aware that the rest of the industry was trying to capture some of their magic. In 1973, CTI signed an exclusive contract with Rudy Van Gelder for his engineering services. All of a sudden, those organists still concentrating on the instrument had lost the services of the man who gave them their sound! Although Lonnie Smith had done a one-shot for the label, the only organist on Kudu was Johnny Hammond, who was by this time moving toward an emphasis on electric piano.

The great CTI/Kudu era began to fade with a decision made in late 1973. The label that had its biggest hit with *Prelude* by Deodato had decided to open some wholly owned branch distribution offices. This was a catastrophic decision since the label had few other hits approaching the magnitude of *Prelude.* Grover Washington Jr. had broken through to be a consistent chart topper. He would have two top 10 pop albums, *Mr. Magic* and *Feels So Good,* during 1975. Even artists such as bassist Ron Carter, drummer Idris Muhammad, and flutist Hubert Laws had chart albums! But it wasn't enough.

Strong-selling jazz albums were one thing, but those sales and the relatively small release schedule of CTI/Kudu did not approach the dollar volume needed to sustain branch distribution. Artists began to leave the label: Freddie Hubbard was the first and was followed by Stanley Turrentine and Johnny Hammond. CTI had brought these men from fame in the jazz community to stardom in the black community. When their contracts came up, there was vigorous competition, and CTI was unable to keep the artists. In 1974, Motown took over distribution of CTI/Kudu. This was an alliance fraught with problems from the beginning and was in no way a success. When the agreement ended, the CTI/Kudu era was near the end. George Benson left for Warner Brothers at the end of 1975, and lawsuits began. The courts would take years to render a judgment, but in the meantime, Benson would have a new career as a million-selling vocalist.

Freddie Hubbard who had five consecutive hits for CTI went to Columbia where he had three more hits into 1976. Stanley Turrentine had greater success after signing with Fantasy and still had hit LPs as late as 1980. Johnny Hammond signed with Milestone and had no more hits. The engineers were catching up as well. Joe Jorgenson and Larry Rosen had thoroughly absorbed the audio style of Rudy Van Gelder.

In 1976, Van Gelder returned to being an independent studio, and Rudy Van Gelder remained the favorite recording engineer of many jazz musicians until his death.

CTI ultimately sank under the weight of its own financial and legal problems and was a nonfactor by the late '70s. The company had been raided and imitated by other labels who managed to sign up the artists, expecting to continue their CTI success. In the majority of cases, the chemistry could not be maintained. Most of the great CTI/Kudu sessions were done by 1975. Those that came later were conducted by arrangers who did not have the stylistic panache of a Don Sebesky or Bob James.

Still, the achievements of Creed Taylor stand up very nicely more than forty years later. The settings he provided in audio, packaging, and context were much better than many of the CTI artists would experience again. And for those artists, such as George Benson, Bob James, Stanley Turrentine, and Grover Washington Jr. who would thrive in the coming years, lessons learned during their association with Taylor would serve them well throughout their careers. These lessons were learned by producers as well. Tommy LiPuma, the next great jazz producer, owed much of his success to the Creed Taylor approach.

CTI/Kudu had been the last great outpost of soul jazz. Fusion seemed to be a better way of describing the methodology utilized by Creed Taylor by the mid-1970s, and indeed, he is identified with that term today.

By the time 1973 rolled around, the players had changed once again. After Prestige was sold to Fantasy, the new ownership continued the soul jazz tradition for a while. They even managed to break a new soul jazz group from Indianapolis, Funk Inc., led by organist Bobby Watley. But by 1975, all the Prestige soul jazz artists, including Charles Earland and Funk Inc., were gone!

In 1971, Frank Wolff, the remaining original Blue Note partner, died. At that point, Blue Note began a slow period of unwinding. The handwriting had been on the wall for some time. After Liberty had been sold to United Artists, the combined jazz roster (which also included Pacific Jazz and the United Artists–owned Solid State) was loaded with organists. Groove Holmes, Jimmy McGriff, Jack McDuff, Reuben Wilson, and Lonnie Smith were only some of the Hammond specialists recording for the combined labels! After Wolff's death, much of the artist roster scattered. The Blue Note operations were soon centered in Los Angeles under the stewardship of Dr. George Butler. Butler was much more at home with the current fusion productions, and with few exceptions, most new projects were pointed in that direction.

As the early '70s advanced to mid-'70s, there were numerous signs that the end was near for soul jazz. The only new labels to sign jazz organists were Groove Merchant, which signed Jimmy McGriff, Groove Holmes, Lonnie Smith, and Reuben Wilson, and Mainstream, which signed Charles Kynard and Gloria Coleman. Each of these labels was fronted by a veteran producer: Sonny Lester at Groove Merchant, Bob Shad at Mainstream. They were unable to sustain activity for very long. By the middle of the decade, each was out of business.

Muse was a label formed by Joe Fields in the mid-'70s. Fields had extensive sales and promotion experience with Columbia, Verve, Prestige, and Buddah. At Muse, he found room for many soul jazz artists among the veteran roster he built. Muse was able to continue operations well into the 1990s before selling out and regrouping as High Note/Savant.

If the history of soul jazz must be told in the music of its biggest stars and most successful performers, it doesn't mean that there were not dozens of others who contributed quality music to the scene. A list of organists fitting that description would surely include the following: Paul Bryant, Henry Cain, Doug Carn, Gloria Coleman, Bobby Forrester, Ronnie Foster, Caesar Frazier, Jennell Hawkins, Jackie Ivory, Charles Kynard, Billy Larkin, Sam Lazar, Perry Lee, Gene Ludwig, Don Patterson, Sonny Phillips, Trudy Pitts, Mel Rhyne, Freddie Roach, Rhoda Scott, Leon Spencer, Chester Thompson, Bobby Watley, Baby Face Willette, Reuben Wilson, and Larry Young. This list, in no way complete, presents players who were recorded as leaders during the soul jazz era and would be very much a part of the scene without having the commercial breakthrough that warrants greater discussion.

The list does not include organists such as Dave "Baby" Cortez, Earl Grant, Billy Preston, or Booker T. who were part of the era but not part of the music. A similar list of guitarists and saxophonists would not be difficult to construct.

All labels were affected by the Arab oil boycott of 1973 that produced shortages in vinyl and forced production stoppage on some jazz albums. The pressing quality of new records from that year was probably the worst of all time. The problem cleared up fairly quickly, but for some, opportunities were lost.

At this stage, overseas labels began to emerge just as quickly as the American labels folded up shop. Among the prominent new arrivals were Steeplechase (Denmark), ECM (Germany), Timeless and Criss Cross (both Holland), as well as Trio, Progressive, and Atlas (all Japan). The only new label with an interest in soul jazz, albeit the older, original concept, was Black and Blue from France.

Organists such as Milt Buckner, Wild Bill Davis, and Bill Doggett found a home there, as did Texas saxophonists Illinois Jacquet, Arnett Cobb, and Buddy Tate. The label was founded by Jean-Marie Monestier and operated by Monestier and Jean-Pierre Tahmazian in a relationship that had several things in common with that of Alfred Lion and Frank Wolff. Black and Blue had an approach both in the choice of artists and the sort of music performed that reflected the views of pioneering French writer Hugues Panassie. The emphasis was on bluesy swing and ballads.

From the beginning, there was an almost equal emphasis on blues; and in the later years of Black and Blue, there were subsidiary labels, Isabel and Blue Phoenix, devoted solely to blues, most often Chicago style. Black and Blue was active from 1968 to 1992, although the last years were devoted to French musicians and touring American bluesmen.

Duke Ellington died in 1974. He had struggled with illness in his last years but managed to keep a regular schedule of touring and recording until the end, although the quality of the band had faded somewhat following the 1970 death of Johnny Hodges. The Duke Ellington Orchestra continued for a time under the direction of Ellington's son, Mercer. But with the death of Ellington, the torch was passed to Count Basie as the last of the great black bandleaders.

Basie's band had been integrated for some time. But the modus operandi had not changed, and newcomers to the band were quickly made aware of Basie traditions. A recording contract with Norman Granz's new Pablo label helped to sustain Basie through the last years, but Granz paid less attention to the Basie band and more attention to Basie, the pianist. The era of great black bands would continue until Basie's 1983 death. But with the death of Duke Ellington, there would be less of a need to keep an arrangement of "Take the A Train," the Ellington theme, in the Basie book. Ellington had kept an arrangement of the Basie theme, "One O'clock Jump," in his library for the same reason. It could be played in answer to a request by an important white person who didn't know the difference between Duke Ellington and Count Basie.

In 1970, the US Supreme Court, in a unanimous decision, reversed a lower court's ruling in the case of *Clay v. United States*. Many people were surprised at the decision. The idea that a black man could receive justice in the United States was a new concept. Within a short time, the draft would be abolished, and the country moved to an all-volunteer military.

Muhammad Ali was free to resume his boxing career and in doing so ushered in another golden era for the fight game. Ali's three bouts with Joe Frazier were among the greatest contests of all time. Ali regained the Heavyweight Championship when he defeated George Foreman in 1974. He remained a hero in the black community, and although he stayed too long in the ring, over time he became a hero to all America. Indeed, white America's embrace of Muhammad Ali that seemed impossible in the mid-1960s was considered routine before the end of the century.

With the fall of Saigon in April 1975, the Vietnam War came to an inglorious end. During this time, Barry White, Al Green, and Kool and the Gang had hot soul singles while Grover Washington Jr. and Ramsey Lewis were battling the Temptations and Harold Melvin and the Blue Notes for soul LP chart supremacy. The fusion era was well under way.

So the end of the soul jazz era came not with a whimper or a bang. It was more like the wheeze of a synthesized string ensemble. Was the end of this era a casualty of integration? Perhaps, but by 1975, the soul era of R&B was also over. Everything was now disco! The small clubs in black neighborhoods were disappearing under the twin assaults of escalating costs (fueled by the Arab oil boycott) and the rise of drugs/crime.

The circuit of clubs that sustained the musicians had disappeared, and many of the key players had deserted what was clearly a sinking ship. Jimmy Smith came off the road, settled in California, and ran his own restaurant/nightclub for several years. Club owners would find that a disco DJ could bring in more patrons than jazz. Disco would be over as a fad by 1979, but the jazz club scene never recovered.

At the same time, a rising tide of drug use and crime in black neighborhoods meant that the jazz club that whites might visit a few years ago was now out of the question. In the late 1970s, the illicit drug business introduced a new product: crack cocaine. It was their most successful by a wide margin. The destruction of entire neighborhoods, the ruination of countless lives, and the spectacular rise in drug-related violent crimes all served as testimonies to its addictive power.

The traveling bandleaders such as Lou Donaldson and Houston Person gave up organ and switched to a piano rhythm section. They had managed to acquire a white following in addition to their core audience. It was the mid-1980s before a new generation of organists, headed by Joey DeFrancesco, Ron Levy, and Lucky Peterson began to appear. These players and others have made fine recordings, but it wasn't the same thing.

Occasional albums appeared that brought back the best feeling of the era; and some communities such as Newark, New Jersey, have openly embraced their connection to the music, although it often seems more like nostalgia than anything else.

Black music departments at the major labels would develop their own stars in new groups such as Weather Report and Stuff, a group made up of studio veterans led by bassist Gordon Edwards and including guitarists Eric Gale and Cornell Dupree. Newly developed stars such as Roy Ayers, Lonnie Liston Smith, and Ronnie Laws came forth with hit albums. Pianists such as Keith Jarrett, Chick Corea, and McCoy Tyner, each of whom was active in the 1960s, would find success in the 1970s with music that was a considerable distance away from what first brought them to attention. Old standbys such as Donald Byrd and George Benson would find places for themselves in the new order of things.

Benson's singing career took off like a shot behind the success of *Breezin'*, a 1976 Warner Brothers album, produced by Tommy LiPuma, which achieved that rarest of accomplishments: #1 hit on *both* pop and soul charts! The key song, "This Masquerade," was a #3 Hot Soul Singles Chart item that cracked the pop top 10. His stardom has continued, and he was still recording hit albums at the dawn of the twenty-first century.

The arrival of international talent began to appear with increasing frequency. Internationally owned labels specializing in jazz continued to thrive, but none of the music related to soul jazz. GRP, a new US label, was a partnership of musician Dave Grusin and engineer/businessman Larry Rosen. GRP would follow the CTI fusion model with first-rate packaging and audio. The label's music would prove to be air-playable while retaining some connection to jazz. The concept of fusion would in time morph into smooth jazz, a hugely successful radio format. Grover Washington Jr., who came out of the soul jazz scene would be a dominant star in this new setting while Stanley Turrentine, whose records would be best sellers, was another who continued to thrive. In time, smooth jazz would develop its own set of stars.

THE 1980s

The advent of MTV and the arrival of a new delivery system, the compact disc, would be the big news of the 1980s. MTV was not immediately accepted, but in short order, it would become the primary promotional vehicle for pop and R&B stars. All major labels would budget for video when undertaking an album project. How you looked became at least as important as how you sounded in this world that did not include jazz of any style. The manufacturing process of pop music was complete to the extent that the music heard on big hit albums often could not be reproduced for live performance. Indeed, karaoke machines now replaced live music in many nightspots.

In time, the major record labels cut their ties to jazz except for the biggest and most successful artists. The smaller jazz-oriented record labels would continue to do their thing, but since most of them were undercapitalized, they were always in danger of closing the doors. The major problem in the decline of CD sales is not the quality of the product but the disappearance of retail record store chains.

The constant price rises by the big labels and the profit margin squeeze on the large chain retailers, such as Tower Records, made their once-mighty presence untenable. There may well be stores to buy jazz CDs in most cities, but many of them also deal in used CDs or other non-music-related products. While Internet locations have taken up some of the slack, there are simply not enough places to buy the music. Today, the vast majority of jazz releases are self-produced projects by musicians who sell most of their albums at their own performances. This is true regardless of the jazz style performed. Downloading and Internet sales can provide some additional revenue, but rarely do those sales amount to enough to sustain a project by themselves.

The organ groups, during their heyday, provided a place to learn one's craft while making a living, an opportunity that no longer exists. In the twenty-first century, a full-time jazz musician has become increasingly rare. The number of traveling bandleaders has shrunk to almost nothing. In the 1970s, most clubs would play groups for an entire week where the rule today is one night. For many artists, touring, apart from the still-vibrant European scene, boils down to working some domestic festivals in the summer months. Teaching is the most popular form of supplemental income, and many musicians give private lessons. Yet the real plum in teaching comes from an appointment to a university jazz program. Jazz is now a college class: something that must be taught. There are dozens of university jazz programs.

Soul jazz repertoire has taken a strange turn. The big hits of Jimmy Smith, Cannonball Adderley, or Art Blakey are often heard in blues bands. They use the instrumentals as warm-ups prior to the introduction of the star performer. Acid jazz, a new term for soul jazz, originated in the dance clubs of London, Paris, and Tokyo in the early 1990s. The original beats invented by an Idris Muhammad or Bernard Purdie were sampled and integrated into new performances. International touring opportunities for soul jazz stars were generated from this revival. Reversing the turn of events in the United States, Lou Donaldson teamed up with Dr. Lonnie Smith for appearances beginning in the mid-1990s that found him bringing his unique brand of happy, old-school soul jazz to white audiences.

NEW ORLEANS

When it comes to the future for jazz, it may be best to consider the city of its birth: New Orleans. While there is a considerable local audience for rap and bounce, seemingly everyone in the Crescent City is familiar with the local music of the past: New Orleans jazz and New Orleans R&B. What is rarely mentioned is that funk has been the jazz-related music most frequently performed by groups for many years. There are young bands playing music in the tradition throughout the city. Often those traditions are mixed up into a hybrid, retaining the best qualities of each idiom. The influence of other indigenous music such as Cajun and zydeco can change up the spice in that musical gumbo. And everyone dances in New Orleans.

In many respects, the most interesting development of the late twentieth century is the revival of the New Orleans brass band tradition. In the mid–twentieth century, such fabled names as the Olympia, the Onward, and the Tuxedo were brass bands that served the needs of the black community from cradle to the grave and had been doing that for many years. The arrival of the Dirty Dozen Brass Band on record in 1984 served to reenergize the entire New Orleans scene.

The Dirty Dozen was the first new brass band to emerge in more than twenty years. The new brass bands also perform for a variety of social functions and can be heard marching and playing in areas throughout the city. Originally eight pieces with a tuba, snare drum, and bass drum, the Dirty Dozen has become more conventional with guitar and a single drummer joining the brass bass. They have also inspired a whole host of new bands such as the Rebirth, the Hot 8, and the Soul Rebels. While not reaching national prominence, key songs by such groups are well known throughout the area. And while there is not an overwhelming national acceptance of these bands, there is a considerable demand for their services in Europe and Japan.

If it is not possible to revive soul jazz in its original form it may still be possible to find room for music that shares a similar feeling. New Orleans music has its own magical cache throughout the world, and if one had to nominate an area that would produce a new musical movement capable of finding its own place in the world of jazz, it would be here.

Grover Washington Jr. 1992 by Joe Rosen

GROVER WASHINGTON JR.

THE KEY CLUB IN NEWARK, New Jersey, had a strange policy for its weeklong musical engagements. A band would open on Monday night and be off the following evening. They would then resume on Wednesday and work through Sunday. While unusual, it was not the sort of problem that a band could not, routinely, deal with. Yet the problem faced by Charles Earland in mid-September 1970 was a unique and vexing one: the tenor sax player he had opened with on Monday had disappeared by Wednesday, and he had a recording session scheduled to be taped live in the club on Thursday night! His solution was to bring in a young saxophonist who had been living in Philadelphia and supplementing his earnings as a musician by working during the day for a local record wholesaler.

There was little time to get things together but the replacement turned out to be a big improvement; and the subsequent album, *Living Black* (Prestige), was not only a hit but also an introduction to the work of Grover Washington Jr. In short order, Washington Jr. became the "house" tenor player for Prestige and made sideman appearances on that label with Boogaloo Joe Jones, Melvin Sparks, Leon Spencer, and, most importantly, Johnny "Hammond" Smith. The importance of Smith's session was not the music played or how successful the album proved to be (*What's Going On* was a modest hit for him) but the fact that it was the final album under Smith's Prestige contract. When he next recorded (for Creed Taylor's Kudu label), he remembered Grover and had him included on the session. Grover also supplied the arrangement for "It's Too Late."

The album *Break Out* was exactly that; it would be the biggest-selling album of the artist's lengthy career. And "It's Too Late" would be the key track from the album. Now known as Johnny Hammond, he would record another hit for Kudu the following year, but by that time, Grover Washington Jr. would no longer be an obscure sideman.

He played on Lonnie Smith's Kudu album and was booked to appear on a Hank Crawford session when word came back from Memphis that Crawford had been jailed because of a large number of unpaid parking tickets. Creed Taylor was loath to cancel a date when careful arrangements had been prepared and musicians had already been hired; so he, in effect, gave the session to Washington Jr. Despite the fact that he had never recorded on the instrument, Grover played alto sax throughout the session. The resulting album, titled *Inner City Blues,* was a huge hit; and his career was off and running. Clearly, Grover Washington Jr. was not slow to get the maximum mileage out of each break that came his way.

Washington Jr. would become *the* new jazz success story of the 1970s. There was competition, to be sure, from George Benson, Herbie Hancock, Stanley Turrentine, and Chuck Mangione; but each of those performers had been a part of the jazz scene for a decade or more before achieving a major breakthrough. Grover Washington Jr. went from zero to sixty very quickly! And he stayed there, building more of an audience with each new appearance and each new recording. He had another eight hits before the end of the decade, including two #1 items on the soul albums chart, *Mister Magic* and *Feels So Good*. Each of those albums made the top 10 on the pop charts. He was now a star.

In 1979, preparing a piece for *JazzTimes*, I drove to Philadelphia to visit Grover whom I had first heard at the Key Club as the producer of Charles Earland's *Living Black* album. During the trip, I reflected a bit on those days in the early '70s when Grover Washington Jr. was an unknown.

The Prestige sessions that Washington Jr. played on were very loose. During breaks, there would sometimes be football games in the studio parking lot; but Grover never participated, preferring to use the time to practice. As a musician, he was a quick study. He functioned ideally in a two-man section and was equally valuable when he was the only horn. He was a genial gentleman who fit nicely with whomever he was playing with, in any context. The musicians enjoyed his company, and he was accepted as one of the guys. There were no airs or attitude from him. Would success spoil Grover Washington Jr.?

When I arrived at the large stately residence in an especially attractive area of Philadelphia, I was greeted by the subject in somewhat battered condition: his right hand was in a cast, and he had a sprained ankle. Still, he was about to begin a tour in a few weeks, so he was practicing. He introduced George Howard who was to be a part of what he hoped would be a new band featuring himself and Howard in a two-reed front line. (That group never got off the ground, but Howard went on to have several hit albums as one of the fusion stars of the '80s.)

We began by discussing the variety of settings he had performed in: blowing sessions, layered situations with multiple overdubs, live recordings, and a self-contained group with all the writing coming from within the band.

"Most of my sideman sessions were done at Rudy Van Gelder's studio. The earliest ones were kind of simple. We'd get a phone call saying to come on in. We weren't told anything about the tunes, but we just went for what felt good without getting too busy. After watching Rudy and Creed Taylor work, I began to get interested in the other side of the glass—what went on in the control room. I gradually built up a modest knowledge of electronics as I moved through these various situations so that I knew what people were talking about when they mentioned mixes, boards, cross-fades, and that sort of thing. One situation seems to lead to another, because as you change—when you learn who you are and where you are going—you acquire certain knowledge. It never hurts an artist to have the broadest possible overview on things. It always seems to help. I learned an awful lot by observing Creed and Bob James on my studio sessions.

"The only session I did where everyone was together in the studio was my second album, *All the King's Horses*. Creed Taylor's operation was extremely well organized. Perhaps a month before the recording session I might begin to confer with Bob James, the arranger. I'd suggest things, and Creed would suggest things. I might rehearse with Bob once or twice before a date, getting keys straight, and then we'd go in with rhythm section only. The sessions could vary in length in that sometimes things would go smoothly and we would need only one or two takes on a tune, whereas other times, it might take three or four hours to get one tune right. But everyone had something to say.

Everyone would contribute. On layered sessions, Creed liked to have the strings and horns there at the same time, which was a good idea. You probably get more control by bringing them in separately, but I always felt that you got more excitement with both sections together."

There are different approaches and different philosophies for recording as a jazz soloist. Many players believe that the inspiration of the moment is all that is necessary. Yet, as Herbie Hancock once mentioned, recordings are facts—permanent documents. Thus, it was not surprising to find that Grover, like many others of his generation who have grown up with the technology, was not averse to replacing his own solo playing and working on a solo until it was finished.

"I like to work on solos until they feel right and really fit with the tune. Perhaps it's selfishness on my part."

Not selfishness as much as perfectionism. Clearly, Grover was aware that his finished product had to meet a considerable standard.

Washington Jr.'s reputation since his arrival in the early '70s had been one of a pop/jazz musician, yet he always found time to include some classic jazz melodies on his albums. There are pop/jazz musicians who have never heard of "Passion Flower," "Body and Soul," or "I Loves You, Porgy" much less have chosen to record them. This is one aspect of his musical persona that links him to an earlier generation of jazz players. Players such as guitarist Kenny Burrell and pianist Tommy Flanagan are celebrated for their subtle musicality. Grover collaborated with each man, yielding memorable results.

While his jazz credentials are impeccable, it is Washington Jr.'s ability to connect with the general public that gained him celebrity. The breakthrough came with the 1974 album *Mister Magic*, which was a gold album. People tend to forget that jazz albums frequently outsold those of their blues and R&B counterparts at this time. Jimmy Smith, Wes Montgomery, and Herbie Hancock were some of his fellow jazz players who achieved gold albums during a period when albums by major R&B performers would struggle with album sales in the low five figures and the singles of some major blues stars wouldn't even be collected in album form! The blues revival of the '60s began to change that; but Stevie Wonder, Aretha Franklin, and Isaac Hayes were among the first R&B artists to sell lots of albums virtually every time-out.

Feels So Good was an album that found Grover the composer, in full flower. "Hydra," "Moonstreams," and "Knucklehead" were his originals. It was another blockbuster as a soul album chart item for thirty weeks.

"I used to have an inferiority complex about my writing because I thought it was too simple. I started writing all kinds of tunes, experimenting with different voicings to see how I could best express myself. I wouldn't even play something of mine until it felt comfortable. Until it said what it was supposed to *say*."

The album, *A Secret Place*, is one that Washington Jr. was less than fully pleased with, and serious problems began to happen with Kudu.

"I came in for what I thought was an overdub session. We had been in the week before laying tracks with my band, but when I arrived, there was a whole new rhythm section. I wasn't even consulted. At that point I realized that I had no control over what I was doing. I'm sure that Creed felt he was doing it for my own good, but I was really disillusioned and angry for a while. But it was now clear that I had to get into the business of music. It was time to say 'I want' instead of 'May I please.'"

While Creed Taylor was listed as producer on his next project, *Live at the Bijou*, recorded in Philadelphia, this was mostly Grover Washington Jr. by this time.

"Creed came down one night, but we actually recorded four nights. He came up to me and said, 'Where did you get this great band?' I told him it was the same band he said couldn't play a year ago."

Quite often, a live recording is looked on as a potboiler, a mark-time project until the next studio album is ready. For Grover, the fact that the LP rose to #11 on the pop album chart was not only vindication for his choice of musicians but also an indication that he had a considerable following for whatever he might choose to do.

CTI, the parent company of Kudu, had been experiencing financial difficulties in the mid-'70s and were briefly bailed out via a distribution deal with Motown. Just as *Live at the Bijou* began to take off, label and distributor were at each other's throats.

"These two companies were fighting between themselves and weren't doing anything for me. I'd ask about support we were promised for one thing or another, and I'd hear, 'Motown's responsible for that' or 'CTI is supposed to do this.' I was going back and forth like a ping-pong ball! And while all this fighting is going on, I've got a record out there that isn't being played. I had to wind up suing both of them. We got a mutual release and settlement."

At that point, Grover Washington Jr. became his own producer and frequently used his own bands as his accompaniment. In time, a number of specially selected vocalists appeared with Washington Jr. on his projects. Among them were Bill Withers, Grady Tate, Nancy Wilson, and Freddie Cole.

After two albums with Motown, Grover went next to Elektra where his major success was the album *Winelight*, which included "Just the Two of Us," with a Bill Withers vocal, which hit #2 on the soul LP chart in a stay that lasted almost a year. Acceptance was even bigger on the pop chart where the album peaked at #5 while the single reached #3. The album was certified platinum.

His third Elektra release, *The Best Is Yet to Come*, from late 1982, contained the last of his four hit singles in the album's title track that featured a vocal by Patti LaBelle.

He moved to Columbia in 1987 and finished his career there. If the spectacular successes of his first decade did not appear as frequently, much of the music is still stimulating. He would, on the one hand, use the most up-to-date technology, including all manner of synthesizers on his jazz fusion albums, and for the next one use a rhythm section of Hank Jones, George Mraz, and Lewis Nash in a program of jazz standards. He would lend his weight to projects by other musicians without regard to their commercial status. The musical challenge always came first.

At a 1990 recording session, as a guest with his old friend organist Charles Earland, he displayed all the fire and drive that was present at the Key Club in Newark those many years ago. Yet it is almost certain that if the Key Club recording session had been scheduled for 1990 rather than 1970, it may never have happened. The economics of the record industry had changed, and few labels would take a chance on an untried substitute when contemplating a live recording. So the achievements of Grover Washington Jr. are somewhat the greater because of his ability to keep the fates on his side. His is a unique story, one without precedent in the jazz world.

When Grover Washington Jr. died suddenly in December 1999, he had just turned fifty-six years old. Along the way, he recorded eleven albums that were substantial hits (two achieved Gold Record status, and *Winelight* had sales of more than one million units). His own playing especially on ballads was celebrated as jazz fusion, something new in the 1970s, and a style that led directly to the smooth jazz radio format.

Smooth jazz was a successful approach to programming from the late 1980s until after the turn of the century and is still found on the dial in many large cities. In 2015, Grover Washington Jr.'s individual CDs don't sell in the quantities they had while he was living, yet Greatest Hits–type compilations of his work still do quite well in the marketplace.

RECOMMENDED RECORDS:

Inner City Blues, with Bob James arrangements, 1971 (Columbia CD); *Mister Magic*, with Bob James arrangements, 1974 (Columbia CD); *Feels So Good*, with Bob James arrangements, 1975 (Columbia CD); *Winelight*, 1980 (Elektra CD); *All My Tomorrows*, 1994 (Columbia CD)

THE PRODUCERS

THE FOLLOWING PRODUCERS ARE MENTIONED frequently in the text. In order that their comings and goings can be sorted out with some accuracy, the following details are offered. This list is not complete and is not intended to represent producers such as Richard Bock, Norman Granz, Orrin Keepnews, Alfred Lion, and Bob Weinstock whose work was done for a label they had owned. Creed Taylor's work for CTI/Kudu is not included here.

TEDDY REIG (1918–1983)

Label affiliations: Continental (1945), Savoy (1945–1951), (Royal) Roost (1948–1966), Coral (1952–1953), Roulette (1957–1962), others

Artists first recorded: Dexter Gordon, Charlie Parker, Stan Getz, Vido Musso, J. J. Johnson, Paul Williams, Fats Navarro, Tadd Dameron, Miles Davis, Leo Parker, Hal Singer, Bud Powell, Harry Belafonte, Johnny Smith, John Handy

Hit singles produced: "Cornbread," Hal Singer, 1948; "35-30," Paul Williams, 1948; "The Hucklebuck," Paul Williams, 1949

Hit LPs produced: *Jazz at NBC*, Johnny Smith 1952; *e=mc2*, Count Basie, 1957; *Sing Along with Basie*, Lambert, Hendricks, and Ross,1958

RALPH BASS (Rafaelo Basso) (1911–1997)

Label affiliations: Black & White (1944–1946), Savoy (1948–1950), King/Federal (1950–1959), Chess (1959–1974), others

Artists first recorded: Big Jay McNeely, Little Esther, the Robins, the Dominoes, James Brown

Hit singles produced: "Open the Door, Richard," Jack McVea, 1947; "Call It Stormy Monday," T-Bone Walker, 1948; "Deacon's Hop," Big Jay McNeely,1949; "Double Crossing Blues," Johnny Otis with Little Esther and the Robins, 1950; "Mistrustin' Blues," Johnny Otis with Little Esther and Mel Walker, 1950; "Cupid's Boogie," Johnny Otis with Little Esther, 1950; "Rockin' Blues," Johnny Otis with Mel Walker,1951; "60-Minute Man," Billy Ward and the Dominoes, 1951; "Flamingo," Earl Bostic, 1951; "Hav' Mercy, Baby," Billy Ward and the Dominoes, 1952; "Work with Me, Annie," the Midnighters, 1954; "Sexy Ways," the Midnighters, 1954; "Annie Had a Baby," the Midnighters, 1954; "Please, Please, Please," James Brown, 1956; "Try Me," James Brown,1958; "All I Could Do Was Cry," Etta James,1960; "At Last," Etta James, 1961

Hit LPs produced: *At Last*, Etta James (1961)

BOB SHAD (1920–1985)

Label affiliations: Manor, Continental, National, and others (1945–48); Sittin' in With, 1948–1952; Mercury (1949–1953); Decca (1953); Mercury/Emarcy (1954–1958); Time (1958–1964); Mainstream (1964–1973)

Artists first recorded: Dizzy Gillespie, Paul Quinichette, Clark Terry, Jimmy Cleveland

Hit singles produced: "Baby Get Lost," Dinah Washington, 1949; "Cold, Cold Heart," Dinah Washington, 1951; "Make Yourself Comfortable," Sarah Vaughan, 1954; "How Important Can It Be," Sarah Vaughan,1955; "Whatever Lola Wants, Sarah Vaughan, 1955

Hit LPs produced: *Sassy*, Sarah Vaughan (1956); *Great Songs from Hit Shows*, Sarah Vaughan (1957); *Sarah Vaughan Sings George Gershwin*, Sarah Vaughan (1957); *Afrique*, Soul Makossa (1973)

FRED MENDELSOHN (1917–2000)

Label affiliations: Regal (1949–1951), Regent (1950–1952), Savoy (1953–1956), DeLuxe (1956–1958), Savoy (1960–1982), others

Artists first recorded: Little Jimmy Scott, Earl King, Lee Allen, Nappy Brown, Wilbert Harrison, Paul Bley

Hit singles produced: "Don't Be Angry," Nappy Brown, 1955; "Johnny Has Gone," Varetta Dillard, 1955; "Candy," Big Maybelle, 1956

Hit LPs produced: *Peace Be Still, Vol. 3*, James Cleveland and the Angelic Choir (1963)

OZZIE CADENA (1924–2008)

Label affiliations: Savoy (1954–1960), Prestige (1962–1964), Prestige (1971–1973)

Artists first recorded: Kai Winding–J. J. Johnson, Cannonball Adderley, Nat Adderley, Donald Byrd, Joe Wilder, Charlie Byrd, Yusef Lateef, Curtis Fuller, Rhoda Scott, Don Patterson, Charles Earland

Hit LPs produced: *Opus de Jazz*, Milt Jackson (1956); *Bad Bossa Nova*, Gene Ammons (1962); *Screamin'*, Jack McDuff, (1962).

CREED TAYLOR (1929–)

Label affiliations: Bethlehem (1954–1955), ABC-Paramount (1955–1961), Verve (1961–1967), A&M (1967–1969), CTI/Kudu (1970–1979)

Artists first recorded: Herbie Mann; Lambert, Hendricks, and Ross; Astrud Gilberto; Deodato; Joe Farrell; Grover Washington Jr.

Hit LPs produced: *Genius + Soul = Jazz*, Ray Charles (1961); *Jazz Samba*, Stan Getz (1962); *Bashin'*, Jimmy Smith (1962); *Hobo Flats*, Jimmy Smith (1963); *Any Number Can Win*, Jimmy Smith (1963); *Getz/Gilberto*, Stan Getz (1964); *Who's Afraid of Virginia Wolf*, Jimmy Smith (1964); *The Cat*, Jimmy Smith (1964); *Soul Sauce*, Cal Tjader (1965); *Organ Grinder's Swing*, Jimmy Smith (1965); *Goin' Out of My Head*, Wes Montgomery (1966); *Tequila*, Wes Montgomery (1966); *Got My Mojo Working*, Jimmy Smith (1966); *California Dreaming*, Wes Montgomery (1967); *Respect*, Jimmy Smith (1967); *A Day in the Life*, Wes Montgomery (1967); *Down Here on the Ground*, Wes Montgomery (1968); *Walking in Space*, Quincy Jones (1969)

ESMOND EDWARDS (1927–2007)

Label affiliations: Prestige (1958–1962), Argo/Cadet (1962–1967), Verve (1967–1969), Chess/Cadet (1971–1975), Impulse (1975–1979)

Artists first recorded: Johnny "Hammond" Smith, Oliver Nelson, Jack McDuff, Eric Dolphy, Larry Young, Odell Brown

Hit LPs produced: *Don't Go to Strangers*, Etta Jones (1960); *Boss Tenor*, Gene Ammons (1960); *Angel Eyes*, Gene Ammons (1964); *Together Again*, Willis Jackson with Jack McDuff (1965); *The In Crowd*, Ramsey Lewis (1965); *Hang On Ramsey*, Ramsey Lewis (1966); *Wade in the Water*, Ramsey Lewis (1966); *Gotta Travel On*, Ray Bryant (1966); *Mellow Yellow*, Odell Brown (1967); *Hard Work*, John Handy (1976).

SID MCCOY (1922–2009)

Label affiliation: Vee Jay (1958–1963)

Artists first recorded: Eddie Harris, Bill Henderson, Wayne Shorter, Louis Hayes, Frank Strozier

Hit LPs produced: *Exodus to Jazz*, Eddie Harris (1961)

JOEL DORN (1942–2007)

Label affiliation: Atlantic (1967–1974), others

Artists first recorded: Hubert Laws, Roberta Flack, Bette Midler, Leon Redbone, Roomful of Blues

Hit LPs produced: *Much Les*, Les McCann (1968); *Swiss Movement*, Les McCann and Eddie Harris (1969); *First Take*, Roberta Flack (1970); *Chapter Two*, Roberta Flack (1970); *Quiet Fire*, Roberta Flack (1971); Roberta Flack and Donny Hathaway (1972); *The Divine Miss M*, Bette Midler (1973); *Killing Me Softly*, Roberta Flack (1973); *Feel Like Makin' Love*, Roberta Flack (1974)

BOB PORTER (1940–)

Label affiliations: Prestige (1968–1971), Westbound (1972–1973), Savoy (1975–1980), Atlantic (1986–1991), others

Artists first recorded: Billy Butler, Melvin Sparks, Idris Muhammad, Leon Spencer, Funk Inc., Hank Crawford–Jimmy McGriff group

Hit LPs produced: *Goodness*, Houston Person (1970); *The Boss Is Back*, Gene Ammons (1970); *Black Talk*, Charles Earland (1970); *Brother Jug*, Gene Ammons (1970); *Black Drops*, Charles Earland (1970); *Right On, Brother*, Boogaloo Joe Jones (1971); *The Black Cat*, Gene Ammons (1971); *Soul Liberation*, Rusty Bryant (1971); *Living Black*, Charles Earland (1971); *What's Goin' On*, Johnny "Hammond" Smith (1972); *My Way*, Gene Ammons (1972); Funk Inc. (1972)

EPILOGUE

DURING THE SUMMER OF 1983, I was visiting relatives in Charleston, West Virginia. One evening while leafing through the local newspaper, I came across a nightclub advertisement announcing the appearance of Winston Walls.

I sat straight up. Winston Walls was a legendary name among organists. I had been hearing stories about him for years. In 1970, while I was working for Prestige Records, a gentleman came to see me with a crudely recorded eight-track tape of Winston Walls. Prestige was loaded with organists on its roster at that time, so I passed. But I remembered the fire and drive that I heard on that tape, and I remembered the name Winston Walls. I knew he was the son of the equally legendary Atlantic Records session pianist Van "Piano Man" Walls.

I went to hear him in Charleston. He was playing a typically dumb gig for those years: Walls, his guitarist, and his drummer were the only black people in the club. There may have been thirty customers, making the room less than half full. A man had been feeding the tip jar and singing the Frank Sinatra songbook with mediocre results. When he finished, Walls announced last call and began playing the blues.

He took the blues through all the keys, building intensity as he went. No guitar solos, no drum solos, but those accompanists were locked into a perfect groove. Walls was sweating, his hands flying over the keyboard, and he was obviously releasing all the pent-up emotions that had accumulated while accompanying the Sinatra Wannabe. Then he started a drone.

The drone allows the right thumb to hold a note while the rest of the right hand improvises. The left hand walks the bass. It creates a powerful groove that is best-exemplified in certain works by Jimmy Smith, notably "The Sermon." The drone was used by virtually all organists to rouse an audience, and it roused this one. As the performance concluded, the room was standing to applaud. I thought that I must meet this man.

Just then the waitress presented the check. After settling up, I looked for Walls. He was gone. Vanished. Disappeared. Poof! I had just witnessed as great a single performance by an organ trio that I could recall by anyone. Was I dreaming? Was this guy a ghost? Nobody would believe what I just heard.

I couldn't wait to tell someone. But then I thought about it. Who would I tell? Ideally I could talk to someone who knew the organ scene. Someone who could relate to the situation. Who would that be?

No. I left it alone. What would likely happen is that even knowledgeable friends would shrug. It was too late. Who cares? Soul jazz, what's that?

ACKNOWLEDGMENTS

THANKS TO SHELDON MEYER FOR the opportunity to write this book. Thanks to Tom Curry for research assistance and encouragement. Thanks to Richard Seidel and Dick Shurman for all kinds of positive suggestions. Thanks to Tony Outhwaite for all that you do. Thanks to Joe Rosen for everything you do. Thanks to Karl Tan, Valerie Mendrez and Sarah Perkins from Xlibris.

Patrons: Armen Boladian, Clive Davis, Ahmet Ertegun, and Bob Weinstock,

Mentors: Gene Ammons, Stanley Dance, Esmond Edwards, Ira Gitler, Illinois Jacquet, and Dan Morgenstern

Inspiration: George Avakian, Nesuhi Ertegun, Milt Gabler, Norman Granz, John Hammond, Orrin Keepnews, Harry Lim, Alfred Lion, Fred Mendelsohn, Teddy Reig, Creed Taylor and Jerry Wexler.

My guys: George Duvivier, Bill Easley, Houston Person, Bernard Purdie, and Melvin Sparks,

Musicians: Johnnie Bassett, Ruth Brown, Rusty Bryant, Bob Bushnell, Billy Butler, Arnett Cobb, Hank Crawford, Sonny Criss, Lou Donaldson, Charlie Earland, George Freeman, Dexter Gordon, Grant Green, Red Holloway, Groove Holmes, Helen Humes, Willis Jackson, Eddie Jefferson, Plas Johnson, Etta Jones, Charles Kynard, Jimmy Lewis, Gene Ludwig, Junior Mance, Pat Martino, Jimmy McGriff. Idris Muhammad, David Newman, Sonny Phillips, Greg Piccolo, Arthur

Prysock, Duke Robillard, Dr. Lonnie Smith, Sonny Stitt, Buddy Tate, Grady Tate, Eddie Vinson, Grover Washington, Jr., Bobby Watley, Paul Williams. Thanks to Rudy Van Gelder for creating the sound.

Colleagues: Malcolm Addey, Mel Albert, Ray Avery, Steve Backer, Richard Bock, Cephas Bowles, Bruce Bromberg, Mark Cantor, David Chertok, Michael Cuscuna, Charles Delaunay, Joel Dorn, Joe Fields, Bob Golden, Maxine Harvard, Van Jay, Jorgen Grunnet-Jepsen, Ralph Kaffel, Karl Emil Knudsen, Bob Koester, Jack Kreisberg, Eric LeBlanc, Ira Leslie, Charlie Lourie, Andy McKaie, Al Pryor, Sylvia Rhone, Bruce Ricker, Al Riley, Michel Ruppli, Ira Sabin, Don Schlitten, Jack Towers, Jerry Valburn, Billy Vera, Malcolm Walker, Nat White, and Noreen Woods,

Messengers: EZ Speed Anderson, Ed Beach, Tommy Bee, Joe Bostic, Frankie Crocker, Yvonne Daniels, Alan Freed, Sid Gribitz, Terri Gross, Rhonda Hamilton, Hunter Hancock, Huggy Boy, Bubba Jackson, Ed Love, Bill Marlowe, Phil Schaap, Sleepy Stein, Martha Jean Steinberg, Vern Stephenson, Billy Taylor, Rufus Thomas, Symphony Sid Torin, Gary Walker, Linda Yohn, and the guy who used to host **The Harley Show** on WBAL, Baltimore.

Insights: Amiri Baraka, Francis Davis, Ralph Ellison, Aaron Fuchs, Gary Giddins, Fred Goodman, Tad Hershorn, Ben Hurwitz, Albert Murray, Hugues Panassie, Mel Schlissel, Bob Ursury, Cornelius Watts, and August Wilson.

INDEX

A

ABC Records, 101, 121, 151
Abramson, Herb, 23, 77–78, 129
Ace, 90
Ace, Johnny, 98–99, 149
acid jazz, 244
Adams, Berle, 18, 61
Adams, Faye, 81, 98, 167
Adderley, Cannonball, 29, 99, 132, 134, 157, 164, 169–70, 176, 183, 189, 194, 215, 219, 222–23, 230
Adderley, Nat, 257
AFM, 6, 20, 59, 172, 234
    recording ban of, 9, 45, 49, 59
Alabama, xiv, 19, 198
Aladdin, 7, 12, 19, 29–30, 39, 49–51, 64, 75, 77, 90–91
Albam, Manny, 71
Albert, Don, 76
albums
    best-selling, 124, 228
    biggest-selling, 248
    gold, 220, 250
    making, 135, 139, 235
    one-shot, 126, 160, 173, 181
    orchestral, 180, 190, 195
    pop, 166, 177, 214, 221, 236
    stereo, 128, 204, 212
    strong-selling, 132, 190, 222

Alfred, Roy, 67
Allen, Annisteen, 15
Allen, Henry "Red," 9, 137–38
Allen, Lee, 89–90, 98, 257
All-Stars, 5, 138
    album of, 127
American Federation of Musicians, 1, 107, 172
Ammons, Albert, 8, 28, 106, 133
Ammons, Gene, ix, xiv, 27, 30, 74–75, 94, 98, 100, 104–12, 157, 164, 167–68, 173–74, 232, 257–59
    albums of, 109–10, 174
    Bad Bossa Nova, 109–10, 112, 168, 257
Ampex Corporation, 45
A&M Records, 153, 194, 204, 219, 235, 257
Anderson, Cat, 2–3, 80, 125
Apollo, 9, 25, 39, 49–51, 171
ARA, 7, 49
Archia, Tom, 29, 47, 107
Argo, 52, 65, 74, 101, 109, 167, 169, 185, 202, 218, 221
Argo/Cadet, 217, 220, 258
Armed Forces Recording Service, 12
Armstrong, Henry, xii
Armstrong, Louis, 5, 21, 40, 127, 136, 138, 186, 214

265

ASCAP, xii, 103
Asch, Moses, 12
Asch Records, 9, 12
Askey, Gil, 72
Atco, 82
Atlantic Records, 30, 53, 60, 64, 67–68, 77–82, 89–92, 128–32, 150–51, 153, 174, 189, 212, 226–30, 259
Atlas, 239
Atomic, 7, 121
Audio Fidelity, 125
Austin, Sil, 72, 95, 98, 136
Avant, Clarence, 166
avant-garde, 157, 228–29
Ayers, Roy, 242

B

Bacon, Trevor, 5
Bagby, Doc, 74, 160
Bailey, Benny, 193
Bailey, Buster, 138
Bailey, Donald, 166
Bailey, Pearl, 70
Baker, LaVern, 80–81
Baker, McHouston "Mickey," 72, 91, 131
Baker, Shorty, 137
Baldwin, James, 195
Ballard, Butch, 71
bandleaders, xi, 1–2, 4, 20, 37, 75, 81–82, 111, 138, 161, 195, 202, 229, 233, 240–41
Barefield, Eddie, 53
Barge, Gene, 89
Barnet, Charlie, 7
Barretto, Ray, 109, 174
Barron, Kenny, 181
Bartee, Claude, 205
Bartholomew, Dave, 90–91, 103
Bartholomew, Gayten, 27, 90
Bartley, Dallas, 18
Bascomb, Dud, 3, 8
Bascomb, Paul, 3, 8, 54, 78, 94

Basie, Count, 2, 14, 25, 29–30, 54–55, 60, 71–72, 97–99, 115–17, 119–21, 160, 162–63, 193–94, 240, 255
Basie band, 50, 117, 119–21, 160, 240
Bass, Fontella, 89
Bass, Ralph (Rafaelo Basso), 22–25, 34–35, 63–66, 75, 85, 256
Beacon, 9
Beale Streeters, 149
bebop, xi, xiii, 8, 10, 23, 31–33, 45, 57–58, 62–63, 103, 107, 111, 158, 189, 191
Bechet, Sidney, 99
Beecher, Johnny, 90
Begian, Harry, 58
Belgrave, Marcus, 152, 155
Bellson, Louie, 61, 70, 99, 122, 180
Bennett, Tony, 117, 121
Benson, George, 92, 107, 153–54, 173–74, 190, 204, 207–8, 217, 219, 237, 242, 248
Bentley, Gladys, 42
Berry, Chu, 8, 35, 48, 53, 58
Berry, Chuck, 84, 124, 142–43
Bethlehem, 74, 137, 140, 178, 183, 257
big band, 1–3, 5–6, 8, 11, 15, 47–48, 54–55, 58–59, 70–71, 73, 93–96, 116–20, 124–26, 166, 178–80
Big Bill Broonzy, 29
Biggs, Howard, 80, 91, 131
Big Maybelle, 61, 132, 193, 257
Billy Berg's Swing Club, 11, 32, 49
Billy Ward and the Dominoes, 256
Birdland Records, 31, 63, 97–98, 108, 116, 123, 127, 161, 194, 201
Bivens, Willie, 205
Black & Blue, 43, 52, 136, 239
Black & White, 7, 23–25, 256
Black, Dave, 71, 122
Black Deuce, 35–36
Blakey, Art, 106, 158, 169, 181–85, 191, 223, 244
Bland, Bobby, 149, 196

Blanton, Jimmy, 122
Bley, Paul, 196, 257
Bluebird, 60
Blue Note Records, 9, 99, 133–34, 164–67, 169, 174–75, 182–85, 187, 190–91, 202–3, 205–9, 217–18, 222–25, 235, 238
blues, 4, 8–11, 24, 29–30, 38–41, 65, 113–14, 119–20, 130, 134, 170, 213, 223, 239, 261
Bluesville, 82, 133, 164
BMI, xii, 68, 103
Bock, Richard, 175, 255, 264
Bohanon, George, 229
Booker, James, 179
Booker T., 239
BOP, 35, 139
Bostic, Earl, 3, 39, 60, 75–76, 94, 98, 100, 152, 235, 256
Boulanger, Nadia, 193
Bowen, Jimmy, 98
Bracken, Jimmy, 134
Bradshaw, Myron "Tiny," 94
Bradshaw, Tiny, 78, 95, 98, 136
Bregman, Buddy, 126
Brooklyn Dodgers, 13, 44
Brookmeyer, Bob, 99
Brooks, David "Bubba," 43, 98
Brooks, Hadda, 19, 28
Brooks, Roy, 182
Brooks, Tina, 183
Brown, Clifford, 73, 99, 154, 181, 199
Brown, James, 110, 203, 205, 211, 256
Brown, Lawrence, 2, 69, 122
Brown, Nappy, 80, 132, 257
Brown, Odell, 219, 258
Brown, Pete, 8, 23
Brown, Ray, 32, 73, 97, 189
Brown, Roy, 28, 41–42
Brown, Ruth, 79, 91
Brown, Wilbur, 152
Brown, Wini, 27
Browne, Samuel, 58
Brubeck, Dave, 135, 191
Bryant, Paul, 175, 239

Bryant, Ray, 218, 258
Bryant, Rusty, 95, 232, 259, 263
Buckner, Milt, 3, 15, 35, 52, 73–74, 122, 159, 162–63, 165, 239
Buddah, 238
Buddy Johnson Orchestra, 115
Bullet, 39
Burrell, Kenny, 173, 175, 183, 185, 190, 208, 211, 235, 250
Butera, Sam, 95
Butler, Billy, 135, 201, 259, 263
Butler, George, 238
Byas, Don, 8–9, 23, 32, 36
Byers, Billy, 121
Byrd, Charlie, 257
Byrd, Donald, ix, 132, 181, 184–85, 224–26, 242, 257

C

Cabrera, Louis, 58
Cadena, Ozzie, 110, 132, 257
Cadet, 173, 190, 212, 218, 221, 236
Cain, Henry, 239
Calloway, Cab, 6, 22, 47–49, 80, 94, 118, 133, 136–37
Campanella, Roy, 13
Campbell, Jo Ann, 142
Capitol Records, 6–7, 9–10, 19–20, 24, 28, 34, 41, 59, 72, 74, 82, 90, 96, 137, 170
Carell Music, 90
Carn, Doug, 239
Carnegie Hall, 2, 12–13, 35–36, 50
Carney, Harry, 2, 81, 123
Carpenter, Charlie, 30
Carter, Benny, 5, 18, 21, 28, 121, 194
Carter, Ron, 5, 21, 195, 236
Carter, Vivian, 134
CBS, 62, 92, 116, 138
Cedar Walton, 184
Chambers, Paul, 194, 223
Chamblee, Eddie, 42–43, 89, 107, 125
Chance, 89

Charles, Ray, 80, 105, 128–31, 149–52, 155, 169–70, 178–79, 196, 234, 258
Charles, Teddy, 99
Charms, The, 43, 98
Chart, 43
Charter, 90
Cheatham, Doc, 28
Checker, 89, 119
Chess/Cadet, 258
Chess Records, 28, 43, 63, 65, 75, 89–92, 94, 107, 109–10, 169, 196, 212, 256
Chico Hamilton Quintet, 229
Chordettes, The, 117
Chudd, Lew, 129
Civil Rights Act, xv, 196, 198
Clark, Sonny, 199
Clarke, Harold "Babe," 67
Clarke, Kenny, 132, 180–81, 183, 189
Clay, Cassius Marcellus, Jr., 197
Clayton, Buck, 2, 12, 138, 162
Clef, 31, 70, 96, 114, 127
Cleftones, 82
Clef/Verve, 120, 125
Cleveland, Jimmy, 73, 193, 256
Clovers, The, 79, 115
Coasters, The, 65, 81
Cobb, Arnett, 3, 15, 27, 29, 35, 39, 47, 54, 66, 78, 95, 98, 161–62, 174–75, 194–95
Cobb, Danny, 93
Cobb, Jimmy, 194, 223
Cohen, Howard, 111
Cohn, Al, 30
Coker, Henry, 28, 50
Cole, Cozy, 8, 138–39
Cole, Freddie, 252
Cole, Nat "King" (Nathaniel Adams Cole), 7, 19–21, 48, 50, 99
Coleman, Earl, 35
Coleman, George, 195
Coleman, Gloria, 87, 238–39
Coleman, Ornette, 131, 169, 228
Collins, Cal, 232

Colpix, 194
Coltrane, John, 30, 82, 128, 131, 169, 186–88, 194, 199, 206, 229
Columbia Records, 1–2, 14, 22, 44–45, 59–61, 114, 137, 139–40, 191, 212, 217–19, 221, 224, 237–38, 252–53
Columbus, Chris (Joseph Morris), 18, 119, 159
Comet, 24
Commodore, 9, 28, 137
Concord, 90, 222
Conn, Billy, 13
Connor, Chris, 129–30
Continental, 9
Cook, Junior, 182
Cooke, Bill, 92
Cooke, Sam, 90, 216
Cooper, Buster, 73
Cooper, Leroy "Hog," 150
Cootie Williams Orchestra, 21
Coral, 37, 61, 75, 116–18, 138–39, 255
Corcoran, Corky, 27
Corea, Chick, 242
Cortez, Dave "Baby," 239
Cosmo Records, 24
Crawford, Hank (Bennie Ross Crawford), 29, 130, 148–56, 169, 177, 207, 235, 248, 263
Crawford, Ray, 166
Crayton, Pee Wee, 41–42
Crescent, 129, 244
Criss, Sonny, 29, 35, 149, 199, 263
Criss Cross, 239
Cromer, Austin, 152
Crosby, Bing, 18, 25, 45, 214
Crothers, Scatman, 80
CTI, 153, 189, 235–37, 242, 251
CTI/Kudu, 153, 236–37, 255, 257
Culley, Frank "Floorshow," 79

D

Dale, 35
Darin, Bobby, 131
Dash, Julian, 3, 17

Davis, Dick, 42, 107
Davis, Eddie "Lockjaw," 23, 41, 71, 110, 121, 133–34, 159–63, 167, 170–71, 175
Davis, Jackie, 74, 160, 178
Davis, Lem, 28, 36
Davis, Maxwell, 12, 89, 91
Davis, Miles, 29, 34, 105, 128, 135, 140, 158, 180, 182–83, 186–88, 194–95, 218, 221, 223–24, 234
Davis, Sammy, Jr., 193
Davis, Wild Bill, 18, 26, 52–53, 74, 120, 158–59, 162, 164, 178, 239
Davis, William Strethen, 159
Davis Sisters, 132
Dawson, Alan, 52, 73
Decca, 1, 3, 5, 9–10, 15–17, 19, 21–22, 25, 27–28, 34–35, 40, 45, 54, 59–61, 139
Dee Gee Records, 96
DeFrancesco, Joey, 241
DeFranco, Buddy, 71
Dells, 134
DeLuxe, 6, 9, 27, 43, 132, 171, 257
Deodato, 236, 258
Derby Records, 6
Dial Records, 36
Dickenson, Vic, 28
Dillard, Varetta, 91, 93, 132, 257
Dirty Dozen, 245
disco, ix, 241
Dixon, Floyd, 90
Dixon, Willie, 91
Doby, Larry, 44
Dockery, Sam, 183
Doggett, Bill, 4, 18, 26, 38, 41, 73–74, 135–36, 159, 165, 178, 201, 239
Dolphy, Eric, 167, 192, 229, 258
Domino, Fats, 79, 90, 98, 115
Donaldson, Lou, 29, 87, 174–75, 183, 202, 207, 211, 216–18, 227, 232–33, 241, 244, 263
Dorham, Kenny, 138, 181
Dorn, Joel, 156, 173, 226, 230, 259, 264
Dorsey, Jimmy, 180

Dorsey, Tommy, 1, 7, 180
Drayton, Charlie, 13
Drew, Kenny, 199
Drifters, The, 80, 90, 98, 115, 129–31
Drinkard Singers, 132
Duke, Doug, 74, 99
Duke/Peacock, 61, 91
Dupree, Cornell, 82, 131, 154, 242
Duvivier, George, 4, 180, 263
Dyett, Captain Walter, 58, 106

E

Eager, Allen, 23, 30, 35
Earland, Charles, 87, 234, 238, 247–48, 257, 259
Eckstine, Billy, 6, 20, 31, 78, 106, 109, 119, 121, 179, 186, 213
ECM, 239
Edison, Harry "Sweets," 2, 52, 77, 137, 163
Edwards, Esmond, 52, 86, 133, 160, 164, 167, 217–19, 236, 258, 263
Edwards, Gene, 178
Edwards, Gordon, 242
Edwards, Teddy, 152
Eldridge, Roy, 7, 11, 52, 55, 58, 97, 127, 138, 180
Elgort, Arthur, 53
Ellington, Duke, 2–3, 14, 40, 50, 58, 61, 69–72, 76–77, 81, 114, 118, 122–24, 126, 191, 240
Ellington and Basie bands, 7, 72
Ellington band, 14, 69–70, 81, 122–23
Elliot, Don, 132
Ellis, Herb, 97, 222
Ellison, Ralph, 195, 264
Emarcy, 89, 99, 256
Embers, 90, 98, 137
End, 82, 194
Epic Records, 61
Ertegun, Ahmet, 77–79, 92, 129, 131, 192, 226, 263
Ertegun, Nesuhi, 128–29, 131, 151, 192, 226, 230, 263

Ervin, Booker, 196, 223
essence, 236
Essence, 236
Evans, Bill, 194
Evans, Gil, 195
Evans, Herschel, 2, 8, 11, 53–54, 82, 162
Excelsior, 7, 38
Exclusive Records, 9, 22, 26, 64

F

Famous Ward Singers, 132
Farmer, Art, 73, 99, 182, 185, 199
Farrell, Joe, 258
Federal label, 65, 75
Felder, Wilton, 231
FEPC (Fair Employment Practices Committee), xiv
Ferguson, Maynard, 98, 180
Fields, Ernie, 36, 155
Fields, Joe, 233, 238, 264
Fitzgerald, Ella, 8–9, 18, 33, 43, 51, 97, 120, 126–28, 159, 161, 213
Flack, Roberta, 259
Flanagan, Tommy, 109, 219, 250
Fletcher, Dusty, 25
Floyd, Buddy, 20
Floyd, Troy, 162
"Flyin' Home," 27, 48–49, 54–55, 99, 124–25
Foreman, George, 241
Forrest, Earl, 149
Forrest, Jimmy, 14, 76–77, 81, 86, 110, 123, 157, 163, 167, 173, 201
Forrester, Bobby, 239
Foster, Frank, 71, 120–21
Foster, Ronnie, 205, 239
Fowler, T. J., 66
Francis, Panama, 4, 118, 131
Franklin, Aretha, 82, 212, 215–17, 250
Frazier, Caesar, 239
Frazier, Joe, 241
Freed, Alan, 42, 68, 78–81, 84, 90, 93, 95, 97, 113–19, 124, 140–44, 264

Freeman, Russ, 32
Fuller, Curtis, 184–85, 257
Fuller, Gil, 33
Fulson, Lowell, 119, 235
funk, 110–11, 189, 203–4, 206, 231, 244
Funk Inc., 238, 259

G

Gabler, Milt, 16, 18, 54, 263
Gaillard, 19
Gaines, Charlie, 17
Gaines, Roy, 21
Gale, Eric, 3, 95, 101, 242
Gale Agency, 3–5, 11, 30, 95, 97, 116
Gant, Cecil, 10, 21
Garland, Red, 74, 194–95, 220
Garner, Erroll, 8, 23, 178, 214
Garrett, Alvin, 42
Garrison, Jimmy, 188
Gastel, Carlos, 20
Gayles, Juggy, 68
Gayten, Paul, 27, 90
Gee, 82, 194
Gelder, Rudy Van, 133, 165–67, 188, 205, 219, 236–37, 249, 264
Gentlemen of Swing, 220
Getz, Stan, 23, 30, 35, 98–100, 107, 127, 178, 180, 220, 227, 255, 258
Gibbs, Terry, 58, 180
Gibson, Andy, 7, 67–68
Gibson, Harry "The Hipster," 32
Gilberto, Astrud, 258
Gillespie, Dizzy, 4, 8, 23–24, 28, 31–33, 35, 57, 62, 82, 96, 106, 138, 180–81, 187, 189–92
Gillespie Orchestra, 33
Gilt Edge, 10
Glaser, Joe, 3, 166
Glenn, Lloyd, 63, 91
Glenn, Tyree, 138
Glover, Henry, 24, 41, 67
Golden Gloves, 197
Goldner, George, 82

Golson, Benny, 101, 183, 185, 194
Gone, 82, 194
Gonsalves, Paul, 14, 82, 122–23
Gonzales, Babs, 100
Gooden, Leo, 202
Goodman, Benny, 1, 3, 5, 7, 14–15, 23, 53, 114
Good Time Jazz, 129
Gordon, Dexter, 3, 12, 23, 30, 35, 48, 106, 111, 134, 170, 179, 186, 199, 224, 255
Grand Award, 138
Grant, Earl, 239
Granz, Norman, 5, 10–12, 27, 31, 34, 49, 51–52, 60, 69–71, 73, 96–97, 114, 120, 126–29, 240
Grauer, Bill, 134
Gray, Wardell, 14, 30, 35, 71, 75, 100, 106, 199
Green, Bennie, 137, 139–40
Green, Charles, 152
Green, Freddie, 121
Green, Grant, 173, 175, 190, 196, 200–201, 203–5, 207–8, 230, 232, 263
Greer, Sonny, 69–70, 122
Grey, Al, 77, 121, 162, 196
Griffin, Johnny, 15, 27, 163, 183, 199, 223
Grimes, 8, 30, 78, 93, 218
Grimes, Lloyd "Tiny," 8, 30, 78, 93, 218
Grissom, Jimmy, 123, 167
Groove Merchant, 177, 238
GRP, 242
Gryce, Gigi, 73
Guilbeau, Phillip, 66–67, 155
Guild, 9, 31, 138
Guitar Slim, 130

H

Haig, Al, 32
Hamilton, Chico, 229
Hamilton, Jimmy, 2
Hammond, John, 23, 217–18, 263
Hammond organ, 18, 158
"Hamp's Boogie Woogie," 3, 73, 124
Hampton, Lionel, 3, 9, 14–15, 25–27, 38, 41, 47–49, 53–55, 69, 72–75, 89, 124–25, 161, 189, 192
Hampton, Slide, 30, 72, 178
Hampton band, 3, 15, 25–27, 48, 73, 124, 161
Hamp-Tone, 39
Hancock, Herbie, 195, 201, 224, 235, 248, 250
Hancock, Hunter, 92, 264
Handy, John, 192, 255, 258
Hardesty, Herb, 90
Hardman, Bill, 183
Harlem, 35
Harper, Ricky, 150
Harptones, 115
Harris, Ace, 17
Harris, Barry, 188
Harris, Bill, 50, 97
Harris, Eddie, 134, 216, 226–28, 232, 258–59
Harris, Wynonie, 5, 37, 39–40, 222
Harrison, Wendell, 152
Harrison, Wilbert, 132, 257
Hartman, Johnny, 188
Hathaway, Donny, 259
Hawkins, Coleman, 7, 11–12, 33, 50, 58, 99, 138, 163, 190
Hawkins, Erskine, 3, 16–17, 21, 38, 54, 60, 90, 95, 102, 118–19, 145
Hawkins, Jennell, 239
Hayes, Edgar, 23
Hayes, Ernie, 131
Hayes, Isaac, 215, 250
Hayes, Louis, 182, 258
Haywood, Cedric, 159
Heath, Jimmy, 82, 179, 186
Heath, Percy, 189
Hefti, Neal, 53, 71, 121
Henderson, Bill, 258
Henderson, Fletcher, 5
Henderson, Joe, 182, 209, 235
Henderson, Wayne, 231

Hendricks, 255, 258
Hendricks, Jon, 121
Henry, Heywood, 3, 28, 102, 118
Henson, Purvis, 16
Hentoff, Nat, 192
Herald, 80–81
Herman, Woody, 21, 107, 180
Herschel Evans, 162
Heywood, Eddie, 28
Heywood, Eddie, Jr., 28
Hibbler, Al, 2, 119
Higginbotham, J. C., 9, 138
Hill, Andrew, 196
Hines, Earl, 5, 31, 137, 139
HIT, 6, 10
Hodges, Johnny, 2, 18, 69–70, 81, 94, 122, 178, 187, 203, 240
Hogan, Carl, 18
Holder, T., 36, 162
Holiday, Billie, 8–9, 28, 30, 40, 97, 159
Holloway, Red, 89–90, 173–74, 179, 263
Holmes, Groove, 76, 169, 175–76, 178, 213, 233, 238, 263
Holt, Red, 220
Hooke, Jack, 118, 141–42
Hooker, John Lee, 59, 134
Hooper, Nesbert "Stix," 231
Hope, Lynn, 75
Hopkins, Claude, 138
Hopkins, Linda, 65
Horace Silver Quintet, 182
Horn, Paul, 229
Hot Lips Page, 8
Howard, Camille, 19–20
HRS, 9
Hubbard, Freddie, 153, 184, 224, 235–37
"Hucklebuck, The," xiii, 67–68, 158, 218, 255
Humes, Helen, 7, 12–13, 263
Hunt, John, 150
Hunter, Ivory Joe, 29, 41, 63, 130
Hyman, Dick, 138, 159

I

Imperial, 58, 64, 79, 90–91, 129
Impulse, 155, 165, 167–68, 174, 178, 184, 187, 189, 235, 258
International Records, 111
Irvin, Monte, 13
"It's Too Soon to Know," 43
Ivory, Jackie, 239

J

Jackson, Benjamin "Bull Moose," 5, 15, 39
Jackson, Milt, 32, 129, 132, 182, 189, 219, 257
Jackson, Willis, 79, 110, 157, 159, 161, 171–72, 178, 233, 258, 263
Jacquet, Illinois, ix, 3, 6, 10–12, 14, 23, 29, 31, 38–39, 46–55, 60, 74, 78, 107, 127–28
Jacquet, Russell, 49
Jacquet band, 47, 49
Jade, 35
Jamal, Ahmad, 169, 196, 218, 220–21
James, Bob, 153, 220, 236–37, 249, 253
James, Etta, 65, 256
James, Harry, 7, 70, 180
Jammin' the Blues, 49
Jarrett, Keith, 229, 242
JATP (Jazz at the Philharmonic), 11–12, 26–27, 30–32, 45, 49–53, 70, 73, 96–97, 114, 126–28, 180
Jax, 35, 68
jazz, ix–xi, 49, 53, 63, 127–28, 132, 145–46, 169–70, 182–83, 192–95, 212–17, 224–25, 227–31, 241–45, 257–59
    modern, xiii, 31, 133, 161, 180, 189, 228, 231, 234
    smooth, 242–43, 253
jazz albums, 82, 177, 225, 239, 250
    best-selling, 178, 194
jazz artists, 9, 132, 153, 166, 168, 190, 193–94, 215, 220, 227, 230

jazz community, 182, 184, 188, 194, 235–36
Jazz Crusaders, 169, 231
jazz groups, 173, 199
jazz labels, x, 113, 166, 177, 212
  independent, 132–33
Jazzland, 134, 163, 185–86, 228
Jazzman record, 129
Jazz Messengers, The, 181–84
jazz musicians, xi–xii, 193, 207, 214, 237
jazz pianists, 123, 222
jazz producers, 41, 71
Jazztet, 185
jazz writers, ix, 168
Jefferson, Eddie, 100–101, 263
Jennings, Bill, 18, 86, 157, 159, 171
Joe Liggins and His Honeydrippers, 22
Joe Louis, xii
Johnson, Bobby, 17
Johnson, Budd, 54, 58, 79, 118, 163, 193
Johnson, Buddy, ix, 4, 9, 16, 38, 40, 44, 72, 89, 95, 98, 118, 125, 140, 193–95
Johnson, Eddie, 26, 75, 107
Johnson, Ella, 4, 16, 115
Johnson, Gus, 119
Johnson, Howard, 152
Johnson, Jack, xii
Johnson, J. J., 2, 23, 50, 127, 132, 140, 195, 255, 257
Johnson, Lonnie, 40–41
Johnson, Lyndon, 196
Johnson, Plas, 89–90, 263
Johnson band, 4, 16, 72
Jonah Jones Quartet, 138
Jones, Boogaloo Joe, 233, 247, 259
Jones, Carmell, 182, 199
Jones, Elvin, 188
Jones, Etta, 137, 167, 213, 258, 263
Jones, Hank, 132, 159, 183, 219, 252
Jones, Ivan Joseph, 232
Jones, Jo, 2, 50, 52, 74, 127, 218
Jones, Joe, 201, 233
Jones, Jonah, 136–37, 139
Jones, Philly Joe, 158, 183, 194

Jones, Quincy, 73, 101, 121, 140, 189, 192–94, 258
Jones, Sam, 183
Jones, Thad, 120–21, 192
Jordan, Duke, 199
Jordan, Louis, 9, 17–21, 25–26, 28, 38, 61, 119, 158–59, 214
Jordan, Taft, 2, 118, 138
Jorgenson, Joe, 237
Josie, 82, 90
Jubilee, 43, 61, 75, 82, 136, 139, 183, 194

K

Kapp, 82
Kay, Connie, 79, 131, 189
Kelly, 37, 194–96, 219, 223–24
Kelly, George, 21
Kelly, Wynton, 37, 194, 196, 219, 223
Kennedy, John F., 196
Kenton, Stan, 20, 150, 180
Kersey, Kenny, 13
Kessel, Barney (pseud. Rock Murphy), 97, 126, 222
Keynote, 9, 30, 137–38
King, B. B., 40, 98–99, 119, 149
King, Earl, 257
King, Freddie, 43
King, Martin Luther, Jr., 198–99, 211
King Cole Trio, 1, 17, 19–20, 48, 107
Kingpins, The, 82, 217
King Pleasure (Clarence Beeks), 90, 100, 106, 216
King Records, 6, 21, 29, 37, 39, 41–43, 58, 60–61, 63, 65, 67, 75–77, 94–95, 160, 208
Kirby, John, 28
Kirk, Andy, 5, 76, 81, 162
Kirk, Rahsaan Roland, 229
Kirk, Roland, 173, 192
Kirkland, Leroy, 17, 80, 84, 91, 102, 117–18
Knox, Buddy, 98
Konitz, Lee, 192

Krupa, Gene, 12, 49, 97
Kudu, 153, 235–36, 247–48, 251
Kynard, Ben, 27
Kynard, Charles, 238–39, 263

L

Lambert, 255, 258
Lambert, Dave, 121
Land, Harold, 186
Lane, Morris, 35
Lang, Eddie, 40
Larkin, Billy, 239
Larkin, Milt, 47
Larkins, Ellis, 4
Lateef, Yusef, 188, 209, 212, 229–30, 257
Laurie, Annie, 27, 37, 78
Laws, Hubert, 236, 259
Laws, Ronnie, 242
Lazar, Sam, 202, 239
Lee, Julia, 19, 28, 41
Lee, Peggy, 20
Lee, Perry, 239
Leiber, Jerry, 129
Leonard, Harlan, 5, 38
Les Paul, 50
Lester, Sonny, 30, 177, 238
Letman, Johnny, 137
Levey, Stan, 32
Levy, Morris, 84, 97, 108, 115–16, 118, 121, 193
Levy, Ron, 241
Lewis, Howard, 101
Lewis, Jerry Lee, 142
Lewis, John, 33, 50, 189
Lewis, Meade "Lux," 13, 43, 133
Lewis, Nolan, 115
Lewis, Ramsey, 169, 218, 220–22, 224, 241, 258
Liberty Records, 185
Liggins, Joe, 7, 9, 17, 19, 21–22
 "Honeydripper, The," 9, 21
Lightnin' Hopkins, 35
Lil Green, 29
Limelight, 189, 226, 230
Lion, Alfred, 133, 169, 185, 191, 202–3, 205, 222, 239, 255, 263
LiPuma, Tommy, 237, 242
Little, Booker, 199
Little Esther (Esther Mae Jones), 24, 38, 64–65
Little Jimmy Scott, 37, 69, 132, 257
Little Richard, 90
Little Willie John, 37, 68
Lloyd, Charles, 170, 229
"Long Gone," 42–43, 93
Longmire, Wilbert, 232
Lorenz, George "the Hound," 92
Lott, Carl, 152
Louis, Joe, xii, 13, 101
Lowe, Sammy, 3, 102, 117
Lubinsky, Herman, 23, 35–36, 66–68, 132
Lucas, Buddy, 75
Ludwig, Gene, 239, 263
Lunceford, Jimmie, 5, 22, 70
Lutcher, Nellie, 19, 28, 41
Lymon, Frankie, 82
Lynne, Gloria, 213

M

Macero, Teo, 192
Magid, Lee, 37
Mainstream, 238
Majestic, 6, 9, 41, 75
Mance, Julian "Junior," 111, 180, 223
Mancini, Henry, 194
Mangione, Chuck, 248
Mann, Herbie, 211, 230, 258
Manor, 9, 23, 256
Marlowe, Bill, 92, 264
Marquette, Pee Wee, 97
Marr, Hank, 232
Marshall, Joe, 131
Martino, Pat, 172, 201, 207, 263
Mayall, John, 89
McCain, Bo, 123
McCann, Les, 169, 175–76, 215, 226–27, 259

McClure, Bobby, 89
McCoy, Sid, 134, 164, 258
McDavid, Percy, 47, 55, 58
McDuff, Jack, 87, 89, 109, 157, 163, 171–74, 178, 190, 202, 206, 209, 217, 230, 238, 257–58
McFadden, Eddie, 166
McGhee, Brownie, 35–36, 44
McGhee, Howard, 8, 35, 49–50, 82
McGriff, Jimmy, 176–77, 238
McLean, Jackie, 183
McLin, Claude, 75
McNeely, Big Jay, 24, 38, 63–64, 78, 256
McNeely, Cecil, 38, 63
McPartland, Marian, 132
McPhatter, Clyde, 80, 115, 130
McRae, Carmen, 218
McShann, Jay, 5, 7, 36, 76, 162
McVea, Jack, 3, 7, 24–26, 35, 256
Melle, Gil, 165
Melodisc, 25
Mendelsohn, Fred, 24, 37, 132, 257, 263
Mercury Records, 6, 9, 12, 19, 23, 27, 29, 58–59, 68–69, 71–72, 96, 99–100, 106–7, 125, 138–39
Merrill, Helen, 137
Merritt, Jymie, 184
MGM Records, 6, 59, 63, 73, 80, 113, 128, 138, 166, 178
Michelot, Pierre, 180
Midgets, 97
Midler, Bette, 259
Midnighters, 98, 256
Midsummer Night's Swing, 47, 54
Mighty Burner, 233
Milburn, Amos, 29
Milestone, 90, 154, 177–78, 223–24, 237
Miller, Glenn, 180
Millinder, Lucky, 4–5, 7, 9, 15–16, 38, 40, 60, 67, 69, 80, 95, 118
Milton, Roy, 7, 19–21, 67, 78
Mingus, Charles, 27, 129, 170, 191–92, 199, 223

Miracle Records, 30, 41–42
Mitchell, Billy, 121
Mitchell, Blue, 138, 182
Mitchell, Freddie, 79, 118
Mitchelle, Jimmy, 3
Mobley, Hank, 181, 183–85, 195, 203
Modern, 7, 60–61, 64–65, 90
Modern Jazz Quartet, 127, 129, 131, 137, 169, 181, 189
Monestier, Jean-Marie, 239
Montgomery, Monk, 73
Montgomery, Wes, 178, 190, 195, 208, 216, 219–20, 224, 250, 258
Moodsville, 109, 133, 157, 164
Moody, James, 94, 100–101, 152, 169, 181, 189, 193
Moondog, 93
Moonglows, The, 95, 101, 115, 124
Moore, Brew, 30, 35
Moore, Dwight "Gatemouth," 29
Moore, Johnny, 19, 28
Moore, Wild Bill, 12, 66
Morgan, Al, 18
Morgan, Lee, 138, 183–84
Morin, Wheeler, 80
Morris, Joe, 15, 27, 30, 67
Morris, Joseph "Chris Columbus," 26
Morris, Leo, 203, 217
Morris, Marlowe, 159, 178
Morris, William, 2
Morty, 35
Motown, 137, 155, 236, 251–52
Mraz, George, 252
Muhammad, Idris, 203, 205–6, 217, 225, 236, 244, 259, 263
Muhammad Ali, 197–98, 241
Murphy, Rose, 41
Muse, 233, 238
Musicraft, 9, 14, 33, 122
Musso, Vido, 12, 23, 255
Mutual, 92
Myers, Bumps, 12
My People, 70

N

Nance, Ray, 3, 123
Nanton, Tricky Sam, 2, 14, 122
Nash, Lewis, 252
Nathan, Syd, 39
National Records, 6, 9, 23–24, 78
Navarro, Fats, 99, 106, 255
NBC, 62, 92, 255
Nelson, Oliver, 86, 166–68, 184, 194, 220, 258
Nelson, Ricky, 126
Newborn, Calvin, 152, 159
Newborn, Phineas, Jr., 152
Newcombe, Don, 13
New Jazz, 133, 163–64, 167, 176
Newman, David "Fathead," 150–51, 155, 167, 169–70
Newman, Joe, 3, 50, 138, 167
Nighthawk, Robert, 94
"Night Train," 14, 76, 201
Nobs, Claude, 226
Norgran, 31, 70, 96
Norman, Gene, 27, 63

O

O'Day, Hank, 149
Ogerman, Claus, 167, 220
Okeh, 28, 40, 60, 159, 162
Oliver, Sy, 80
"Open the Door, Richard," 24–25, 256
Orioles, 43, 63, 99
Orrin Keepnews, 134, 255, 263
Ortega, Anthony, 73
Oscar Peterson Trio, 97, 127–28, 222
Otis, Johnny (John Veliotes), 7, 19, 21, 24, 37–38, 64–65, 256
Ousley, King Curtis, 81–82, 141, 163, 167, 173, 212, 217
Ousley, King Curtis. *See* Curtis, King
Overall, Floyd, 105
Owens, Jimmy, 152

P

Pablo, 240
Pacific Jazz, 169, 175–76, 178–79, 183, 219, 229, 231
Page, Dave, 27
Page, Patti, 99
Paige, Leroy "Satchel," 44
Painia, Frank, 101
Panama Francis, 4
Parker, Bobby, 68
Parker, Charlie, 23–24, 29, 31–33, 35–36, 57, 62, 78, 96, 100–101, 106, 114, 139, 158, 180, 191–92
Parker, Leo, 35, 50, 94, 106, 134, 199, 255
Parker, Weasel, 14
Parlan, Horace, 199, 203, 223
Parrish, Avery, 3, 17
Patterson, Don, 228, 239, 257
Patton, Big John, 175, 201–2
Patton, John, 169, 175, 179, 201–2, 209
Payne, Percival "Sonny," 119
payola, 115–16, 144–45, 215
"Perdido," 27, 50–51, 70
Person, Houston, 111, 154, 176, 206, 233, 241, 259, 263
Peterson, Lucky, 241
Peterson, Oscar, 73, 126, 128, 190, 196, 222
Pettiford, Oscar, 199
Phillips, Flip, 50–51, 97, 127
Phillips, Sonny, 239, 263
Pitts, Trudy, 239
Playhouse Four, 223
Ponder, Jimmy, 236
Poppa Stoppa, 92
Porter, Bob, iv, 259
Porter, Cole, 126
Potter, Jerry, 118
Powell, Bud, 29, 99, 180, 192, 194, 255
Powell, Jesse, 14, 82
Pozo, Chano, 33
Premium, 75

Prestige Records, 82, 99–100, 108–10, 112, 133, 136–40, 159–61, 163–65, 167–68, 171–76, 178–79, 186–87, 232–34, 237–38, 257–59
Preston, Billy, 154, 239
Price, Lloyd, 89
Price, Sammy, 8
Progressive, 239
Prysock, Arthur, 4, 16, 61, 72, 78, 94, 213
Prysock, Red, 78–79, 94, 115
Purdie, Bernard, 82, 154, 244, 263
Putnam, Bill, 94

Q

Quebec, Ike, 23, 80, 133–34, 164, 169, 176, 199, 201, 203
Queen Records, 10, 39
Quincy Jones Orchestra, 193
Quinichette, Paul, 30, 71, 162, 256

R

Race Charts, 15, 17–18, 40–42
race music, 1, 10, 18, 29, 39, 45, 57, 65
Race Records, 2–5, 9, 21, 26, 36–38, 40, 60, 73
Rainey, Chuck, 82
Rama, 41, 82, 194
Randle, Bill, 63
Ravens, 23, 43, 63, 78
Ray, Johnny, 61
R&B (rhythm and blues), xiv, 57–65, 67–69, 74–79, 81–82, 92–95, 99–101, 115, 129–32, 135–36, 170–71, 176–78, 215, 217–20, 231
RCA, 1, 14, 19–20, 22, 25, 33, 45, 48, 51, 53, 59–60, 90, 95, 137, 140
RCA Bluebird, 21–22, 40, 80
RCA Victor, 2–3, 10, 14, 28, 32–34, 50, 78, 139, 187
Rebennack, Mac "Dr. John," 204

Rebop Six, 32
recording ban, 4, 7, 34–36, 58–59, 66, 77–78, 107, 139
Red, Tampa, 42
Redbone, Leon, 259
Ree Boppers, 31
Reed, Jimmy, 134
Reed, Lula, 43
Reese, Della, 213
Reese, Lloyd, 48, 55, 58
Regal, 28, 257
Regent Records, 132, 257
Reid, Irene, 213
Reig, Teddy, 22–23, 35–37, 44, 66, 68, 84, 98, 118, 121, 132, 255, 263
Rene, Leon, 21
Rhodes, Todd, 39, 42
Rhyne, Mel, 239
rhythm, xi, 10, 12, 15, 19–20, 25, 31, 53, 57, 72, 91, 98, 103, 149, 158
Rice, Charlie, 160
Rich, Buddy, 73, 97, 99, 125–26, 180
Richardson, Jerome, 160, 193
Ridgely, Tommy, 130
Riverside Records, 133–34, 138, 164, 169, 176, 184, 187, 189, 191, 219, 223–24, 230
Roach, Freddie, 169, 196, 239
Roach, Max, 99, 180–81, 183, 186, 192, 235
Robey, Don, 101
Robins, The, 65, 256
Robinson, Frank, 172
Robinson, Jackie, 13, 44, 102
Roche, Betty, 173
Rogers, Shorty, 129
Rollins, Sonny, 180, 186–87, 199
Roost, 36, 160, 194, 255
Rosen, Larry, 237, 242
Ross, 121, 255, 258
Ross, Annie, 121, 159
Roulette Records, 41, 52, 98, 121, 125, 137, 160, 194, 255
Rouse, Charlie, 123, 140, 191
Rover Boys, 117

Royal, Ernie, 3, 107
Royal, Marshall, 3, 48
Royal Roost, 36, 68, 118
Rushing, Jimmy, 2, 38
Russell, Curly, 180
Russell, George, 33
Russell, Ross, 36

S

Sample, Joe, 231
Sanders, Pharoah, 229
Sarge Goes to Washington, 25
Savoy Records, 3, 9, 23, 30–31, 35–37, 39, 44, 47, 50, 58, 60, 63–68, 132, 137–38, 255–57
Schifrin, Lalo, 181, 220
Schmeling, Max, 13
Schwartz, Thornel, 166
SCLC (Southern Christian Leadership Conference), 198
Scott, Clifford, 73, 135, 176, 179
Scott, Rhoda, 169, 199, 239, 257
Scott, Shirley, 41, 74, 133, 157, 160–61, 163, 167, 174
Screamin' Jay Hawkins, 142
Sears, Al, 3, 69, 76, 80–82, 84, 98, 117–18, 163
Sears, Zenas, 92
Sebesky, Don, 153, 220, 237
Seeburg Company, 60
Sensation, 30, 39, 42
SESAC, xii
Shad, Bob, 22–23, 34–35, 78, 99–100, 139, 238, 256
Shakey Jake, 173
Shavers, Charlie, 7, 27, 97, 138
Shaw, Artie, 1, 7, 95, 101
Shaw Artists Guild, 11, 37
Shearing, George, 74, 98
Shepherd, Leo "the Whistler," 27
Shihab, Sahib, 199
Shorter, Wayne, 183, 185, 195, 234, 258
Silver, Horace, 151, 154, 170, 181–82, 185, 195, 224

Simpkins, Jesse "Po," 18
Simpkins, Lew, 24, 42, 93–94
Sims, Zoot, 30, 159
Sinatra, Frank, 261
Singer, Hal, 35–37, 75, 78, 82, 159, 161, 199, 255
Slim, Memphis, 29, 41, 94, 119
Slim Gaillard, 7, 19, 24, 32
Sly Stone, 203
Smalls, Tommy "Doctor Jive," 92
Smiley Lewis, 98
Smith, Bobby, 3, 17, 80
Smith, Floyd, 159
Smith, Huey, 203
Smith, James Oscar, 164
Smith, Jimmy, xiv, 163–68, 177–78, 183–85, 190, 196, 201, 208, 216, 219–20, 235, 241, 244, 250, 258
Smith, Johnny "Hammond," 109, 176, 233, 236–37, 247–48, 255
Smith, Lonnie Liston, 217–18, 236, 238, 242, 244, 248
Smith, Major N. Clark, 58
Smith, Stuff, 8, 136
Smith, Tab, 4, 8, 75, 94
Smith, Willie, 7, 11–12, 18, 27, 49, 70, 97
Solid Senders, 20
Solomon, Clifford, 73
soul jazz, i, iii, x, xiii, 157–60, 163–64, 169, 175, 178, 211, 213, 217, 228, 231, 237–39
soul jazz activity, 175, 177
soul jazz era, 76, 239, 241
soul jazz groups, 158, 199, 212, 231
Spaniels, 134
Spann, Les, 138, 180
Sparks, Melvin, 154, 233, 247, 259, 263
Specialty (Juke Box), 7, 58, 60, 90–91
Specialty Records, 22
Spencer, Leon, 239, 247, 259
Staple Singers, 134
Staton, Dakota, 213
Stax Records, 103
Steeplechase, 239

Stewart, Billy, 91
Stewart, Rex, 2, 138
Stewart, Slam, 8
Stidham, Arbee, 41–42
Stinson, Albert, 229
Stitt, Sonny, 75, 89, 105–9, 111–12, 127, 168, 173, 180, 194, 227–28, 264
Stoller, Mike, 129, 131
Stone, Jesse, 80, 90, 117, 131
Stormy Weather, 6, 49
Stovall, Don, 9
Strozier, Frank, 258
Sulieman, Idrees, 199
Sullivan, Ed, 171
Sultan, 42
Sunset Royals, 80
Sutton, Percy, 215
Swan Silvertones, 134
Swingville, 133, 164
Sykes, Roosevelt, 21–22, 29, 94
Symphony Sid, 62–63, 97, 100
Szabo, Gabor, 229

T

Tadd Dameron, 33, 255
Tahmazian, Jean-Pierre, 239
Tampa, 90
Tarrant, Rabon, 25
Tate, Buddy, 2, 22, 58, 110, 161–62, 218, 239, 264
Tate, Grady, 252, 264
Tatum, Art, 8
Taylor, Art, 109, 180–81, 183, 199
Taylor, Cecil, 228
Taylor, Creed, 153, 178, 188, 206, 219–20, 235, 237, 247–49, 251, 255, 257, 263
Taylor, Floyd, 66
Taylor, Gene, 182
Taylor, Koko, 89
Taylor, Little Johnny, 196
Taylor, Sam, 4, 16, 79–82, 98, 136, 141
Tee, Richard, 82
Teenagers, 82, 100

Terry, Clark, 7, 71, 193, 256
Texas Tenor, 47, 53
Tharpe, Rosetta, 4–5
Thiele, Bob, 117, 188, 192
Thigpen, Ed, 223
Thomas, Joe, 5, 58
Thomas, Leon, 229
Thompson, Charles, 4, 16, 35, 50, 159, 178
Thompson, Chester, 239
Thompson, Dickie, 159
Thompson, Hank, 13
Thompson, Lucky, 2, 32, 35
Thompson, Sonny, 39, 42–43, 93
Thornton, Willie Mae "Big Mama," 65
Three Blazers, 19, 28
Til, Sonny (Earlington Tilghman), 43
Timeless, 239
Timmons, Bobby, 157, 183, 223
Tiny Grimes Quintet, 78
Tizol, Juan, 50, 70
Tjader, Cal, 132, 178, 196, 258
Toast of the Town, 51, 171
Towles, Nat, 36, 162
Trotman, Lloyd, 79, 84, 118, 131
Tru-Sound, 82, 133
Turner, Big Joe, 7, 39, 78, 80–81, 90, 95, 115, 130–31
Turner, Milt, 152
Turner, Pete, 235–36
Turner, Titus, 37
Turrentine, Stanley, 153, 163, 165, 174, 184, 203, 208, 211, 235–37, 242, 248
Tyler, Jimmy, 14
Tympany Five, 1, 17, 25–26
Tyner, McCoy, 185, 188, 242

U

Ulmer, James "Blood," 232
United Artists, 167, 182, 205, 208, 212, 238
United Music, 68

V

Vanderpool, Sylvia, 91
Vaughan, Sarah, 14, 34, 98–99, 121, 213, 256–57
Vee Jay, 64, 68, 89, 134, 162, 164, 185, 224, 227, 258
Ventura, Charlie, 23, 35, 49, 139
Verve Records, 31, 55, 70, 109, 112, 120, 126–27, 138, 153, 165–67, 173, 178, 189–90, 219–20, 257–58
Vick, Harold, 173
Vinson, Eddie "Cleanhead," 6, 29–30, 47, 187
Vitacoustic Records, 42
Volstead Act, 7
Voting Rights Act, xv, 196, 199

W

WABC, 143
Waldron, Mal, 199
Walker, Earl, 27
Walker, Junior, 82
Walker, Mel, 65, 256
Walker, T-Bone, 7, 24, 41, 48, 65, 256
Waller, Ben, 20
Waller, Fats, 17, 160
Walls, Van "Piano Man," 79, 131, 261–62
Walls, Winston, 261
Warner, Little Sonny, 64
Warner Brothers, 64, 135, 178, 224, 237, 242
Warren, Quentin, 166
Washington, Dinah, 3, 8, 15, 25–26, 41, 43–44, 65, 89, 99, 119, 141, 193, 198, 213, 256
Washington, Grover, Jr., 236–37, 241–42, 247–53, 258
Washington, Laura, 17
Watkins, Doug, 109, 181
Watley, Bobby, 238–39, 264
Watson, Paula, 41
Watts, Noble, 95
Webb, Chick, 17, 118
Webster, 34, 76, 123, 236–37, 241–42, 246–48, 251–53, 258
Webster, Ben, 3, 8, 53, 58, 69, 76, 97, 122–23, 176, 199
Webster, Freddie, 4, 34
Wein, George, 123–24
Weinberg, Ralph, 101
Weinstock, Bob, 98, 108, 110, 133, 160–61, 163, 172, 201, 204, 212, 233–34, 255, 263
Wells, Dickie, 2, 162
Wess, Frank, 71, 109, 121, 167, 189
Wexler, Jerry, 57, 92, 128, 131, 263
White, Barry, 241
White, Kevin, 211
Wiggins, Gerry, 159
Wilcox, Eddie, 5–6
Wilder, Joe, 137, 257
Wilkerson, Don, 130, 134, 170
Wilkins, Ernie, 71, 117, 119, 121, 132
Willette, Baby Face, 201, 203, 239
Williams, Cootie, 3, 6, 10, 21, 29, 69, 78–80, 85, 122, 136, 138, 158, 171
Williams, Devonia, 19
Williams, Jody, 91
Williams, Joe, 98, 119, 121, 213, 223
Williams, Larry, 142
Williams, Mary Lou, 8
Williams, Paul, 35, 66–68, 85, 93, 155, 255, 264
Williams, Tony, 195
Williamson, Sonny Boy, 59
Willis, Chuck, 61, 89, 130
Willis, Ralph, 35
Wilson, Carl, 172
Wilson, Gerard, 7, 152, 179
Wilson, Nancy, 170, 196, 213, 232, 252
Wilson, Phil, 53
Wilson, Reuben, 205, 238–39
Wilson, Shadow, 13, 50
Winchester, Lem, 167
Winding, Kai, 132, 140, 178, 257
Withers, Bill, 252

Witherspoon, Jimmy, 196
Wolff, Frank, 87, 104, 169, 200, 205, 238–39
Wonder, Stevie, 215, 250
Wood, Mitchell "Booty," 15, 27, 79
Woods, Phil, 193
Woodyard, Sam, 122, 124
World Transcriptions, 9
Wright, Billy, 132
Wright, Jimmy, 82
Wright, Leo, 173, 180
WWII (World War II), ix, xii, xiv–xv, 1, 6, 23, 33, 45, 67, 75, 94, 119, 133, 186

X

X, 60

Y

Young, Eldee, 220
Young, Larry, 163, 169, 201–2, 228, 239, 258
Young, Lester, 2, 8, 10–12, 20, 30–31, 38, 50, 53, 58, 63, 97, 100, 106–7, 127, 199
Young, Trummy, 35

Z

Zawinul, Joe, 222, 234

Lightning Source UK Ltd.
Milton Keynes UK
UKHW011331060521
383248UK00001B/114